The Bottlenecks of Business

The Bottlenecks *of* Business

THURMAN W. ARNOLD

BeardBooks
Washington, D.C.

Acknowledgments

THANKS are due to the following sources for permission to reproduce material in this book: To Theodore Kreps and The Macmillan Company, for the chart of income levels on page 8, taken from *Social Education;* to *The New Republic,* for an editorial and for an article by Walton Hamilton; to the *New York Mirror,* for an editorial; to Bruce Catton and the N. E. A., for a syndicated article appearing in many papers; to Walter Lippmann and the *New York Herald Tribune,* for an article of Mr. Lippmann's.

Contents

vii

CONTENTS

Introduction

THIS book is dedicated to the men in the Antitrust Division of the Department of Justice whose anonymous work during the past two years has been responsible for the revival of interest in breaking down the barriers of trade in this country. I cannot say too much about the quality of their services. It has required intelligence and energy of a high order. It has also required the sacrifice of personal interest by men who believed in the job they were doing. Men in the Division have frequently turned down higher salaries because they were in the midst of cases for the Division which they were too loyal to abandon. Because sufficient travel funds were not appropriated, men in the Division have been asked to pay their own expenses while they conducted investigations or cases away from Washington. There was no way of compelling them to make this sacrifice, yet there wasn't a man who refused to take an assignment in the field at his own expense. I quote from a letter from one of them:

Assuming that I receive per diem for thirty days up to the middle of May (which Johnston Avery said would be the case, although I have not yet put in a voucher), I should estimate that my financial contribution to the success of the fertilizer case, for which I shall have received no reimbursement in any manner, will amount to something in excess of $500.

Similar sacrifices have been made by other members of our staff, but we have not been overly voluble in our complaints, because we so greatly enjoy the opportunity of working together with such a congenial and talented group of lawyers under the direction of so skillful a chief as Mr. Pearce. Consequently, the morale of our force is still very high, notwithstanding any impediments in the operations of the quartermaster's department.

In addition to all this, the men of the Antitrust Division have gone without vacations. They have worked long hours. They have treated the cases which they were working on as more important than any personal interest. They have been real soldiers in a cause in which they believe.

This book is written in an effort to prevent the work of these men from going for nothing because of a lack of public understanding of what they are trying to do. Although it is printed during a political campaign, no political issues are raised or intended to be raised. There is no attempt in its pages to raise disputes irrelevant to the purpose of the book by praising or blaming any political party or any political figure. The Sherman Act belongs to both political parties.

The emphasis of the book is on the interest of the consumer. The reader will find no discussion in its pages of the various proposals for reform or humani-

INTRODUCTION

tarian legislation now current. The reason is not that I am opposed to reform or to humanitarian legislation, but that such a discussion would confuse the issue here. Every kind of society, whether it be an Indian tribe, an army, a dictatorship or a republic must give reasonable social security to the great mass of its citizens. Every society must compromise with the pure logic of its institutions. The Sherman Act is not a social or a legislative program. Its function is to maintain the economic background essential to any such program in a democracy. Therefore, this book is not addressed to conservatives or liberals as a class, but to those whether on the left or on the right who prefer writing their social programs in a democracy to putting them in effect under the discipline of a regimented economy.

I wish to acknowledge particularly my indebtedness to Wendell Berge, Administrative Chief of the Antitrust Division, who went over the manuscript in detail, to Charles H. Weston, Chief of the Briefing Section of the Division, who prepared the appendix, to George Comer, Chief Economist, and to Holmes Baldridge, Chief of the Trial Division, and finally to Professor Walton Hamilton of Yale.

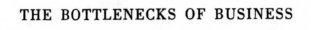

THE BOTTLENECKS OF BUSINESS

I.

The Basic Problem of Distribution

THE purpose of this book is to explain to the consumer what can be done for him to increase the distribution of goods under our existing laws and by pursuing our traditional ideals of an economy of free and independent enterprise. It is written on the assumption that there is no substantial political group in the United States which will support drastic changes in our economic structure. We are committed to a system of distribution of goods through private enterprise. The success of that system depends upon the ability of the consumers of America to use the instruments of government which they have at hand to get the maximum distribution of goods in a free market.

The problem of the American consumer, who depends on private enterprise to give him goods at competitive prices, is intensified by the crisis in national defense. That crisis has created a gigantic new consumer, coming into our market with mass buying power and artificial credit, to compete with the ordinary American who wants food, clothes, and houses. It would appear, for the present at least, that we have

1

plenty of goods to satisfy this new giant. He will cause men to be employed and purchasing power to be increased and some organizations may gain unprecedented riches. Yet if we do not understand the situation, or if we are unprepared to meet it, this new purchasing power and these new riches may hinder instead of help the American consumer. They may even create a permanent dislocation of our economy of distribution for the next twenty-five years.

What happened to the ordinary consumer in the boom which followed the outbreak of the war in 1914? When the war first broke out there was a drop in prices and general distress. Then came the war inflation which robbed productive industry for war boom industry, resulting in complete unbalance of prices. We were confronted with the spectacle of the Southern farmer going hat in hand to the newly-created millionaires and asking them for charity's sake to buy a bale of cotton. There were no controls. Real wages went down one-third while thousands of new fortunes were made. Wilfred I. King estimated that in the United States alone enough money was transferred from the pockets of labor and consumers to the pockets of manufacturers and promoters to make forty thousand new millionaires.

There is no reason, in the nature of things, why this need happen again. We have somewhere around ten million unemployed—more men than in the entire Allied armies. We have vast reservoirs of idle capital. This is a colossal waste. Putting this labor and capital to work at *anything*, at least until there is an actual shortage of labor and productive capacity, should raise instead of lower the standard of living in this country, at least until there is an actual shortage of labor and productive capacity.

It is cheaper for the country to put idle labor and idle capital to work at *something* rather than to permit them to rot away through disuse. Skills disappear and capital is destroyed when we fail to put them to work. Therefore, the necessity of preparation for national defense, regrettable though it may be as compared to an ideal alternative, does have the hint of a silver lining, provided war industry is not permitted to destroy peace-time industry.

The problem we face on the eve of great expenditures for national defense is, therefore, not essentially different from the problem we faced during the depression when we had to spend huge amounts for relief and subsidies. We must see that these expenditures are made in a free market. We must see that the distribution of peace-time necessities of life, which are now produced by private industry, is not handicapped. More than ever today the American consumer needs protection against fixed prices and inefficient, non-competitive methods of distribution. More than ever we need to guard against the private seizure of power over a free market. In order to better understand the problem that is ahead, and how to meet it, we should be familiar with the pattern of restraints that have been clogging the market in the past.

Most of the books in the past on the antitrust laws have been written with the idea that they are designed to eliminate *the evil of bigness*. What ought to be emphasized is not the evils of size but the evils of industries which are not efficient or do not pass efficiency on to consumers. If the antitrust laws are simply an expression of a religion which condemns largeness as economic sin they will be regarded as an anachronism in a machine age. If, however, they are directed at making distribution more efficient, they will begin to make sense, and, incidentally, they will also solve the problem of bigness wherever bigness is blocking the channels of trade.

A nation's economic wealth consists of its productive capacity. Its income consists of the goods and services which it is capable of getting around to consumers. When farmers and laborers cannot get goods, national income goes down. When national income goes down, it is harder to live in peace and it is also harder to prepare for national defense. National income is ordinarily given in terms of dollars, but this dollar value can only be given to goods or services that people can buy. Idle productive capital has no dollar value; it is a liability because it requires upkeep. Idle labor cannot produce national income; it is a liability because it requires relief. Goods which are unsalable lose their dollar value, and those who possess them become bankrupt. No one gets these dollars that the owner of the goods has "lost"; they simply go out of existence. At the same time the manufacturing plants which produce the goods that cannot be sold lose their dollar value. Their owners also become bankrupt. And the farms that produce the food which no one can buy become worth less than the mortgages even though they are better farms than they used to be.

The economic problem that faces an industrial democracy, therefore, in both war and peace is whether private enterprise is able to distribute to consumers the food, clothes, houses, and other commodities which they need. Theoretically, private enterprise can do it because competition always will force prices down to meet purchasing power. This theory is called the law of supply and demand. Let us see how it has been working since the great depression.

The Brookings Institution estimated that during the twelve-year period from 1922 to 1934 this country could have produced in goods and services 248 billion dollars more than it did produce.[1] This means that $8,000 in goods and services were withheld from each of our thirty million families. This is more than ninety per cent of them could save in a lifetime. Such a situation seems senseless. It is a dangerous kind of waste because it advertises to the ordinary man in the street that our industrial economy is not efficiently distributing the goods which our engineers and technicians are able to produce through modern methods of mass production.

The history of distribution of goods in the United States since 1850 may be pictured by the following chart.[2] It shows the national income expressed in dollars which have been weighted against fluctuations in currency value. It is, therefore, a shorthand way of expressing the amount of goods and services distributed each year since 1850.

5

UNITED STATES NATIONAL INCOME

TOTAL

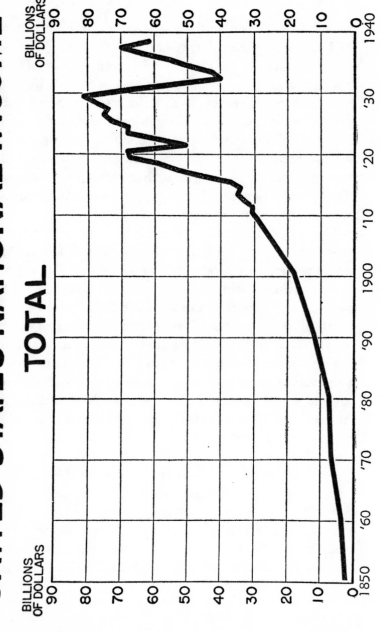

THE BASIC PROBLEM OF DISTRIBUTION

This chart shows a constant increase in the material income of the American people from 1850 to the depression. The lines on the chart prior to the year 1920 do not show the intervening ups and downs because they have been figured in ten-year periods. The chart indicates that at the end of each of these ten-year periods the American people had more material income than in the preceding decade. During the war the income rose enormously in spite of the fact that war is supposed to be wasteful. It continued to rise until the depression. Then, for the first time in the history of America, in the face of plenty, national income dropped. The end of the chart shows our national income below the level of 1920 in spite of the fact that we have a much larger population and a greater productive capacity than we had twenty years ago. The chart gives us a picture of a system of distribution that has somehow gone wrong—that is not operating the way it used to operate. It is from such charts that radical economic planners get ammunition to support sweeping changes.

The same thing may be illustrated in another way by presenting a picture of the distribution of income among our thirty million families. The following chart,[3] prepared by Theodore J. Kreps from figures compiled by the National Resources Committee, represents the best available data regarding the distribution of income with government aid eliminated.

There is no way of checking the figures on this chart with anything approaching absolute accuracy. They represent the best guess that skilled men can make. But

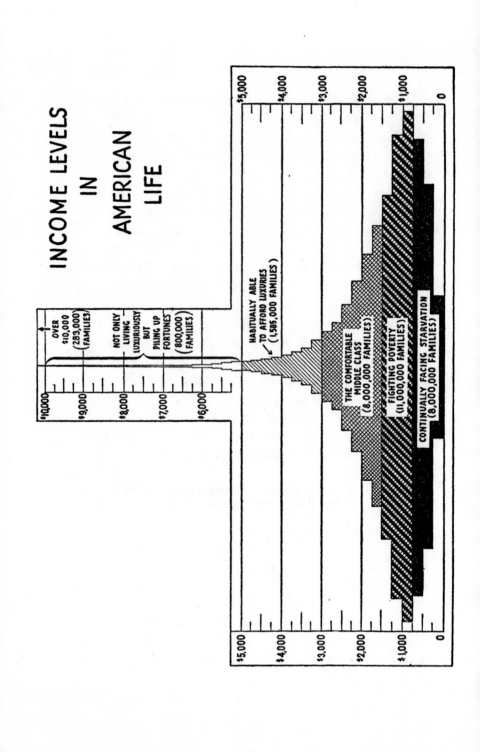

INCOME LEVELS IN AMERICAN LIFE

OVER $10,000 (283,000 FAMILIES)

NOT ONLY LIVING LUXURIOUSLY BUT PILING UP FORTUNES (800,000 FAMILIES)

HABITUALLY ABLE TO AFFORD LUXURIES (1,585,000 FAMILIES)

THE COMFORTABLE MIDDLE CLASS (8,000,000 FAMILIES)

FIGHTING POVERTY (11,000,000 FAMILIES)

CONTINUALLY FACING STARVATION (8,000,000 FAMILIES)

assuming that they are fifty per cent inaccurate, the income distribution picture still looks like the Eiffel Tower.

The minimum on which a family of three can purchase a fair share of the goods advertised over the radio and in our better magazines is approximately $2500 a year. Families with that income or over comprise only thirteen per cent of our population, or about the population of the State of New York.[4] The chart, therefore, shows that our productive plant, equipped to make goods for a country of 130 million people, can distribute its production only to thirteen per cent of that population without some form of government aid. Under these circumstances it is not surprising that, when the wheels of industry start turning, it is only a short time before goods pile up on shelves and the wheels have to stop.

Figures and charts of this kind are compiled in abundance in the first volume of the hearings of the Temporary National Economic Committee.[5] The general observations set out here are proved there with elaborate detail by distinguished economists. Ten years of experience since the beginning of the great depression have demonstrated that we have made extraordinary strides in invention and in the efficiency of organized production. It is the economic machinery of distribution which is stalled. And this raises the problem which puzzles American consumers today.

To sum up, these charts show an economic machine which is either in reverse or which has brakes that are stronger than its engine.

9

THE BOTTLENECKS OF BUSINESS

Some people think that we can throw the machine away and buy a new one. The trouble with that notion is that there do not seem to be any new machines on the market in which the American people like to ride. There is nothing about the European models that appeals to us. Therefore, we are faced with the absolute necessity of making our own machine run. We have got to fix it with the tools presently at hand.

The Basic Problem

Broadly speaking, human society has found only two ways of distributing goods and services. One is the army system, by means of which a commanding officer passes out the goods in the supply house to the troops in proportion to their needs. The other is by a system of exchange in a free market. As organization increases, free exchange necessarily becomes more limited, so that neither the army system nor the free market system of distribution ever entirely disappears from any society. Even in the most pioneer society the State always has to distribute *some* goods and services to its citizens. And, on the other hand, even in the most highly organized army, the soldiers can trade their pocketknives and buy whiskey with their pay.

In a society where individual freedom is the prevailing ideal, the *main* method of distributing goods and services must be by free exchange in a free market. It is not a particularly orderly process. It is not a planned economy. Nevertheless, it is the only process which relies on the independence of the individual as a person rather than on his efficiency as a cog in a machine. It is the only process which does not become static by freezing at the top a dynasty of men who have the means of keeping new enterprise from coming to the surface. It is the American ideal because the existence of industrial democracy is the only basis on which political democracy can rest.

The maintenance of a free market, therefore, becomes the first concern of every political democracy. It is not a difficult problem in an agricultural economy where men can obtain the necessities of living by their own hard work and where each farm is an independent unit. It becomes more difficult in a machine age as mass production and distribution of necessities develop. The reason for this is that when industry becomes highly organized, it gains the power to control prices which the people must pay. The exchange of raw materials and services by unorganized groups for the products of organized industry becomes more and more a one-sided bargain. When this happens a farm problem always arises because the farmers cannot buy. Then an unemployment problem becomes acute because the manufacturers cannot sell. Then an investment problem appears because no one wants to put money in an enterprise that cannot sell its goods. Then the unorganized groups, who cannot exchange their raw materials and services for necessities of decent living, have to demand that the government buy these necessities for them. Then a budget-balancing problem takes the center of the stage and people begin to worry about taxes to pay for subsidies.

THE BOTTLENECKS OF BUSINESS

This has happened in every business civilization whenever prices were fixed by great industrial organizations so high that consumers could not buy. The bread and circuses given to the poor in Rome were the same kind of thing as relief and WPA theater projects are today. They were not given because politicians foolishly followed wrong economic principles. Government subsidies have poured out and always will pour out when the free exchange of goods and services for manufactured products breaks down.

This is what is happening in America today. Let us examine the economic situation which is back of farm subsidies and relief. The great mass of our population sell their goods, services, and labor in a competitive market. They buy their necessities in a controlled market. Thus our economic structure consists of two separate worlds. The first is a world of organized industry; the second is a world of small unorganized business men, farmers, laborers, and consumers. In the first world, there is the power to maintain high prices no matter how much the demand for the product falls off. When this power is exercised, purchasing power is curtailed, production drops, men are laid off, and this in turn lowers purchasing power and makes demand drop still further. A vicious downward spiral is set in operation. In the second world, unlimited competition still exists and cannot be controlled. In this world live the farmers, retailers, and small business men who supply the consumers with both goods and labor. Here, when the supply increases or the demand falls off, prices drop to the bottom, but the people go right on producing as

12

much as the conditions of the market will permit. In the first world we have concentrated control, which makes possible high and rigid prices. These, in turn, lead to restriction of production and wholesale discharge of labor. In the second world, we find competition, low flexible prices, large production and labor standards often at starvation levels.*

The trouble with the system is that the first of these worlds works at cross-purposes with the second. In the first world, organizations, great and small, keep up prices and lay off labor. The labor so laid off has no power to purchase the consumers goods furnished by the second world, but that world is not organized to restrict production and maintain high prices in the face of falling demand. Unmarketable surpluses therefore pile up.

In the business decline of 1937, our troubles were laid to the accumulation of huge inventories which could not be distributed. Industries had speeded up production and enlarged their productive capacity without any realization that price policies should be inextricably linked with productive capacity. Productive capacity was planned on a ten-year basis. Price policies were planned on a three-month basis. With the expanding market, most industries attempted, by raising their prices, not to distribute the most goods but to obtain the largest share of that expanding purchasing

* The dividing line between these two worlds is not necessarily between big and little business. Small groups in little business often succeed in organizing to raise their own prices at the expense of distribution. The cumulative effect of a lot of little price-fixing organizations is as bad as a few big ones.

power. The result was that we became choked with our own wealth. We are coming to realize the absurdity of people going without goods because inventories of these very goods have become too large.

So, today, we are forced to face the price and distribution problem because the organizing genius of the American people will not tolerate a series of depressions which are caused principally by the fact that we have too much undistributed wealth. The American people will not submit to going without goods which they see piled up on every side of them simply because industrial management is unable to distribute the wealth which industrial technicians are able to produce in such quantities. We have the materials, the factories, the men and the money. The problem now is to unleash the productive forces for the benefit of consumers without taking the short and easy road to industrial autocracy.

The ordinary man has little understanding of economic structures. He can only understand what he sees in front of him. When he observes an industrial management which for no understandable reason is unable to distribute the goods that it makes, he turns to the government. Here, at least, there is practical relief, and he feels that he has nothing to lose. Preaching and denunciation of totalitarian systems of industrial control is as useless to stop this process as preaching against disease.

There are two ways of running industry to capacity and distributing all of its product. One is to establish conditions under which competitive independent industries can maintain themselves. The other is for the state to regulate the centralized industrial power which has been allowed to develop. The former method is represented by an economy like that of Sweden, where the government function is concerned with the means of giving the privileges of free and unrestrained competition to independent business. The latter method is represented roughly by the model of the collective states of Europe in which centralized industry is controlled by the iron hand of government and effective distribution of goods is thus insured.

The inevitable result of the destruction of competitive domestic markets by private combinations, cartels, and trade associations is illustrated by Germany today. Prior to the First World War that country had no antitrust law, but industrial self-regimentation was counterbalanced by a strong centralized government, ready to adopt necessary socialistic legislation. There was a practical compromise that worked.

In the depression that followed the war, a weak government in Germany permitted the self-regimentation of industries to proceed without restriction. That system of industrial concentration without public responsibility failed disastrously. Public discontent forced the enactment in 1923 of a decree similar in purpose to our antitrust law.[6] But unfortunately for Germany its tradition of free enterprise was too weak. The law was never enforced. The year 1927 witnessed the last gasp of free enterprise in Germany. An economic commission was appointed to study the monopoly problem. It sat for three years and produced nearly forty volumes.[7] The activities of this commission are interesting because the arguments for the cartel system were identical with the arguments now being used to oppose enforcement of our antitrust laws. First, there was the theory that enforcement of the antitrust laws created uncertainty in business. Then the socialist planners of Germany argued that out of their enforcement no planned economy could result. The trade associations insisted on protection against the chiseler. The unions believed that higher wages would come from large and prosperous cartels. So the commission ended on the note of letting business combinations alone.

With this encouragement German business regimentation drifted to its logical conclusion. Industrial Germany became an army with a place for everyone, and everyone was required to keep his place in a trade association or a cartel. Here was arbitrary power without public control and regimentation without public leadership. That power, exercised without public responsibility, was constantly squeezing the consumer. There was only one answer. Germany was organized to such an extent that it needed a general and Hitler leaped into power. Had it not been Hitler it would have been someone else. When a free market was destroyed, state control of distribution had to follow.[8]

In discussing these questions we should remember that there is nothing new about this problem of restraints of trade. It is as old as business civilization. From the days of ancient Corinth down through the business empires of Venice and Florence to modern times, the disappearance of a free market for consumers has been the first step in the decline of every business civilization,—the beginning of its absorption into a centralized government.[9]

Inventory booms and artificial surpluses in times of real scarcity are not new. They have been intensified by the machine age, but they can be observed in the decadence of business civilization long before mechanized production was dreamed of. They appear whenever private monopoly chokes off its home markets. The most convenient modern illustration is again found in Germany. Prior to Hitler, food was relatively scarce in Germany. Manufactured products were relatively plentiful. Indeed, at one time it was feared that the German industrial machine would flood the world with cheap goods under pressure to pay reparations. Yet in this situation of plentiful manufactured products and scarce food, a farm problem developed. The farmer found that he could not exchange his produce on a parity basis for the products of industry which he needed. An unemployment problem followed in spite of the fact that there was a vast reconstruction job to do and not enough labor to do it.[10] The consumers of Germany woke up, and there is much evidence of their activity during the decade from 1923 to 1933 to establish competitive prices in a free internal market. But the movement failed, perhaps because there were so many economic planners in Germany—so many believers in the rationalized state—that it was impossible to gain wide acceptance for the idea of forcibly preventing the growth of the great cartel, or to devise any method of checking it.

THE BOTTLENECKS OF BUSINESS

The disappearance of competitive enterprise in Germany and the rise of a powerful industrial autocracy occurred under pressures which we have never had to face in this country. And yet we can observe a few disquieting symptoms of the same sort of process in this country. In 1920 the American farmer got 50¢ of each dollar spent by the American consumer. He was spending that 50¢ to buy manufactured products. Today he gets only 30¢ of each consumer's dollar.[11] He cannot buy the same proportion of manufactured goods. He has lost 40 per cent of his proportionate purchasing power. That loss expressed in dollars is $1,800,000,000 each year. The manufacturer did not get this money. It has simply disappeared. This means that the farmer cannot buy so many goods, and therefore less manufactured products will be distributed to farmers. How is the farmer making up that loss? He is getting a $1,000,-000,000 subsidy from the government. But he is still $800,000,000 short if we keep to these rough figures. And the budget is unbalanced. And everyone is beginning to worry about the government taking over the distribution of goods which should be the function of private enterprise.

At this point the economic thinker can go in one of two directions. He can begin to talk about a general planned economy and start the long struggle with private enterprise, which naturally does not wish to subject itself to government dictation. The result of that struggle will be the chaos of last ditch battles when general economic planning is thrown against the stubborn resistance of private enterprise. He will be in for years of struggle, legislative sabotage, judicial controversies, and the bitterness of extreme theoretical positions. We have been going through much of that chaos in the past eight years. If, however, limited planning for specific industrial problems is thrown against a broad background of free enterprise, he can argue its merits in terms of the particular need of a particular industry. Some planning is unquestionably necessary. We are getting used to the idea that in certain areas the State must step in and perform functions which private enterprise cannot effectively do. But this limited planning for particular needs can only be made to work if competitive forces are freely allowed to distribute the maximum of the goods and services on which we live.

II.

How Restraints of Trade Affect Your Standard of Living

Restraints of Trade in Peace Time

GENERALIZATIONS about a free market and restraints of trade have become a drug on the market. What consumers really want to know more concretely is how the evils of monopoly affect their daily lives. The best way of presenting that picture is by giving a kaleidoscopic series of actual examples. In this way the reader may observe the cumulative effects of such restraints in destroying free trade between the states. He can see how the unbalance of prices which they cause creates the need for relief and subsidies. He will understand how government spending, imposed on a controlled market, ends by raising prices still higher and thus compels more spending.

Let us start with the distribution of automobiles. Here is the industry which has been the most competitive in its growth and, therefore, the most efficient of any in our economy[1] in distributing goods to the consumer. It has made the automobile a more widely distributed product than decent houses. It has changed motor fuel from a luxury to a necessity. Let us examine how a series of growing restraints in the field of motor distribution can hamper the distribution of other commodities such as food.

We will begin with the man who lives across the road from my house just outside Washington. He has been having a hard time for the past few years. He has a few acres, but he is always behind on the rent because he has no cash income. His cow and pigs do not give him a balanced diet. His children are not getting an even start in this world. His family is poorly clothed and his house is in bad condition. He is a burden on the State because from time to time he has to rely on relief or on charity.

For a while he was fortunate enough to have a job on a construction project. He saved fifty dollars. One day I was astounded to find that he had paid fifty dollars down on a shiny, new, second-hand car, priced at $400. The balance was on installments. I felt indignant at such improvidence. If the poor act like this how can they expect the taxpayers to help them? I therefore considered it my duty as a citizen and a taxpayer to tell him what I thought.

He replied, "I had to buy that car because I am losing my job." This answer seems absurd until we analyze what is back of it. When he lost his job he had to apply for relief. He told me that he would be willing enough to save his fifty dollars for a rainy day if he could use it to eke out the miserable standard of food and clothing for people on relief. "But they won't let me on relief so long as I have fifty dollars," he explained. "They will let me on relief if I have a car that isn't paid for. Anyway, I can get more for my fifty dollars by buying this car than if I buy anything else."

Of course he will never pay for that car. Sooner or later it will be taken back, when there is some other place to put it. It will absorb this man's fifty dollars and such installments as he can pay. Then it will take up someone else's thirty dollars and next a third person's twenty-five dollars. On its way to the junk yard it will act like a piece of blotting paper, soaking up money that should go to the producers of food and clothing,—competitive industries which are trying to sell their goods in an organized market.

But how is it possible for a man who can't pay for a car to buy one? The answer is that great finance companies issue a kind of fiat currency, called installment paper, which can be discounted at banks. Back of this paper is a long procession of cars on their way to the junk yard, but each individual car is so far away from the promissory note which it secures that nobody knows or cares who has it. The second-hand cars support the automobile installment currency just as the gold buried in the Kentucky hills supports the national currency. Everybody believes it is there—and that confidence is sufficient.

There is another important angle. Suppose you offer cash for one of these second-hand cars. You will find that ability actually to pay for the car gives you no advantage over the man who cannot pay for it. There is practically no competitive market in second-hand cars for those who want to buy. The whole machine is geared to keep up the price of second-hand cars. Installment selling is an important factor in keeping up the price of second-hand cars. If the cars had to be sold for cash, obviously prices would have to come down to move them. Installment sales at high prices are desired by the industry in preference to cash sales. The reason is that if second-hand cars were sold at really competitive prices they would sell so low that they would compete with new cars. This would mean that the prices of new cars would have to come down or else the automobile companies would have to get out a cheaper and more efficient car—a new "tin lizzie" that would get you there and get you back with less fuel.

Reliable automobile engineers tell me that it is possible to make an excellent light car to sell for $300 which will go forty miles on a gallon of gasoline. Such a car would give the consumer cheaper transportation. It would also give the farmer a greater portion of the consumer's dollar (because consumers would then have more money to spend for things the farmer raises), so that it would take less government subsidies to keep the farmers afloat. But such a free market would cause a loss of millions to the great automobile manufacturers by forcing them to change their present highly organized processes in order to put out the $300 car.

Therefore, it is only natural that the automobile manufacturers should try to put a floor under the price of second-hand cars so that they will not absorb the cash which goes into new cars.

THE BOTTLENECKS OF BUSINESS

I do not wish to raise here any question as to the legality of combinations which have secured for automobiles such strategic advantages in the national market that the poor go without proper diet and housing to buy them.* Nor do I wish to blame the automobile for a situation which no one in the industry intentionally created. (Railroads are now selling vacation tickets on installments.) I use the automobile industry only to illustrate how domination of the market in the distribution of one important product may finally reach a stage where it unbalances our entire distribution system. The automobile industry has grown up under free competitive forces. That growth has been marked by efficiency of production and distribution. It is now in a position of power where the balance wheel of competition has become less effective. General Motors, today, is reaching out toward market domination in every type of automobile, in refrigerators, and in motor fuel. This constant expansion is accompanied by a like increase of its already vast powers over consumer finance. It is tak-

* The question of the legality of the control of finance companies by automobile manufacturers was raised indirectly in the criminal prosecution in which Ford, Chrysler, and General Motors were indicted on the charge of coercing dealers to use exclusively the finance company affiliated with the manufacturer. Ford and Chrysler entered into a decree in which they agreed to abandon their control of financing under certain protections against impositions by loan sharks. General Motors declined to enter into such a decree. It was convicted of violating the antitrust laws at South Bend, Indiana. The case is now on appeal. If a conviction is sustained, the Government expects to bring a suit to dissolve the combination of General Motors and the General Motors' finance company. Until the Supreme Court decides the case, it is impossible to state the law with any finality.

ing mortgages on the consumers' dollars of the future. How many such mortgages may be taken without unreasonably restraining trade?

The determination of that question is the function of the antitrust laws. In this situation an antitrust investigation would compel a choice between two policies. The first policy would be to attack in court as unreasonable the power over consumer finance now exercised which gives the motor industry such advantages over distribution. The second policy would be to refer the situation to Congress in order to develop consumer finance in other lines so that home building would be on a competitive basis with automobiles. Because it compels that choice, an antitrust investigation is the best method for focusing attention upon an industry whose power is approaching the danger point. It compels us to devise remedies for such situations not in the abstract but case by case in the light of the particular facts of each industry.

But there is another reason why even the efficient and reasonable use of enormous size and power must be watched, and that is to prevent others from using such an industry as the springboard from which to exploit the consumer. With this in mind, let us look at the oil industry from which the man across the road must immediately buy since after he has once bought his car gasoline becomes a necessity.

Therefore, when gasoline becomes a necessity control of the market is in effect the power to tax. The poor will go without a proper diet in order to ride. The lords of the gasoline market can take away cash income from the farmer and send him to the government begging for subsidies, (which he must spend for more gasoline) , simply putting a floor under the price of motor fuel.

Suppose, therefore, we examine the marketing of motor fuel which the man across the road must buy. We find that the distribution of 85 per cent of all the motor fuel in the United States has been controlled by a combination of the Ethyl Corporation and the refiners. Here we may speak more positively about the illegality of the combination (in which General Motors had a part) because it has been recently condemned by the Supreme Court of the United States.[2] It was worked in the following way:

The Ethyl Corporation was jointly owned by the Standard Oil Company of New Jersey, the General Motors Corporation, and the Du Pont interests. It had a patent on a fluid called "Ethyl" which made gasoline much more efficient for high compression engines. To make ordinary anti-knock motor fuel (called regular gasoline) required only one gallon of this patented fluid for forty-two hundred gallons of unpatented gasoline.

The Ethyl Corporation got its profits by selling the fluid, but it also had a patent on the motor fuel made by mixing the patented fluid with ordinary gasoline. Thus it was able to control the distribution of 4200 gallons with one gallon of Ethyl fluid. Under this patent it gave away free of charge to 123 refiners the right to make and sell this motor fuel. The refiners agreed in return that they would sell only to persons who were licensed by the Ethyl Corporation. The Ethyl Corporation then followed a policy of refusing to license those who did not follow the "marketing policies and posted prices" of the major oil companies or their market leaders. Thus was the system of distribution controlled.

There was also direct price fixing. The refiners agreed that they would establish a fixed differential of two cents per gallon in price between regular and high test gasoline. The difference in cost is much less than that. In this way the patent was used to maintain an open price-fixing scheme which took away money which might have been spent for farm products and gave it to the refiners.

The decision declaring that the patent licensing system of the Ethyl Corporation was illegal had far reaching effects because the same method of eliminating competitors was familiar throughout American industry. Patents were used to fix prices and control the whole distribution of a commodity. There are 153 patents on one type of wallboard used in building houses.[3] The American Telephone and Telegraph Company controls 15,000 patents. The General Electric Company controls between 8,000 and 9,000 patents. The money which the government spends for war materials is spent in a series of industries where prices are controlled by a similar use of patents.

Let us see how this same type of patent control works in another field—the spectacle industry. There is a pat-

THE BOTTLENECKS OF BUSINESS

ent on a spectacle frame which is in common use. Through that patent the price to the consumer of both frames and lenses is controlled. The device was the same as that used by the Ethyl Corporation, *i.e.*, to refuse to license distributors who want to cut prices. There is no economic reason why the ten-cent stores should not sell spectacles. The argument is made that it is necessary to the health of the public that good optometrists be employed. However, Woolworth's is in as good a financial position to hire a good optometrist as is anyone else. The fact is that merchants who are willing to distribute spectacles cheaply have been unable to get hold of the best type of product. The only spectacles which they could sell were made from inferior Japanese lenses with inferior frames.

Spectacles are a necessity. It is estimated that 21 million people in the United States need them. The tax on low income groups by fixing the price of spectacles is enormous. And again it is also a tax on the farmer because the family of $1500 a year who pays $10 too much for a pair of spectacles must take it out of the budget for diet or for clothes.

It seems a far cry from spectacles to Ethyl gasoline. Yet the decision of the case against the Ethyl Corporation led directly to a reduction of the cost of spectacles in Washington. The story is told in two full-page advertisements which appeared in the *Washington Daily News* on April 19 and June 3, 1940 shortly after the decision in the *Ethyl* Case.

The first advertisement reads as follows:

28

THE BOTTLENECKS OF BUSINESS

A week after this advertisement, the dealer received a call and was told to stop cutting prices. He complained to the Department of Justice. Shortly after that four indictments were handed down.[4] Then followed a second full-page advertisement, shown opposite.

Such situations are easy to deal with if there is an organization in the Antitrust Division able to take care of complaints, and to watch the distribution of the principal necessities of living. If that organization is on the job ripples of one antitrust investigation will spread in all directions. Offhand there seems to be as little connection between the price of gasoline and the price of hosiery as there was between gasoline and spectacles, and yet the revolutionary decision of the Supreme Court of the United States in the Ethyl Case had the following interesting results in the distribution of hosiery.

The Du Pont interests are one of the principal owners of the Ethyl Corporation. They have also developed a new thread called Nylon which they control by patents. It is supposed to make a better stocking than has ever been made before. At the time the Ethyl decision was handed down, Du Pont was proposing by a patent licensing system to control the price at which stockings made from Nylon would be sold. If Nylon hose fulfills expectations, it may revolutionize the stocking industry. Other processes may become obsolete. Capital will be lost. Men will lose their jobs. Such technological change in the long run will work to distribute more goods provided the savings of the new process are passed on to the consumer. It may mean a temporary

loss of capital and wages in the industry made obsolete by the new product, but the farmer and the laborer will gain in the long run because a smaller proportion of the dollars consumers spend will go for stockings. Therefore, the man across the road can get a better diet and make his house warmer for the winter even though his wife insists on silk stockings. Unorganized industry will have a better chance to get a part of the consumer's dollar than before the invention was made.

But suppose that Nylon does succeed in destroying the manufacturers of other stockings *without distributing the savings to consumers.* The farmer will still have to pay *almost* as much for his wife's stockings. He won't have any extra money to buy her a new dress. And the people who made the old type of stockings and have been put out of business can no longer buy his farm products. This is exactly what the Du Pont Company proposed to do. After the Ethyl decision and at the suggestion of the Department of Justice the Du Pont Company voluntarily dropped its proposed plan of control. It was a simple case of policing economic traffic without the necessity of calling anyone to court, made possible because the Antitrust Division had an economic section on the job, watching the development of key industries. Suppose that these men had not been available. On the 15th of May, 1940, the licenses would have gone into effect. If complaint had been made years later, after the lines of control had been consolidated and vested interests had become intrenched, innocent investors might have suffered. The moving picture cartel grew up under government neglect. It is going to take years of expensive litigation and loss to stockholders to straighten it out.

But there is another aspect to price fixing which few people realize. It does not necessarily mean more profits because it creates wasteful and more expensive distribution. When great organizations succeed in putting a floor under prices, they still compete with each other for the greatest share of the market, without dropping prices. The competition takes the form of adding unnecessary luxuries to the distribution system. This raises its cost. It forces a luxury system of distribution on low income groups.

Take the oil companies as an example. The major oil companies aided by the Ethyl Corporation had put a floor under prices. There is no difference in motor fuels because they had become standardized. Competition has become a race to see which company could put out the most expensive hokum. Millions have been spent in advertising different brands that were in fact all the same. Filling stations more luxurious than the homes of most of the customers appeared on every corner. Maps were given away free. Unnecessary services were added. Men were hired to smile at poor customers and say "Happy Motoring." All this meant that a greater share of the customer's dollar was going into gasoline. The government relief checks filled the gap and helped pay for that hokum.

The effect on the efficiency of distribution was this:—
On an average throughout the country major costs of both refining and transportation have been 6 cents a gallon. The average cost of getting the gas through ten

feet of hose into your car has been 6 cents a gallon. Thus the savings from an efficient technological process were all absorbed by a wasteful system of distribution. They were not passed on to the consumer.

Take tobacco as another example. There is no price competition among the companies dominating the industry. There is plenty of competition at rigid prices. This means that most tobacco advertising is expensive hokum. Cigarettes have become a necessity. Yet the ten-cent cigarette packet cannot get a foothold in a market where half the family incomes are under $1000 a year.

Let us turn from the things the man across the road must buy and look at an example of a great new enterprise trying to get a chance to sell more modern and better equipment in a controlled market.

Within the last few years the design of sleeping cars has improved enormously, partly through the ideas of a new competitor of Pullman, the Budd Manufacturing Company. In a competitive market Pullman would have been compelled to scrap its old equipment in order to compete with Budd. But Pullman has a virtual monopoly on the operation of sleeping cars, and it is able to force the railroad to use its old equipment by threatening withdrawal of all sleeping car service if the railroads themselves buy new equipment from Budd.* This is a familiar monopoly device. It resembles block

* In July 1940 an antitrust proceeding was begun against the Pullman Company in the United States District Court in Philadelphia charging generally the facts set out in this paragraph.

booking in movies, or full line forcing in the liquor industry. It was effective in keeping Pullman cars of obsolete design in service. However, we are concerned here with the economic effect of throttling a new competition in the car field. The continuance of the old equipment made it unnecessary for the Pullman Company to manufacture new cars until the old ones had worn out. It prevented Budd from hiring more labor to make better cars. It relieved Pullman of the necessity of hiring more labor to build cars to compete with Budd. The labor that was not hired could not buy houses or food. Taxpayers had to dig up to keep it on W.P.A. projects or relief.

This is only a single example of the kind of thing that happens over and over again in great industries. Let the reader use his imagination as to the cumulative effect of the repetition of this kind of restraint of trade throughout our economy. It is easy to prevent if there is an adequate force to patrol the road—but if it is let alone it grows like weeds in a tropical garden.

Thus far we have seen from this kaleidoscopic picture how restraints of trade in one industry draw purchasing power away from other industries, causing loss to consumers and to business, labor, and agriculture. There is no one industry that has suffered more under a multiplicity of restraints of trade than the building industry. Therefore we will discuss in some detail the way they operate in that industry.

THE BOTTLENECKS OF BUSINESS

Restraints of Trade in the Building Industry.

Dr. Isadore Lubin, in his testimony before the Temporary National Economic Committee,[5] stated that we needed 525,000 new housing units per year for the next ten years in order to maintain even our present inadequate percentage of housing in the United States. It appeared from the testimony given before the Committee that there was little chance of getting these units under the restraints of trade then existing. In order to get any houses built the government has had to step in with various kinds of subsidies and housing projects— and this spending has not yet primed the pump.

Let us examine the market in which the government had to spend its housing money. The problem of unreasonable restraints in the building industry is not primarily one of whether a concern is big or little. It is as unreasonable for a small organization to prevent the use of standardized products, which can only be produced on a large scale, as it is for a large organization to eliminate the competition of small organizations which offer lower prices. Indeed, the boycott of standardized materials produced by large organizations is one of the principal types of restraints of trade found today in the building industry. The stoppage of the flow of competing materials and services in commerce is equally illegal, whether it be done by manufacturers, distributors, contractors, labor, or by vertical combinations of all of them, or whether it be accomplished through municipal ordinances and state laws many of

36

which in reality are not building regulations but protective tariffs against other parts of the nation.

In the building industry we are confronted with a series of restraints, protective tariffs, and aggressive combinations which has practically stopped progress. No one knows how a house ought to be built or what materials are the most economical or how they should be distributed. Because of the existence of aggressive combinations, experimentation in housing can proceed only by compromise with various gangs. Both standardized equipment and experiments with standardized methods are limited in large scale housing projects largely because of these compromises.

The building industries have frankly given up half their job. They take for granted that it is impossible, as things are today, for them to build houses without public aid and sell them cheaply enough that the lowest paid half of the population can afford to live in them. This has been true for four reasons: that financing costs were high; that taxes were high; that land was high; and that the costs of construction were high. The government stepped in to help on the financing. It provided cheap credit and even subsidies. But the easing of this difficulty only afforded an opportunity for costs of construction to go still higher.

Let us examine why pump-priming on the housing market failed to start the pump. It will add to our kaleidoscopic picture of restraints of trade because a house is a tangle of goods and services. No single heavy industry, nor the distributors of its products, nor the contractor who installs them, nor the labor that works

on them can do anything alone to affect the final price
of the house. If any one of these groups competes, it only
handicaps itself for the benefit of others. Like a number of dogs who have hold of the same piece of meat,
none of them dares let go. Housing is the kind of
industry in which all the restraints must be prosecuted
at the same time in order to get any economic effect. To
make this clear let us summarize the kind of restraints
of trade the Antitrust Division has discovered in the
building industry.*

I. Producers of building materials

Producers of building materials have fixed prices
either by private arrangement or as the principal activity of trade associations. Owners of patents on building
materials have used them to establish restrictive structures of price control, control of sales methods, and
limits upon the quantities sold, in direct contradiction
of the broad intent of the patent laws to encourage,
through inventions, the development and spread of new
productive methods. Some of these patent holders have
taken advantage of their control over patented products to require their licensees to give them control of
unpatented products also. By the use of basing point
systems, and zone price systems, various building material industries have established by formula a rigid
structure of uniform prices throughout the country;

* The material which follows is taken from the author's
testimony before the Temporary National Economic Committee. *Id.* at 5144-5162.

and in some of these industries such price formulas have encouraged the wasteful location of industrial plants and the wasteful shipment of products to great distances. The use of joint selling agencies has been another means by which some of these groups have undertaken to maintain their prices. In some groups the various producers have subscribed to the theory that every member of the industry should have a definite share of whatever business there is to be done, and that no concern should try to get more than its share by price competition.

Supplementing these various devices for keeping the prices of building materials high have been a series of other devices used to discipline competitors who are unwilling to play ball. In one industry the means is cutting off the supply of raw materials. In another it is starting a series of harassing lawsuits. In a third it is the harassment of distributors by selling through the seller's own factory branches at prices lower than those at which the distributor is permitted to resell. In a fourth it is the maintenance of orthodox channels of distribution by concerted refusal to sell to groups representing new methods of sale or new price policies.

Overlying this mass of practices, often as a result of the pressure placed upon the weaker and smaller competitors, there is a growing concentration of control in many of these industries. For the most part the increase in the size of the business unit has not been the necessary result of more machinery and bigger plants; it has come about by the merger of competing enterprises which continued after their union to pro-

39

duce in very much the same way as before. Its chief significance has been an increase in the power of the particular business unit and greater ease in reaching an understanding with the two or three other large concerns in the industry.

II. Distribution of Building Materials

Various groups of distributors of building materials engage in two kinds of restrictive practice. First, they try to raise the price of their services by establishing a fixed mark-up between the price they pay the manufacturer and the price at which they resell. For this purpose they collusively determine their mark-up or their selling price, and sometimes agree among themselves to boycott manufacturers who will not cut off supplies from price-cutting distributors. Sometimes they conspire with manufacturers' groups to establish a joint price control binding upon the manufacturers' and the distributors' organizations alike.

The second type of restraint by distributors arises from the effort to see to it that all business passes through their hands and that no new methods of distribution are introduced which may dispense with their services. The great weapon in this field is the boycott. Groups of wholesale distributors may boycott those who sell direct to retailers. Groups of retailers may boycott those who sell direct to mail order houses or direct to the ultimate consumers. Sometimes the members of a distributors' organization will boycott any manufacturer who sells in their territory to non-members. To secure freedom in methods of distribution, some manufacturers have found it necessary to pay the distributor a commission on sales even when the customer and the manufacturer have dealt direct and the distributor has had no part in the transaction.

III. Contractors

Contractors who erect buildings add their own systems of restraint. Many contracting groups maintain bid depositories in which copies of all bids and estimates are supposed to be filed prior to the award of the contract. In some of these depositories the bids are opened before the contract is let and the information thus obtained is used to coerce low bidders to withdraw or raise their bids. Other contractor groups maintain central estimating bureaus which calculate the cost of the job and supply the various contractors with the bids they are to make. In still other groups a central bureau determines the specifications for materials and labor to be included in the bid, and the contractor is expected to apply standard prices and labor rates to these specifications and thereby to arrive at the same bid as everyone else. Some bidding rings determine in advance which contractor is to get the job and arrange their bids so that everyone else bids higher than he.

In addition to these efforts to control their charges for services, many of these groups set up little closed markets from which they exclude outside contractors or new types of services. They may try to keep all the contracting work for local contractors or for contractors

THE BOTTLENECKS OF BUSINESS

who are members of the association. They may refuse to use materials which have been bought from any source of supply other than themselves. They may insist that prefabricated products be not used in the buildings they work in. They may cooperate with contractors interested in other materials, so that no contracting group will work on a building if a product assembled at the factory is used contrary to the wishes of some other group.

IV. Labor

The building trades unions often participate in these policies of restraint and add new restraints of their own. In recent years they have frequently been used as the strong-arm squads for collusive agreements among contractors, refusing to supply labor where the contractors' ring wishes labor withheld. In other cases the unions themselves have refused to permit the use of new products or new processes because of their fear that the new method might make it possible to erect a house with fewer hours of labor than the old.

V. Legislative Restraints on Trade

Such practices crystallize and lead to legislative restraints on trade. Many building regulations are, in reality, protective tariffs. The licensing and registration of contractors by boards of contractors affords a means of discipline over contractors. In one state, a contractor who must take out a license, is one who un-

42

dertakes "to construct, alter, repair, add to, subtract from, improve, move, wreck, or demolish any building, highway, road, railroad, excavation, or other structure, project, development, or improvement, or to do any part thereof, including the erection of any scaffolding, or other structure, or works in connection therewith."

To this broad class of work, which includes practically everything, the statute applies a method of rating bidders according to vague standards interpreted by the contractors themselves. It then puts handicaps on out-of-state contractors and out-of-state products. This is not an isolated example.

On top of legislative restrictions are added municipal ordinances designed to restrain competition. They start out from the fact that there must be protection from fire and safeguards of minimum health requirements. They develop into legally established boycotts, particularly relating to walls, roofs, electrical work, and plumbing. I am reliably informed that the plumbing which is good enough for the magnificent Department of Justice building in Washington, D. C., cannot be used in private homes in many cities.

I do not need to elaborate the significance of these restraints, particularly during a time of huge expenditure for war materials. Most of them are intended to raise or maintain prices and have been successful in doing so. Although the decline in the volume of construction was conspicuously greater than that of most other industries during the depression which began in 1929, the level of building materials prices and of building costs fell less than that of other prices. When

THE BOTTLENECKS OF BUSINESS

building recovery began, the effect was just the reverse. By 1936 the volume of construction, including public work, had recovered from the four billion dollars of 1933 to about eight billion. From 1936 to 1937 it rose less than half a billion dollars, and in the latter year totaled not quite eight and a half billion dollars, a little less than two-thirds of the volume to be expected at prosperity levels. Urban residential construction rose about 27 per cent during the year, but was still only 40 per cent of the 1929 level. Nevertheless, during that year the cost of constructing a small house rose more than 10 per cent throughout the United States and in some large cities rose about 25 per cent. Building costs have proved flexible upward but not downward. The aggregate effect of the restraints in the building industry appears to be a gigantic stairway of prices and costs on which the height attained during the period of rising prices becomes the taking-off point for mounting to the next period.

In a free market subsidies and relief should have acted as a temporary stimulus. In the controlled market of the building industry they actually tended to perpetuate the vicious system which has kept the price of housing up and made subsidies necessary. They operated actually to raise prices instead of to lower them. Taking New York City as an example, we find the volume of building doubled under government subsidy and credit in 1936 and 1937. Theoretically, since there was no scarcity of goods or materials, this greater volume should have lowered prices. Actually prices rose 25 per cent. As a result the ordinary man had to pay

44

for these subsidies three times, once in taxes, once in prices when he built his own house during that temporary boom, and a third time in loss of wages when that temporary boom collapsed. Under such circumstances the building boom choked itself off and the subsidies became only a bonus for inefficiency. This is typical of what happens to plans to stimulate industry when there is no free market. And thus in an economy where free markets are choked we are presented with the absurd spectacle of the poor riding around in cars and paying fixed prices for gasoline while the government has to keep their children fed and a roof over their heads.

You can't spend relief money in a market like that without subsidizing inefficiency and thus raising both prices and taxes. Neither can you spend national defense money effectively in that kind of market.

III.

How Restraints of Trade Unbalance the National Budget

WHERE restraints of trade are let alone they grow like weeds because they are profitable. After they have become established, they are capitalized—that is, given a value in dollars and cents. Investors put their savings into them. Even charities and colleges become dependent on them. They become part of the so-called "capital structure." This gives them enormous power to maintain themselves against the more efficient new organizations which would destroy them in a free market. The sudden deflation of an artificial price structure is always painful. It creates pressures that are usually strong enough to compel the government to step in to ease the shock. But the pressures to protect the capitalized restraint of trade continue during the period of adjustment. Those who have invested in a wasteful system of distribution come to regard it as part of the nation's wealth. They demand the indefinite continuance of a price structure which will pay them dividends, even though it is beyond the purchasing power of consumers. If they succeed in their demands, the government is

46

called on to subsidize consumers. As long as this situation exists the national budget can never be balanced.

No one would deny that a cushion must sometimes be provided against too sudden deflation of a capitalized restraint of trade which would otherwise destroy the savings of a vast army of people. It may be likened to giving a local anaesthetic while a tooth is being pulled. But to give a series of such local anaesthetics without pulling the tooth will soon cause trouble over the entire body of the patient. With this sort of treatment the patient may begin with a sore tooth and end a permanent invalid. Price fixing is a most dangerous economic opiate. It should never be freely dispensed by private groups without public responsibility. And even where it is administered by the government it needs the utmost scrutiny and safeguards.

Perhaps the most plausible excuse for using the economic drug of price fixing is found where it is used to protect *small* business against what is called ruinous competition, because the public sympathizes with the troubles of the small business man. This was the excuse given by the major oil companies when they were convicted for putting a floor under prices in the mid-continent field.[1] In the argument before the Supreme Court of the United States to reverse that conviction, the attorney for these companies argued that stabilizing prices was the "human thing to do." He meant that the majors were protecting the independents. But for every dollar that the independents got by this price-fixing method, the public was forced to pay four dollars to the major companies. No more wasteful and expensive way of keeping the independents in business could be imagined.

But this economic drug has other consequences. It is an indirect expense to the government. It also destroys the market for other products whose prices are not fixed. This may be most conveniently illustrated by spelling out the effects of price-fixing in a comparatively small combination among the gasoline filling stations in Washington.

Washington is supported practically entirely by the government. There are no productive industries there. The government must pay salaries high enough so that its employees can live. Higher living costs in Washington mean higher salaries. Already these costs are far above many sections of the country. The Washington salaries are also higher, but because Washington is an expensive place government employees are unable to live as well as in cities with lower salaries. Neither the government nor the consumer is getting any benefits from these higher salaries, but they go on our tax bills just the same.

As this chapter was being written the Washington filling stations got together to end competition—which they referred to as a price war—and to fix gasoline prices high enough so that all the filling stations could survive. The Antitrust Division estimated that the increased price would cost the consumers in Washington $2,000,000 a year. This $2,000,000 a year would have had to come out of the United States Treasury because it is the only source of income for Washington.

The Antitrust Division immediately called a grand

jury to prosecute the conspiracy. Indignant friends of poor filling station proprietors flooded us with protests. They said, "Some of these fellows running filling stations will practically starve to death without this price rise. They are not making a fair profit even if they get the extra 2 cents. Why do you pick on them?"

In order to see how expensive this kind of subsidy is let us assume that the government by means of relief or otherwise must give these indigent filling station proprietors a living. Let us assume that these indigent filling stations sell about one-third of the volume of gas (an estimate which is probably too high).

In order to give them $600,000 the government must pay out $2,000,000 through this method of putting a floor under their prices. This is a fantastically expensive way of giving relief to the poor filling station proprietors even if we agree that they should be paid for performing an unnecessary service. It is inconceivably worse than any kind of boon-doggling. It is not only useless but it costs three dollars to the government for every one dollar paid to the gasoline boon-dogglers. A rich nation may be able to afford this sort of thing in peace time. It cannot afford it when it is straining every effort to prepare for war.

But this is not all. If this money were paid directly for boon-doggling it would take one dollar out of taxes and add one dollar to consumers' purchasing power. The farmer would get some of it. When it is collected by means of a fixed price on a necessity, the government clerk getting $1800 a year has twenty-five or thirty dollars added to his gasoline bill. Since rents will not come

down there is only one place the clerk can take this
thirty dollars from and that is from his diet. The farmer
loses a $2,000,000 market for his goods. But even
this is not all. Food costs go up in Washington because
it takes gasoline to transport food, and this adds further to the spread between the farm and the table. This
is how price fixing of necessities not only costs the
government money but makes the farmer less able to
pay the taxes to supply that money.

But it took only a few dollars to clean up this situation because there was a policeman on the job. Here is
how it came out (*Washington Post*, June 26, 1940):

NEW GASOLINE PRICE WAR LOOMS IN D. C.

Dealers' Organization Dissolved; No-Discount Agreement Banned

The District's 700 gasoline retailers last night were
faced with the possibility of a new price-cutting war as the
Justice Department announced the dissolution of the retailers' association and the rupture of a program which
ended a 2-cents-a-gallon discount for cash.

The Justice Department's statement revealed it had sus-
pended an investigation of the alleged price-fixing program as a result of a move by the Washington Retailers,
Inc., to break up its organization.

On May 20 a meeting of the retailers voted to halt a
price war and stop the practice of allowing a discount of 2
cents a gallon for cash sales.

This agreement, the Justice Department maintained,
was a violation of the Sherman Antitrust laws.

With the no-discount agreement banned by the Justice

Department, and its organization dissolved, the retailers were threatened with a renewal of the price war which for the past several years forced 75 per cent of the filling stations to sell gas at the cut-rate price.

Effect of the discount has been disastrous for the retailers, according to James D. Gouldin, former president of the association. "The cut rates cost the retailers $1,800,-000 a year," he said.

On the other hand, the Justice Department declared on opening its investigation, that the end of the discount system virtually raised the price of gas by 2 cents, at a cost of $2,000,000 to local consumers.

In a letter to Thurman Arnold, Assistant Attorney General in charge of the antitrust division, the retailers' association said:

"It has always been the purpose and intent of our association to act within the letter and spirit of the law. After conferring with members of your staff, we have decided to discontinue . . . the program. Steps will be taken forthwith to effect the dissolution of our corporation . . ."

In a vigorous industrial democracy no one expects his profits to be guaranteed against competition of any sort. It is a race to the swift. That is what makes it the most efficient way of distributing goods. When private groups are allowed to protect themselves against competitive forces, industrial democracy grows soft and finally ends by becoming completely dependent on government, while at the same time it fears government. Let us see how this happens.

Suppose you are a small merchant. You have worked all your life to build up a business which you think is worth about a hundred thousand dollars in good will

and inventory. Suppose that your town has stopped
growing because of a flattening population curve and
on top of that because the incomes of three-fourths of
the families are under $1500. What has actually hap-
pened is that your store has ceased to be worth a hundred thousand dollars. But you do not want to admit
this. If you did this the savings of a lifetime would appear to be gone. Therefore, you join with the other
merchants in the town in order to fight the cheaper
methods of distribution, which you think are destroying your savings. You organize to keep cut-rate stores
out of the town. You boycott cheap products from other
states. I know of one town where this practice has made
building prices 26 per cent higher than in another town
across the state line only 40 miles away.

Even though you keep prices up you still do not
make any money, since in the long run prosperity does
not come from restraining trade. You then turn to the
legislature, or the City Council and seek stronger methods of protection against competition you think is destroying your savings. You get ordinances passed which
make it difficult for outsiders to ship goods in. You get
state laws passed which are protective tariffs. And thus
the Balkanization of the United States proceeds.

You still do not make any money. You see a lot of idle
men in your town who cannot work because the channels of trade are blocked. You think the only thing to
do is to get money into your town somehow, and so you
write your Congressman to back this or that local subsidy. Of course, you are a solid, substantial citizen, and
you are in favor of balancing the budget for other peo-

ple and in other sections of the country. Nevertheless, you send wires and letters to your Congressman and Senators telling them that you need a new government project in order for *your* town to survive. This is the explanation of the constantly recurring phenomena which we see in our legislative halls, *to wit*: long speeches in favor of the principle of budget balancing coupled with off-the-record votes which increase the spending by pure log-rolling methods on the part of different communities and different groups. The real cause is the absence of a free market.

When the spending mounts up you begin to worry about taxes and so you try to cut everybody's subsidies but your own. The result of this is that the unorganized groups who need the subsidies worst lose out in the shuffle, and the stronger groups who need the subsidies least get them. No better example of this is found than in the huge subsidies which are given to the silver-mining industries which employ only 8,000 men. I will not pause to give other examples.

The following headline from the *New York Times* of April 4, 1940 tells a story that is repeated over and over again as the result of such pressures:

SENATE GROUP PADS FUNDS
FOR RIVERS DEFYING PRESIDENT

$25,000,000 for 50 Projects Is Added
Despite Warning Against Increases

You can make out your own additional list of these local subsidies. They are intended to stimulate busi-

THE BOTTLENECKS OF BUSINESS

ness. The point is that there can be no rational adjustment where spending is needed to stimulate business unless it is imposed on a free market. The cause of spending to prime the pump is the destruction of a free market, and at the same time it is the reason why such spending never does prime the pump according to expectations.

The impotence of current criticism of subsidies to prevent both political parties from voting them is so plain that he who runs may read. Picking up the *Washington Post* on Easter Sunday, 1940, I find the following editorial:

Critical Weakness

The Senate's approval of the agricultural supply bill authorizing the expenditure of more than $1,000,000,000 is an utterly irresponsible act. In effect, the Senate has said that borrowed money must continue to pour from the Treasury into the pockets of the farmer, regardless of what the budgetary situation may be.

Apparently the road to bankruptcy has no perils for a majority of the Senators when they see prospects of reaping political harvests along the right of way next November. They came face to face with one of the gravest problems that can arise to plague a democracy. But instead of meeting the issue courageously, the Senate yielded to the philosophy of Mr. Wilkins Micawber without a record vote.

I do not happen to agree with the current criticism of all farm subsidies. Indeed, I see no escape from them in the present condition of national exchange between farm products and manufactured goods. But whether I am right or wrong about this, it is apparent that neither political party dares oppose them today. The reason is sharply outlined in the following headlines in the *Washington Star* on the same Sunday as the editorial just quoted:

FARMER'S CASH INCOME FAR ABOVE YEAR AGO IN TWO MONTHS

Beneath it, however, is the rest of the story:

*More Than Half of Big Gain Comes
from Benefit Payments*

Turning back to the *Washington Post*, I find a special article dealing with unemployment, the headlines of which read:

PUBLIC WEIGHS RESULTS OF 9-BILLION EXPENDITURE

*Benefits of Road-Building, Airport and
School Constructions, Lunches to
Needy Are Debated*

Is the editorial going to stop this kind of thing? Certainly not while the chart of income distribution set out on page eight is within shooting distance of accuracy. Gestures for economy, operating against economic forces too powerful to be resisted, accomplish only small and perhaps disastrous cuts in needed government services. This is illustrated by another editorial

THE BOTTLENECKS OF BUSINESS

in the *Washington Post* of March 28, 1940, only a few days after the budget balancing editorial first quoted:

Coming on the heels of the Person committee report, requesting replacement of numerous obsolete and worn out schools, the slash in funds allowed the Board of Education is very discouraging. Year after year plans for modernization of the District's school system are made, only to be brushed into the wastebasket by the appropriations subcommittee.

Failure to grant funds for any additional policemen, too is a strange response to the crime wave rampant here in recent months. When the White House recently asked that its police force be increased from 60 to 80 men the House passed the bill by unanimous consent. Such discrimination between national and local interests in the Capital City makes an extremely bad impression.

The *Washington Post* believes in budget balancing. So do I. But the result of preaching budget balancing without doing anything to destroy the pressures which cause deficits is to cut schools and police while subsidies continue.

These clippings are sufficient to illustrate the point. The farmers have settled down to the conviction that they need subsidies; no responsible political group contends that low-cost housing can be built without government aid; relief is to be with us as long as the unemployment problem remains; social security is a settled issue. The pressures of these popular demands have been strong enough to force the Republican Party (with appropriate denunciation of the Democrats) to adopt practically all of the New Deal policies. The pre-convention trial balloon platform of Glenn Frank and his hundred stalwarts approved of New Deal parity price policies, social security policies, farm subsidy policies, and housing policies. This occurred in the face of a drive for economy supported in theory, at least, by the great majority in Congress and by the entire press. Yet the forces against it have been sufficient to over-ride the Administration itself in increasing budget estimates.

When the money comes back from Washington to be spent in your town you get a new feeling of hope and so you try to recoup your losses of the past year when you didn't have any money. The only way you know of doing this is to get together with other merchants and raise prices still more. And so it happens that the consumer has to pay for the subsidy once in higher taxes, and again in higher prices. The boom which the subsidy started is thus choked off.

In the meantime the unorganized groups who have nothing but farm products or services to sell in this controlled market get poorer and poorer off. As a protection, they in turn, get together and seek to raise their own prices and their own wages. This means that they must organize boycotts against low price areas of the country, or low wage areas.

The thing which this hypothetical small merchant tries to do is identical with what the large corporation tries to do when it seeks to protect its inventories, its good will, and its system of distribution by excluding its competitors. Physicians band together to destroy low-cost systems for the distribution of medical care. The Ethyl Corporation uses its patents to prevent "destructive" price cutting in the sale of gasoline. The chemical industry does the same thing. The cement industry, and the rubber tire industry get in the habit of making identical bids. The makers of spectacles freeze a system of high-cost distribution to keep out the chiseler. It is not surprising that under these conditions labor unions feel their only salvation consists in doing the same thing.

The thing winds up, usually, with big business, little business, farmers, and labor all getting together in order to exclude from the market less fortunate members of their own class and thereby to keep up inefficient systems of distribution in which they have a vested interest. And thus our economy becomes divided against itself—half organized and half unorganized, separate, defenseless units, unable to buy or to sell without government aid.

And so we close our kaleidoscopic picture of how the uncurbed activities of private groups who have seized control of our economic toll bridges have been destroying the free market in this country since the depression. We could go on and on with our examples, but those which we have given should be enough to show how the destruction of a free market affects the consumer. One restraint leads to another. Every aggressive combination compels others to combine in self-defense. The total effect of all these various restraints is the unbalance of prices which has been the principal cause of the failure of our economy to get on its feet in the last eight years.

Industry is now awaiting the stimuli of war expenditures. Therefore, in the next chapter we will talk about the restraints of trade which affect consumers in wartime and about spending for national defense.

IV.

A Free Market In Time of National Emergency or War

THE antitrust laws must constantly defend the ideal of industrial democracy against all sorts of pressures. These pressures increase when the government is suddenly forced to buy huge quantities of defense materials from closely controlled sources of supply. The temptation to exploit consumers and the government through the domination of a suddenly expanding market is almost irresistible, and usually prevails unless it is curbed.

For that reason the need for consumer representation in national industrial policy is intensified whenever government spending on a large scale becomes necessary. In such times the fear of rising prices is felt in every home. Consumers demand protection. The pressure of that demand compels the government to put a consumer's representative on every committee of importance that directs the expanding industrial production which is the aim of the government expenditure. During past crises, however, such representation has usually been quite ineffective because it has had no real tools to work with.

For example, during the days of the NRA when there was huge government spending, the pressure of consumers compelled the setting up of committees to look after their interests. Unfortunately, these committees did not know what to do, they had no concrete program and no enforceable powers, and they were swept aside by the influence of the special interests bent on maintaining price levels against deflation. Inevitably the consumers responded by turning against the NRA itself.

Today the defense program forces on us another huge increase of government expenditures. Again a directing committee to advise on industrial expansion is appointed. Again representatives of the consumer's interest have been put upon that committee. Thus the consumer movement as usual obtains its initial place in the sun. The only question is whether these representatives are to be figureheads or whether they will have enough power to give effective protection to the great mass of low-income groups they are supposed to represent.

The pressures against consumers are already making their appearance. They are illustrated in an account in the *New York Times* of a hearing on a bill to eliminate competitive bidding and substitute negotiated contracts on a cost-plus basis in government purchases of war materials. This measure may be necessary when vast supplies have to be bought suddenly. However, the tendency to use such a proposal as a springboard to obtain unwarranted advantages for war industries is shown by the underlined passages of the *New York Times'* story:

WASHINGTON, June 19—Profits growing out of the nation's armament program caused a stormy debate today behind the closed doors of the Senate Naval Affairs Committee. The committee was "shocked," according to Senator Walsh, its chairman, to learn that the Navy Department has prepared some $1,000,000,000 worth of shipbuilding contracts on the cost-plus-10-per-cent basis which was used in the World War.

This disclosure was made by Rear Admiral Samuel M. Robinson, chief of the Bureau of Engineering, as a part of his testimony regarding the possible effect of a limitation of 7 per cent on profits from the manufacture of naval vessels and airplanes for the army and navy. The committee has reported the Naval Expansion Bill to the Senate, having added to the House draft a limitation of 7 per cent to take the place of the present limitation of 10 per cent on ships and 12 per cent on airplanes.

Competitive Bids Are Barred

The Walsh-Vinson bill, which is an Administration measure intended to expedite the shipbuilding program during the next fiscal year, would permit negotiated contracts to replace competitive bidding. Mr. Walsh said it was never the intention of Congress to permit guaranteed profits of 10 per cent, and that such a figure had been written into law as an absolute ceiling.

Mr. Walsh indicated that his committee would take steps to amend the law so that such practices would end. He added that a proviso would be written into the bill, similar

A FREE MARKET IN EMERGENCY

to the one Representative Vinson, chairman of the House
Naval Affairs Committee, put into the $4,000,000,000 Two-
ocean Navy Bill his committee reported yesterday, to forbid the disposal of naval vessels, in existence or building,
without the consent of Congress.

These provisos are intended to prevent such action as
the release of twenty torpedo boats to the British Navy
under an agreement whereby the United States Navy
waived its right to the contract in favor of later delivery or
presumably improved models.

Appear Against 7 Per Cent Limit

The argument over armament profits started when Fred
Eaton and Captain Sidney Krause, members of the staff of
the Defense Advisory Commission, appeared this morning
before the Naval Affairs Committee to testify against the
7 per cent limitation.

According to Mr. Walsh, virtually all the committee
members were indignant at the implication that American
manufacturers were seeking unwarranted profits. Members
asked the witnesses whether there had been any intimation
to them or the commission that armament plant expansion
and supply would be hampered if profits were limited to
7 per cent.

Captain Krause and Mr. Eaton replied, according to Mr.
Walsh, that there had been no direct complaints by manufacturers, but that the limitation would tend to make them
"less eager" to cooperate in the necessary production. Their
present attitude might become one of hesitancy or resistance, the witnesses said, if the profits problem were to be
attacked too vigorously.

THE BOTTLENECKS OF BUSINESS

Here is the old idea, so familiar in the last war, that national defense requires leaving the market to the control of the patriotic instincts of businessmen instead of utilizing competitive forces.

About the same time this story appeared, the tentative draft of a bill which would authorize the Attorney General to waive the antitrust laws in specific situations where the appointee thought it was necessary for national defense was submitted to the Department of Justice. This was the NRA all over again, excepting that a single individual without any hearings or public notice could approve of any private combination which without his approval might be doubtful under the law. These are only straws that show the direction of the wind which is just beginning to blow.

We have already gone through one experience of spending in so much of a hurry that we took no thought of the kind of market we were buying into. That was when we poured into a closed market the huge farm subsidies, the huge relief appropriations, and the huge W.P.A. appropriations which the depression forced us suddenly to provide. This need for unexpected spending on a large scale was used as an excuse to permit private groups to dominate the market.

When the depression created the necessity of bolstering up the money value of inventories in order to avoid national financial collapse, the NRA had a useful emergency function to perform. But because antitrust enforcement was abandoned it got so completely out of hand that it performed that function with maximum dissatisfaction. The economic history of those few years is fantastic when viewed in retrospect. Industrial combinations in no danger of bankruptcy used the Act as a cloak to fix prices against the consumer. Order and consistency became impossible. The pot simply boiled over and had to be taken off the stove.

This was not the fault of General Johnson. No man worked harder than he to get some sort of order out of that gold rush of frightened businessmen toward higher prices. The feat was impossible because there was no balance wheel which limited the NRA to the purposes for which it was passed, *i.e.,* the attainment of maximum production and employment. Code meetings went wild. Every inefficient industry demanded protection. Industries worked night and day shifts to produce goods before code provisions went into effect so that they could sell this surplus at the higher code prices when the code was adopted. Then they stopped work just when employment was needed. No one thought of indicting such conduct as an unreasonable use of organized power. We were using emergency legislation without defining the limits or the necessities of the emergency. Something might have been done to limit codes to their legitimate function had the Antitrust Division been active and known where it was going. The NRA would have achieved entirely different results if it had been balanced by vigorous antitrust enforcement. The failure to provide any brake whatever let the whole thing get out of control.

Of course during the NRA period no one thought of the Sherman Act as a protection to consumers or as a means of limiting the use of a legislative privilege.

THE BOTTLENECKS OF BUSINESS

During forty years of private enforcement the Act had been translated into an attack on trusts or big business, merely because it was big. This made it appear as opposed to efficiency, and therefore something which should be thrown overboard when times were bad. The revival of the antitrust laws since NRA makes us better prepared today for a similar emergency—the expenditure of vast sums in a hurried preparation for defense.

The need for national defense is starting the wheels of industry turning at greater speed. This means that more men will be employed; purchasing power will increase; dollar income of the country as a whole will go up; consumers will have more dollars to spend. The task before the consumers' representatives in this situation is to see that real wages do not go down when money wages are rising. Real wages did go down one-third in the boom which preceded our entry into the last war. Labor suffered. The farmers suffered. The white collar workers suffered. These are the great bodies of consumers which need protection today.

These consumers need protection not only on their own behalf but in the interest of the government's getting its money's worth. If there is a housing shortage, the government must pay higher wages to give its workmen houses. If the price of milk is maintained at artificial levels, more money must be paid to workmen to provide milk for their families. The race between higher wages and higher costs of living was the chief contributor to unduly expensive military preparation in the last war.

A FREE MARKET IN EMERGENCY

I do not contend that the necessities of national defense may not create the need for various types of concerted action among businessmen. In time of emergency such as war, combinations may become reasonable because of the necessities of national defense. But the Sherman Act recognizes those necessities. Its function in such periods is first, to prevent such necessary combinations from being abused by an unnecessary or incompetent industrial feudalism, and second, to keep alive the philosophy of industrial democracy by preventing the seizure of emergency power by private groups.

There will be no difficulty recognizing the necessities of national defense under the Sherman Act whenever a responsible government department is willing to go on record that any particular combination or agreement is essential. Whether a particular combination or agreement is essential for defense purposes is a question of fact. It should be decided by those most expert on such questions of fact. It should not be left to the *sub rosa* action of private groups. The sole function of the antitrust laws in such situations is to prevent the necessities of national defense from becoming a cloak for schemes which are motivated only by desire for undue private profit. The antitrust laws are the front line of defense against the unreasonable use of industrial power.

During the last war the monopolistic combinations of war industries levied a tribute on the American consumer so wasteful that it led to proposals to draft capital in the next war. The same kind of thing can happen

67

again today. Basic war materials are still dominated by small groups. Every combination in war industry needs constant scrutiny as to how it is using its organized power.

The deterrent effect of such scrutiny is a tremendous protection. For example, at the outbreak of the present war in Europe antitrust proceedings were pending in court against supposedly competing national tire manufacturers who had been submitting bids to the Treasury identical to the last cent. The war in Europe imperilled the rubber supply. Rubber products rose generally, except tires which for a time actually dropped in price. I submit that it is a fair assumption that this peculiarly reasonable attitude on the part of the tire producers was in part at least induced by the knowledge that the government knew the state of their inventories and that they would soon be called to account as to whether they were using their organized power reasonably or unreasonably.

In contrast to this, I shall cite an industry essential to national defense whose activities had never been investigated under the antitrust laws prior to 1940. I refer to the optical goods industry. I use this industry as an example because it also illustrates how a foreign government, by having a hand in the control of American domestic corporations, may hamstring our ability to produce defense materials rapidly in a sudden emergency.

When the United States entered the World War in 1917, it was suddenly discovered that large portions of war industries were in the hands of the Germans because of their control of American patents. This was particularly true of optical glass necessary in fire control apparatus, torpedo directors, binoculars, and anti-aircraft detectors. When we tried to buy optical glass we found there was not a single factory in the United States equipped to manufacture it. The government was forced to call on the public to contribute their private opera glasses and field glasses.

How did this happen? In 1906 no one manufactured optical glass in the United States. We were dependent upon Germany. When the war began, we suddenly found there was no optical glass produced in the United States. Since Germany was an enemy, our main source of supply was gone.

Our consternation at this discovery is a matter of history. Scientists of the Bureau of Standards, and army and navy technicians, were rushed to assist Bausch & Lomb to create a source of supply which their agreement with Zeiss had heretofore prevented. The Alien Property Custodian confiscated the Zeiss Optical Company's patents. That, however, made little difference for the simple reason that the productive capacity had to be created from the bottom. We were without trained technicians or physical equipment necessary to make an adequate supply of good lenses. This was an absurd situation for the most productive and mechanically skillful country in the world to be confronted with. It could have been prevented by even a superficial antitrust investigation of monopolies in defense materials.

After the war, with no antitrust enforcement, the

same thing happened all over again. In 1921 the
Bausch & Lomb Optical Company and Zeiss of Jena,
Germany, entered into an agreement which provided
that all new patents in the military line should be acquired in the name of Bausch & Lomb and held for
the exclusive use of Zeiss. Under this arrangement our
Navy Department had to pay Zeiss a royalty for the
privilege of arming our ships. Again the world market
was divided between these two monopolies. Bausch &
Lomb was prohibited from selling outside of the
United States. Zeiss was obligated not to compete
within United States territory. This, with the patent
control, gave Bausch & Lomb a monopolistic position
in this country. One of the paragraphs in the 1921
contract read as follows:[1]

B. & L. (Bausch & Lomb) obligate themselves not to
sell, directly or indirectly, military instruments to countries outside of the United States of America, and vice
versa Carl Zeiss obligate themselves not to sell such instruments directly or indirectly to the United States unless the
parties have come to an agreement regarding the conditions of sale and the prospective territories of distribution.

In paragraph 9 of the same contract Bausch & Lomb
and Zeiss agreed to conceal the existence of the contract
from third persons, and (so far as practicable) not to
disclose the contract even to their own employees.

In 1926 Bausch & Lomb was advised that the agreement was in violation of the antitrust laws. The agreement was changed in form but the performance
remained substantially the same. In 1940 the Anti-

trust Division called a grand jury to investigate Bausch & Lomb control over lenses. On March 27, 1940, an indictment was returned against Bausch & Lomb, three of its officers, Carl Zeiss of Jena and Carl Zeiss of New York, the American Zeiss representative. The indictment charged a conspiracy in restraint of trade with respect to the distribution of military optical equipment resulting in arbitrary, unreasonable, and noncompetitive prices.

Then followed the typical reaction of a private cartel. The Navy Department was building two new cruisers. Bausch & Lomb was the sole bidder for optical equipment because it controlled the supply. It informed the Navy Department that it would have to delay furnishing the range finders for these cruisers for six months because of the antitrust indictment. Bausch & Lomb thus threatened to tie up the construction of battleships while it contested its right to retain monopoly power. The threat, however, was unsuccessful. On May 21, 1940, the Bausch & Lomb Optical Company submitted to the maximum fine of $40,000 imposed on the company and its indicted officers and withdrew its suggestion to the Navy Department that the cruisers' equipment would have to be delayed six months.

The reader should not be unduly critical of Bausch & Lomb. The real fault lay in the lack of antitrust enforcement since the war. Granted an acquiescent government, such situations are bound to occur. Bausch & Lomb is cited only as a typical instance of what has been happening in every highly organized industry, particularly in war industries. Businessmen had become so accustomed to using patents to control distribution that it had become a commonplace.* To a close student of law the Ethyl case only reaffirmed an old principle that a patent could not be used unreasonably to restrain trade. To many businessmen it came as a rude awakening.

The optical situation is only one of many.[2] Limitations on production, price and distribution in particular geographical areas imposed by agreement with foreign interests have curtailed our productive capacity in respect to many important defense materials. One of the most frequently used devices is the patent privilege. The head of a large company wrote one of his subordinates in 1928:

A great many of the patents which we are operating under are very weak and if we wished to, we could break them ourselves and not pay royalties, but good business judgment, I believe, justifies the idea of paying royalties even on weak patents in order to maintain a price control picture that is helpful.

This is the kind of market in which the Army and Navy were buying year after year.

The Antitrust Division is now on the trail of similar impositions. It can clear them up provided the funds and the men are available to make prosecutions hazardous for those engaged in such practices. But nothing short of real enforcement of the Sherman Act will serve. Preaching and parades were not effective in the

* For example, note the methods by which Hartford-Empire controlled the entire glass container industry in the United States. See page 173, *infra.*

last war. They were not effective during the NRA. They will not be effective in the present emergency.

The necessities of national defense will not be jeopardized by the enforcement of the antitrust laws. If in any case the War or Navy Departments, or other appropriate government agencies, find as a fact that any particular combination or agreement is necessary for national defense, such finding would have great weight in determining the reasonableness of such combination or agreement; indeed it would be hard to find a better test of reasonableness. Or, if any industries on their own initiative are able to show that any plan they submit is essential to the defense program, the test of reasonableness is again met. The antitrust laws are not aimed against necessary preparation for defense. They are only aimed against combinations which cannot show on the particular facts that their plans of combination are reasonably necessary for defense.

The mere public submission of such plans under the regular procedure of the Antitrust Division, which will be described in detail in Chapter VII, is in itself an insurance against most of the abuses of the last war.

The defense emergency caught the Antitrust Division unprepared in men and travelling expenses. In the various prosecutions in the interests of consumers which preceded the emergency, over 1500 persons and corporations had been indicted in 87 major prosecutions. No additional funds had been granted by Congress to go into new fields on any comprehensive scale. Yet the Antitrust Division soon discovered persuasive evidence that monopolistic practices by both foreign and domestic companies, which vitally affect our national defense, had resulted in the following situations:

1. Throttling American capacity to produce essential war materials by foreign ownership and control of patents;
2. Cartelization of certain industries with price and production control in foreign hands;
3. Transmission to foreign companies of American military secrets;
4. Division of markets, fixing and restricting of price of materials essential to military preparation;
5. Collusive bidding on contracts for the Army and Navy.

Three problems arise out of our present need to spend billions for defense. The first problem is the military and naval problem of what kind of defense is necessary. This is the business of military and naval experts.

The second problem is that of insuring that the government gets its money's worth in purchases of defense materials. This is especially necessary to protect the taxpayer, whose burdens are going to be heavy enough anyway, against paying unnecessary tribute to small groups in control of war boom industries. This problem has already been discussed.

The third problem is how to protect labor, the consumer, and the farmer against rising prices of necessities caused by combinations large and small which attempt to take advantage of the war market. Though few people realize it, this constitutes a direct charge on national defense.

Let us examine antitrust enforcement in the field of materials which are equally necessary for war and for peace time use, and which therefore are apt to react in price like the old time "war babies." Potash is such a material. It is a necessary component of fertilizer. In the last war it rose to about $400 a ton. At present we have developed a greater national supply than in the last war but there is still a domestic shortage. The entire supply is closely controlled by four companies.

The problem here is not to destroy these four companies but simply to compel them to justify their organization as essential to the economic distribution of potash. If one individual controlled all the potash in this country, there is no law at present on the books which would prevent him from raising the price as high as he desired. However, fortunately no individual has that control of any necessity. A corporation is not an individual—it is an organization which restrains trade. The validity of the exercise of its organized power must, therefore, depend on whether that restraint is reasonable in the interests of efficiency, the savings of which are passed on to consumers.

Recently the four potash companies were indicted because the government charged that they were using their organized power unreasonably to fix prices. As a result of that pressure, the potash companies voluntarily entered into a decree which cut the price of potash to the farmers at a time when there was a speculative opportunity to increase it, since war had been

THE BOTTLENECKS OF BUSINESS

declared and there was an actual 12½ per cent shortage of potash in the United States.

The potash companies voluntarily proposed that they would refuse to sell to the speculators or take advantage of opportunities to sell to exporters at an increased price. They also altered their transportation charges so that farmers in Missouri may save $3.00 a ton on fertilizer. The government felt that where the four companies which controlled the supply acted in this way there was no reason for attempting to dissolve them. A decree in the federal courts was entered to this effect.

American businessmen, when faced with the necessity of justifying any particular organization in terms of efficiency and showing that the savings of that efficiency are actually passed on to consumers, are not unwilling to pay this price for continuance in power. It is absurd to expect directors of corporations to act in this way unless there is some outside compulsion. Without such compulsion the businessman who acts reasonably is penalized because of his own desire for public service. He is dropped from the Board of Directors unless he moves in the direction of the greatest short-run profit. We are not faced with a group of malevolent businessmen. They are patriotic and loyal to the government. But they are subject to pressures which alone and unaided they are unable to resist. Antitrust enforcement should see to it that farsighted and patriotic conduct is not paid for by competitive disadvantage.

The reason why pressures of this kind actually work

is that there are plenty of men within organized American industry who will take a long-run view of price policies if they can get into control of the industry and get some help from the outside. Antitrust enforcement in actual effect operates to put such men in power on boards of directors and in executive positions. The absence of antitrust enforcement results in their advice being disregarded in favor of short-run profit taking.

Figures on what antitrust enforcement actually saves are necessarily based on an estimation of what the prices would have been without an investigation. They are useful only as guesses. However, it is significant that during the period when all commodities the supply of which is affected by the war were rising, the particular war products under investigation by the Department did not increase in price. It has been estimated that investigations of newsprint, potash, nitrogen, and steel, which cost a total of about $200,000, have saved the consumers of this country $170,000,-000.*

Can a Democracy Prepare for War?

Today the defeat of France and the peril of England have created doubts whether a democracy is able to prepare itself for war against a totalitarian state. Writers compare the enormous release of revolutionary energy in Germany with the lack of industrial co-ordination in France, and blame the democratic form

* These figures are, of course, based on speculation, but they are the only way of putting at least a dollar value on the kind of service that antitrust enforcement gives to the public.

of government for France's defeat. This is a good deal like attributing the success of Napoleon's revolutionary armies to the weakness of democracy.

During the depression we wondered whether a democracy could distribute goods. Now we wonder whether a democracy can build up an army.

The answer is that an *industrial* democracy *can* distribute goods. It *can* defend itself. It is only an economic feudalism masquerading under the name of democracy that is unable to unite to serve a common national end.

It is not a new problem which democracies in the grip of private feudal combinations face today. The idea of a totalitarian state is not the original contribution of Hitler or Stalin. It was Napoleon who gave the nineteenth century the notion of a levy *en masse*, a totalitarian conscription of national resources. Theoretically, the monarchies of the 18th century had such power by divine right. Actually these monarchs were controlled by the monopolies which they themselves had created. They could not maintain an army without consulting their money-lenders. They could not relieve the farmer because private groups had taxing power, as today they have the pricing power.

Those who worry about the ability of a democracy to prepare for war fail to understand that the movements led by Napoleon and Hitler would be impossible against a vigorous industrial democracy. By this I mean a democracy able to work at full industrial capacity, since it could distribute goods to its own people instead

A FREE MARKET IN EMERGENCY

of piling them up in huge surpluses because prices do not respond to purchasing power.

A few years ago, everyone was saying that Hitler must fail because he was stifling initiative. Had the charge been true, he would have failed. But today we see that it was industrial feudalism and not Hitler that was stifling initiative. A glance at the cruelly efficient German military system discloses the fact that it is the younger men, rising out of the masses of Germany, competing on a basis of sheer cold efficiency who give the German military machine its overwhelming competence. There were plenty of people in England who knew the power of tanks. Indeed, tanks were a British invention. The failure of England to use them may be accounted for only by failure to encourage new ideas and initiative by men of superannuated ideas frozen into power. There is no system that keeps down initiative more than a set of business cartels.

Let no one worry about the long-time efficiency of the totalitarian army state. It is only effective during the periods of its sudden growth. Napoleon rose because he freed the energies of the French people. He fell because he forced these energies into a static pattern—the pattern of war. Had Napoleon been able to demobilize his army, he might have solidified a large portion of Europe. But he could not demobilize it. He had no balance wheel against that army. Totalitarian military states expand until they are destroyed. They arise only in times when the energies of free people who oppose them are frustrated. They fall because war cannot be continued indefinitely, and there is no other

79

end to which they can possibly direct the organization which they have built.

Democracy is more permanent than any military organization, because through the freedom of opportunity given to different types of organizations a balance is struck. In the long run it always reestablishes itself because men cannot stand the sacrifices of long-time regimentation when the thrill of victory dies away. Figures like Hitler and Napoleon can rise only when democracy is blocked by the seizure of power by private groups who are unchecked by competitive institutions and who are unable to use that power for national unity.

Napoleon lasted only long enough to break the power of the private groups who were preventing national development in Europe. He was conquered by the forces which he liberated. A similar pattern exists today. England has been in the grip of a static civil service and a set of industrial cartels. Even after Munich, these cartels were busy pursuing their own private interests and actually arming Germany against England. England could not prepare because she had delegated too much power to private groups whose interests did not coincide with national defense and who could not realize its necessity. Churchill shouted his warnings in vain to these men. It was not the British democracy which refused to prepare. Indeed, it was the British democracy which rose in anger against the refusal of the British industrialists to recognize the national need. But the cartel system had frozen so many

incompetent men into strategic industrial positions
that it required a war to shake them out.

There is only one *sine qua non* for the efficient operation of a democracy and that is that it remain an industrial as well as a political democracy. When power
over the market is seized in private hands political democracy becomes a mere shell. The decline and fall of
a democracy does not occur when political democracy is
pushed over. It occurs long before that when freedom
in the market place is destroyed. When that occurs it
is no longer possible for a political democracy to mobilize its forces either to distribute goods or to protect
itself in times of war emergency.

A Guess as to the Future

Only a free domestic market can give us the mobility
we need to face the problems which state monopolies
in Europe will offer us if Germany wins the war. We
can only guess at such problems, and guesses vary.
However, let us take Walter Lippmann's guess as a
starting point. In a column of advice to the Republican
party on June 22, 1940, he said:

The two American parties are nominating candidates
whom they hope to make President during the next four
years. Has it dawned upon the platform makers and party
managers at Philadelphia that the next President of the
United States is going to administer our affairs in a world
where the whole commercial system we have known has
broken down, in a world in which private property and

THE BOTTLENECKS OF BUSINESS

private enterprise have been replaced by a regime of military socialism?

Do they realize what this is going to mean? That when an American businessman wants to sell or buy in Europe and Asia, he will not be trading with other businessmen but with monopolies administered by dictatorial governments? That when he competes in the few free markets which may be left, say in South America, he will be competing not with foreign businessmen but with a European government monopoly?

Do they realize that the American farmer and the American producer of raw materials will be able to sell to this monopoly only if this country will take in payment the manufactured goods of Europe? Have they grasped the fact that these goods are going to be produced by highly skilled labor which is paid the wages of sweated labor and, so far as the conquered people are concerned, the wages of slave labor? Have our labor leaders grasped the fact that the trade union movement in all other industrial nations is dead, and that they will be competing in the American market and in all other markets with workers who have no rights and have a standard of life lower than any white men have known for much more than a hundred years? Have our manufacturers and bankers and shareholders and bondholders grasped the fact that this European government monopoly of industry will not only rest upon sweated labor and slave labor but that it will have no financial overhead to burden the costs of production? For the capitalists of Europe will have been expropriated, the Germans in fact though not perhaps in appearance, the conquered capitalists completely?

Has it occurred to the Republican leaders in Philadelphia what it will mean to compete with such an industrial

82

machine as that? Do they realize that no existing tariff, no subsidy, no system of labor laws, no system of trade union agreements can protect American agriculture and industry against the inroads of such a system? For if they let in the imports from such an industrial machine, how can American producers survive in competition? And if they shut out the imports, how can American surpluses be disposed of?

The situation which Mr. Lippmann foresees boils down simply to this: The totalitarian states are going to flood us with cheap goods which we cannot distribute because our price structure is so inelastic that we cannot stand the plenty which they offer. There is both an economic and a military significance to this problem.

Let us take up its economic significance first on the theoretical side, then from its practical angle. If we were actually at war, if we had armies in the field, the idea of someone flooding us with cheap goods would be a pleasure instead of a pain. It would relieve pressure on our own productive capacity. We will probably not be at war but will be bending every effort to spend unimagined sums in national defense. In such a situation why will not the cheap goods which Europe sends us give us more time and more labor for that national defense? If Hitler should suddenly flood us with cheap armament we could scarcely complain. Why, then, do we suddenly tremble at the thought of his flooding us with the materials which our people can use while they are making armaments? Theoretically, in an absolutely free market a supply of cheap goods will benefit the consumer. It will have the same effect in dislocating industry that a technological improvement has. But in a free market that effect would soon be translated into a higher standard of living because more purchasing power would be released for national defense.

Now let us examine the same problem practically. Unfortunately, we do not live in such a theoretical world, with theoretically perfect competitive markets. Sudden dislocation of industry on a large scale requires painful adjustment because we cannot stand too much deflation of too many industries all at once. This problem of adjustment to cheaper world prices is, therefore, a real problem, but its difficulty will be in direct proportion to the number of rigidly maintained prices and capitalized restraints of trade which we allow to grow up in this country during our national defense program. If we have many of these rigid price structures which cannot be broken without widespread insolvency, the dislocation caused by the influx of cheaper goods will be terrific. If we have only a few, the number of subsidies required to relieve financial distress will be smaller. And hence a free *domestic* market becomes even more important when we are threatened with the necessity of absorbing cheap foreign goods.

Let us look at the international problem posed by Mr. Lippmann. At present we do not want the agricultural products which South America can produce in such abundance. If we keep them out, their only market will be the totalitarian states. Trade with South America means power in South America. That power must not fall into the hands of the very nations against which we are arming.

Much serious thought is being devoted to this problem. The difficulty is to bring the price levels of the Western Hemisphere into some sort of balance so that economic ties (which are the only enduring ties) may be built up. If our prices at home are so unbalanced that we cannot distribute our own agricultural products this difficulty is immeasurably increased.

Let us examine one plan, a summary of which I quote, from an article by Howard J. Trueblood, in the *New Republic* of July 1, 1940:

As an emergency measure in the economic and political defense of the Western Hemisphere against a Nazi-dominated Europe, establishment of an Inter-American Marketing Board, with full control over the foreign trade of the Western Hemisphere, might be a key feature of the new Pan-Americanism. Such a board—of necessity financed in large part by United States capital, perhaps through the intermediary of the Inter-American Bank—would preferably represent all twenty-one American republics, although almost inevitably control and responsibility would devolve upon the United States.

The first task of such a board would be to shift United States imports to Latin America in so far as possible, apportioning purchases among the individual Latin American countries in accordance with previous production or exports of the specific commodities involved. The board would also be empowered to acquire and market all other Latin American export products. Such exports would be used to fill the demands of the United States and other American republics, while the surplus would be disposed of in accordance with both the political policy of the New World and the economic needs of the Old.

How much would it "cost" the United States to underpin the Latin American export market? Assuming, under the circumstances outlined, an immediate increase of at least $200,000,000 in this country's Latin American imports, there would remain—on the basis of the 1936-38 average—a surplus of about $1,000,000,000 worth of goods normally sold outside the Western Hemisphere. This surplus, in the single year 1938, included approximately 10,000,000 bags of coffee, 700,000 tons of meat, at least 5,600,000 bags of sugar, 200,000 tons of wool, 1,500,000 bales of cotton, 200,000 tons of hides and skins, 1,950,000 tons of wheat and 2,737,000 tons of corn, to mention only a few major commodities. For economic reasons, an Inter-American Marketing Board could not throw these products on the United States market without serious internal repercussions on the price structure and normal trade channels. On the other hand, Latin American products bought in the interests of defense would include many commodities now bought in part elsewhere: for example, wool, hides and skins, cacao, fibers, various nuts, waxes and vegetable oils and a number of minerals—including tin, provided smelters are established. Presumably a board with the powers contemplated would find opportunities to dispose of most surplus Latin American products without subjecting the individual countries to the danger of dealing directly with Germany. Even if the $1,000,000,000 were pure loss to the United States, moreover, it would still be a small price to pay for strengthening Latin American resistance to Nazi economic penetration.

If we had a free market for all our products in this country both manufactured and farmed, we would not

86

have the enormous surpluses * to dispose of in the first place, and such surpluses as we would have would be held at price levels which would permit us to penetrate the South American market in competition with totalitarian countries. In addition, under a free internal market, we could absorb a vast amount of South American products and thus counterbalance German economic penetration.

However, we must first face the facts. We do not have such a free market. Therefore some plan of controlling export surpluses to prevent German economic control of South America must be studied. All such plans to control export surpluses involve to a greater or less extent buying those surpluses. After they have been bought they must be distributed. Adjustments must then be made to take care of the sudden deflation which comes from sudden plenty. This we must face even though it be costly.

But during that period of adjustment we must bend every effort to free our market so that emergency subsidies do not have to become permanent ruinous policies. We can afford subsidies only for a short time while we are developing a free market to take care of the surplus automatically. I am not here advocating any particular plan. The antitrust laws do not in themselves solve any of our national defense problems. What they do is to provide a background which makes their solution possible by democratic methods. Only a free mar-

---

* Manufacturing "surpluses" usually take the form of low capacity operations instead of piling up the actual goods such as occurs in agricultural production.

ket can give democracy the elasticity to bend to the necessities of war preparation without breaking.

There is discipline and there is efficiency in a business economy which has accepted the yoke of a totalitarian state. There is a better discipline and efficiency in a business economy which is willing to accept the hazards of competition that is really tough and which does not demand that anyone guarantee its profits against lower prices to consumers. But there is neither discipline nor efficiency in an economy that is half way between. And so we close this chapter with the most poignant illustration of all, an article from the conservative British publication *The Economist* of June 15, 1940, written in an attempt to appraise the reasons why poverty-stricken Germany was able to outstrip in production and distribution the most powerful commercial empire of Europe.

MANY very dearly cherished notions have been swept aside by a month of *Blitzkrieg*. We no longer believe that we have only to sit tight to win; that Germany's effort of production has been no greater than our own; that the war can be fought without the utmost sacrifice of blood and treasure; that a single scrap of virtue resides in caution. In these and in many other ways we have awakened and are now, at last and at length, setting ourselves with all our strength to the task of production.

But there is another set of ideas, just as false and as enervating, which has not been abandoned, partly because its roots lie deeper in self-interest, partly because the proofs of its failure, though decisive, are not publicly apparent. This is the set of ideas that has been the dominant

A FREE MARKET IN EMERGENCY

economic philosophy of the Conservative Party in the past
nine years, the set of notions that sees its ideal of an economic system in an orderly organization of industries, each
ruled feudally from above by the business firms already
established in it, linked in associations and confederations
and, at the top, meeting on terms of sovereign equality
such other Estates of the Realm as the Bank of England
and the Government. Each British industry, faithful to
the prescription, has spent the past decade in delimiting its
fief, in organizing its baronial courts, in securing and en-
trenching its holdings and in administering the legal
powers of self-government conferred on it by a tolerant
State. This is the order of ideas that has transformed the
trade association from a body of doubtful legality, a conspiracy in restraint of trade, into a favoured instrumental-
ity of the State, until membership in such a body has become as necessary to the businessman who wishes to be
successful as an old school tie has been to the ambitious
Conservative politician. It is the order of ideas that led to
the Import Duties Act being drafted in such a way as to
put a premium on self-seeking monopolies and a discount
on the public interest; that turned "high profits and low
turnover" into the dominant slogan of British business;
that raised the level of British costs to the highest in the
world. It is a set of ideas that is admirable for obtaining
security, "orderly development" and remunerative profits
for those already established in the industry—at the cost of
an irreducible body of general unemployment. It is em-
phatically not a set of ideas that can be expected to yield
the maximum of production, or to give the country wealth
in peace and strength in war.

Nevertheless, when the war broke out and it became
obvious to all but the purblind that maximum production

had become the one object that superseded all others, this anti-productive system was carried to its highest point. The noble army of controllers was recruited from organized industry; the rings, from being tolerated, became endowed with all the power of the State. The result has been what could have been, and was, predicted—not so much an unfair advantage to certain private pockets as a sluggish tempo of advance and a low limit to what was considered possible. British industry, by and large, has, until recent weeks, been making the maximum effort compatible with no disturbance to its customs now or to its profit-making capacity hereafter. There is no accusation of unpatriotism in this; on the contrary, businessmen, placed in an impossible position of divided loyalties and contradictory intentions, have done their best. But the result has been what we see—a startling inadequacy of production. What was formerly prophecy is now fact: the men who run the existing organizations of their industries have not been the best men to organize their industries for war. The best of them have been only partial successes; the worst have been failures. Both in tanks and in aircraft—to take only the two outstanding cases) the existing rings have failed to produce the goods and, nine months too late, outsiders have had to be brought in.

V.

An Elastic Procedure Backed by Tradition to Prevent the Private Seizure of Industrial Power

So MUCH for a survey of the necessity for a free market to distribute goods in a democracy in war or peace. The next question is, what practical action can we take to maintain a free market in this country? What do we have to work with?

We have at present only one instrument which can accomplish any practical results in freeing the channels of trade—that is the Sherman Act. The reason is that it permits us to use methods to which we are accustomed and which do not depart from the traditional rôle of democratic government.

This practical advantage has received little attention from liberal economic thinkers—even from those who argue the necessity for a free market. The formula of the Sherman Act lacks certainty and precision. Therefore, to a forward-looking liberal, who likes to see all things proceed according to a logical scheme, the idea of a new administrative tribunal to do the work of the

Sherman Act in a nice, neat manner is most appealing. This has been characteristic of academic thinking in all ages. The practical reformer always has to fight not only reactionary opposition to reform, but also the politically impractical ideas of liberal economic planners. In the world of theory, a new broom always sweeps cleaner than an old one. In a world of fact, old governments are unable to use new brooms without worrying themselves to death in the process.

No social institution, whether it be a political party, a great industrial organization, or even a university, ever develops the single logical course advocated by a particular group of wise men. Social institutions respond to pressures, not to logical thinking. They are like human personalities. The direction they take depends on the necessity of adjustment to outside forces. If you are going to make that adjustment easier and less painful, you must use methods which do not create fear and distrust by attacking revered traditions. And there lies the strength of the Sherman Act. It is a symbol of our traditional ideals.

The practical reformer gains his ends with the least possible dislocation of existing institutions and the least possible shock to existing ideals. This does not produce a logical government, but it does get practical results. It is an art which is more familiar to the practical politician than to the student of government.

Their failure to understand how human organizations actually grow and change explains why liberals generally have not understood the practical utility of the Sherman Act to maintain the free market that alone gives vitality to industrial democracy. A prominent, liberal economist said to me recently, "You can't govern this country by antitrust litigation. You must have a broader plan than that." What he wanted was some new administrative tribunal working after someone had removed politics from politics, and the courts had ceased from troubling and reaction was at rest. He had solved the problem by throwing away all the tools which were immediately at hand in order to fix his eyes, like a flint, Zionward. I said, "You can't get backing for any comprehensive administrative plan out of either of the parties in the present Congress." He replied, "We need a new political party." I said, "Which new one do you like, Phil LaFollette's or John L. Lewis' combination of the CIO, the negroes, and the youth movement." He said, "None of these. We need a new party in which thoughtful, liberal, humanitarian men are all united."

That type of thinking was strikingly illustrated in a college student contest for the best essay on political reform, conducted by the *New Republic*. I quote from their summary in the issue of April 22, 1940:

College Contest: First Heat

The 258 entries we received in our contest for college undergraduates have been given a first reading and the winners will be announced within the next few weeks. Meanwhile, we have made an analysis of all the manuscripts, which affords an interesting straw vote on what college youth is thinking. American democracy was by far the most popular subject of the 258 entries. One hundred and thirty-two students chose it, sixty-two reporting on its failings, seventy speculating on its fate. Their conclusions were almost unanimous: democracy is on the skids; only a shift to collectivism can save it; the alternative is fascism. Fascism's role of villain was sinister and clear. "It's a Bengal tiger in the bulrushes, awaiting the moment of attack," said one contestant darkly. "It's creeping up like the five-o'clock shadow on a man's face," brooded another.

Most papers were rather vague about the best way of preventing its advent. The need for a planned economy was assumed but its blueprints did not clearly appear. A few papers, to be sure, set up bureaus whose sway was benevolent and far-reaching: A National Institute of Social Scientists, "so that an alert public can act on the basis of social scientific opinion"; an Advisory Council System, "to foster closer relations between legislators and people"; a National Planning Board, to salvage our whole economy; a Federal Consumers' Commission, to test and perhaps take over production if it discovers that the public is being short-changed. The majority, though, were more cautious. They agreed that Russia's failure to keep her record clean was no reason to shelve a movement for socialism here. And some, reluctant to give up the Late United Front, said far-Leftists would be welcome in such a movement too. Liberals, they thought, could hold the reins if they tried, but no one equals a Communist for energy and organizing genius.

There is not a cough of practical reform in a carload of this kind of thinking. It does not even consider using the instruments at hand to which we are accustomed and which, for that reason, do not arouse our traditional suspicion that our form of government is being changed out from under us. We cannot suddenly put into operation a new kind of government or any new instrument of government. If we want results rather than debates and oratory we must use the machinery we have.

The machinery we have at hand consists of a government of checks and balances. These checks and balances are controlled by people who do not think alike, who fight each other a large part of the time, and who never get in sufficiently close touch with each other so that they can move for very long in a direction which departs from tradition in a consistent way. A war can unite them on military objectives, but it throws them into a devil-take-the-hindmost policy of economic organization during war.

Added to the inertia inherent in a democratic form of government there are in this country artificial obstacles which make even the democratic process slower than it otherwise would be. The United States is composed of many states whose boundaries have no relation to economic areas. The States cannot solve their own economic problems because their geographical sovereignty does not extend far enough. But there is little chance today of any state giving up its sovereignty merely because it might seem *economically* sound to do so. There is too much emotional steam behind the traditional idea of states' rights to make surrender of state sovereignty a practical possibility. You may or may not like this, but your likes and dislikes are unimportant. It is a political fact, and political facts are far more important economic facts than anything any professor thinks up in a classroom.

Practical action must follow traditional lines and gradually adapt them to changing conditions. New government activities or plans have to become part of our tradition before they will work at all. When in times of stress we create new government organizations which run counter to tradition, they quickly bog down, exhausted by the expenditure of energy which has been necessary to start them. It takes years of emotional struggle to get even such a simple idea on its feet as government guarantees for old age security. We are still quarrelling about the extent of the national government's responsibility for distribution of goods to the unemployed to such a degree that it is being accomplished by fits and starts. Every activity of government which departs from traditional lines has to face a long struggle. This prevents its efficient administration for years. This struggle, this delay in practical effectiveness of new government activities, proves that sudden departure from tradition in the United States means a long period of backing and filling before the new activity involved in the departure can run smoothly and efficiently. A new idea must appear to be an old idea before it will work at all. Such is the price we must pay for a democratic form of government. There is no doubt that democracy is worth that price, but it is necessary constantly to remind ourselves that the easiest remedies for a democracy to apply are those which do not depart too far from tradition. We have enough wars to prepare for as it is, without starting a new philosophical civil war on our own home front.

In our democracy there is only one idea on which everyone can agree and that is that the market must be free from the *private* seizure of power. *Public* seizure of power over the market by various groups will always be a matter for debate in particular cases. Responsible economists will point out that this or that organization needs special protection. Other economists will heatedly contest. However, no one contends that private persons, without running the gamut of our system of checks and balances, should seize power over the market in a *sub rosa* manner.

It is the fact that the Sherman Act bars the way to private seizure of industrial power that gives it its continuing force and its constant public acceptance. Every political party has recommended its enforcement for the past half-century. It has been evaded, ignored, and unenforced, but no responsible group has refused to give it at least lip service. It has the strength of a precept or a canon of constitutional law. It is for this reason that it can be used in times when legislative ideas are in complete confusion. Various groups may attack particular cases brought under the Sherman Act, but no one dares attack the philosophy of the Act itself.

The fact that violation of the Sherman Act was made a crime is a testimonial of the strength of attitude against private seizure of power over the market. It is a crime ordinarily committed by our most respectable people. When the doctors, or the presidents of great oil companies, are indicted, sympathetic editorial writers protest with outraged anguish at the insult to our best people. Yet even our admiration of business leaders has not caused us to repeal the provisions for criminal indictment as the penalty for reckless business aggression. Even in the days of the NRA, when our legislative policy seemed inconsistent with maintaining a free market, we refused to abandon the threat of indictment under the Sherman Act.

It is these very revered traditions which make the Sherman Act so difficult to amend. I can think of many amendments which might make enforcement easier. I have, at times, suggested them to Congress. I have always found that even the slightest amendment is treated as an amendment to a prayer book would be treated by the House of Bishops of some established church. Every procedure of the Act is so rooted in tradition that someone arises and asks the woodman to spare that particular tree. This tradition, though it makes the Act more clumsy in its operation, nevertheless is the thing that gives it its strength.

To the critics of the Act, therefore, I say: If you know of a better instrument to maintain a free market, go to it. Get political backing for it. Then get Congress to pass it. Then get the Supreme Court of the United States to sustain it. Finally, get the businessmen of the United States used to it, so that it is not in constant danger of repeal because of a philosophical attack by the never-say-die what-are-we-coming-to-ists, who see plotters against our system of government under every bed. At the end of that period you may have something that will work. Until that time, however, practical men who really want to accomplish something to prevent the Balkanization of America will have to use the Sherman Act.

The reasons why the Sherman Act is more effective to enforce the broad ideal of a free market on a nation-wide scale than any administrative tribunal lie deep in the psychology of the government itself. On the face of it the judicial process is clumsy and covered with barnacles which would not exist on a shiny new administrative machine. Therefore, someone is always rising in meeting to claim that it is an antiquated way of maintaining a free competitive market; that the federal courts are not experts; that they do not know economics; and that a neatly-planned administrative tribunal could do the job much better. Such arguments have sabotaged judicial enforcement of the antitrust laws during their entire existence. They have led to the substitution of special tribunals for courts of general jurisdiction to enforce the law. These special tribunals have been unable to do the job.

In 1914 the Federal Trade Commission, an administrative tribunal, was made the spearhead of anti-trust enforcement, while the Department of Justice was starved with respect to funds and personnel. The great concentration of industrial power prior to and since the depression grew up in the face of the Federal Trade Commission—not through its fault but because it could never get the power to make effective enforcement possible. It had to appeal to a court even to enforce its own subpoenas. It could make reports. It could issue cease-and-desist orders. It could contribute excellent studies and surveys of industrial problems. But it could not act as the spearhead of a drive to maintain a free market for consumers. This was due simply to a traditional deep seated attitude against trusting administrative tribunals with power except in very narrow fields.

The formula of the Sherman Act is a good deal like the formula of due process. It covers every field. It is a background from which exceptions must spring. Only courts of general jurisdiction can express the philosophy of such a background. Administrative tribunals are not protected by the reverence induced by judicial robes. The public will not accept their pronouncements on broad fundamental principles.

We can illustrate this by imagining what would happen if an administrative commission were set up to enforce the due process clause of the Constitution by administrative orders. Such a commission would find itself hampered at every turn. Each order would be the beginning of a controversy instead of the end of it. Nothing final can be said on such fundamental subjects until the courts speak. Therefore, the commission would end as an inconvenient fifth wheel between the complainant who wanted due process enforced and the court.

On narrower lines the Federal Trade Commission has been able to work effectively. Its positive action on trade practices has been effective. But only courts of general jurisdiction can ever express the philosophy of government. Commissions do not have protective symbolisms which enable them to escape attack in applying a broad formula to business in general. When fundamental principles are not enforced by appropriate judicial ceremony, clumsy though it may be, thoughtful, forward looking men feel that they are in the clutches of bureaucracy.

I have discussed the psychology that makes the court the only body which can effectively apply a broad general formula in a former book *The Symbols of Government*. It may be useful to quote a part of that discussion here:

Thus, in spite of their cumbersome way of approaching problems, courts appear to have found a way of acting which has brought them overwhelming prestige and respect. They seem to have induced the feeling, even among persons who know nothing of court methods and have never been inside a courtroom, that there they will find protection. Even when they fail miserably to give protection to someone who seeks it, such is their demeanor and attitude that he—or at least his friends—feels that it was not the fault of the court that protection failed. Perhaps it was the fault of the legislature, perhaps of the jury—at least the court did the best it could; and had it done otherwise it would have, in some mysterious way, imperiled the whole system of protection to others. Commissions, composed of experts, can be violently criticized by editorial writers. But if the matter is appealed to a nonexpert court, sitting on the same question and using the same criteria, it appears to be settled in the only way possible under the law. . . .

From this we may reach our final definition of just what courts, commissions, and bureaus are.

THE BOTTLENECKS OF BUSINESS

1. A court is a body of judges whose decisions are either (a) right, (b) caused by the fault of someone else (usually the legislature), or (c) unfortunate but unavoidable accidents due to the circumstance that no human system can be perfect.

2. A bureau is a body which, if it happens to make a wrong decision, has no one to blame but itself, and if it happens to make a right decision, offers us no assurance that it will do so again.

3. A commission with quasi-judicial powers is halfway between a court and a bureau.

In other words, a court is a body toward which we take an attitude of respect because we use it to symbolize an ideal of impersonal justice. A bureau is a body which has little symbolic function, and which therefore is entitled to no greater respect than are the individuals composing it. A court escapes criticism just as the church used to escape criticism, because it cannot be criticized without seeming to attack the whole governmental structure. Since its functions are primarily dramatic, the court is necessarily compelled to escape as far as possible from actual contact with society. It succeeds in doing this by elaborate procedural rules, and by isolating appellate courts through a system of appeals which are difficult and expensive. Such a process automatically compels the arbitration of many disputes—and more important than that—it compels the establishment of commissions toward which we do not take the attitude of reverence due a court, wherever efficiency rather than ceremony is desirable. This is not a conscious process. It is the result of a climate of opinion in which courts which become practical and efficient cease to look like courts.[1]

PROCEDURE TO PREVENT SEIZURE

The difference in attitude toward courts and administrative tribunals which enables the courts to exercise effectively broad powers involving freedom may be illustrated by a single case. In the case of *Jones* v. *Securities & Exchange Commission,* a speculator was attempting to manipulate the market. The SEC was prevented from entering into a thorough examination of his practices on the grounds that it was an administrative tribunal trying to set up star chamber proceedings. The case is typical. Administrative tribunals are never able to apply principles which we regard as fundamental in such a way as to escape constant and harassing judicial reviews. In such situations the administrative process does not save time; it wastes it.

Compare what happened in the *Jones* case with the grand jury proceeding, a part of our traditional judicial process. Grand juries may not be experts but they are practically immune from this kind of harassing attack. A real investigation without artificial limitations can be conducted in secret before a grand jury. This is a faster and far more efficient process than is possible before any commission. No one argues that the defendants are being deprived of due process, because the judicial system is the symbol of due process itself.

In the field of maintenance of free markets there must be a concrete application in every industry of a broad general ideal. For such a purpose the court is the most important symbol of government. Those who do not understand this are constantly setting up plans to simplify the judicial proceeding. These plans look well on paper, but they fail in practice. When they are introduced in Congress they are distorted by amendments which arise because of the fear of allowing a bureaucracy to enforce what we regard as our general common law. If the bill is passed, every procedural step is subject to attack on account of the same fear. It is the magic of the judicial process which makes the courts, in spite of the clumsiness of judicial procedure, the most effective tribunals to penalize unreasonable restraints of trade.

Where the conditions of a specific industry require special treatment, on a narrow line, an administrative regulation or control will work. Let us take the Bituminous Coal Act as an example. That act set up the Bituminous Coal Commission to supervise prices in the chaotic soft coal industry. Here was a specific job to be done regulating competition in a particular industry. It departed from the broad conception of a free market because of special circumstances.

The history of the Bituminous Coal Act followed the regular course which seems psychologically necessary in the establishment of administrative tribunals. There was the inevitable attack on the Bituminous Coal Act as an unconstitutional delegation of power to regulate and restrict a free market in coal. The Supreme Court found that the delegation was not too broad,[2] and the Bituminous Coal Commission is now free to operate in its limited field.

It is interesting to note that the decision sustaining the powers of the Bituminous Coal Commission to fix prices in a special situation was written by the same Justice of the Supreme Court who had stated in a

104

sweeping decision announced just two weeks before in the Madison oil case [3] that general price fixing by private agreement was illegal. These two decisions clearly illustrate the relationship between the Sherman Act, which is our economic common law, and legislative departures from that common law. The power to approve combinations by restraint of trade, *in general,* cannot be delegated to any administrative tribunal, however laudable the purpose. Only the courts can determine the reasonableness of a combination on such a broad scale as this. Yet Congress, in a special situation, may take into consideration facts which permit a limited exception to these broad principles without improperly delegating its authority. The court then remains in a position to apply the Sherman Act against the unreasonable use of the new legislative privilege for purposes which it was never intended to serve.

Thus a philosophy of government is set up which firmly establishes a free market as the common law of an industrial democracy. It allows Congress to take care of special situations, but not to delegate sweeping powers to control the market. The Sherman Act deals broadly with restraints of trade where no specific legislative situation has been delegated to a commission. The effect is to compel Congress to take up one industrial situation at a time, to center its attention on particular industries, and to limit the administrative power it grants to the specific needs of those industries.

To sum up, enforcement of the broad formula of the antitrust laws, in federal court, has the following

THE BOTTLENECKS OF BUSINESS

advantages which can never be obtained by the administrative process:

1. It gives us the elasticity of the common law method in dealing with particular situations. This elasticity prevents the Sherman Act from freezing into a static, technical rule to govern a changing economy.
2. It preserves the philosophy of a free market without denying the right of Congress to take special action in special cases.
3. It permits industry to take emergency action in time of crisis without making that action a precedent for controlling the market when the crisis is past.
4. It subjects special privileges, which are inconsistent with a free market, to the checks and balances of the democratic process. It prevents them from establishing themselves or continuing without public approval.
5. It restricts any special privileges which may be granted to the purposes for which they were intended.
6. It prevents Congress from throwing away democratic control by too broad a delegation of power.
7. In other words, under the protection of a philosophy of industrial democracy, it allows us to mobilize and demobilize our industrial combinations according to the actual necessities of the day.

There is only one end to industrial cartelization and that is eventual government control. The purpose of

the Sherman Act is to see that this does not take place
on too broad a front and that each instance of necessary
combinations is specifically guarded by the checks and
balances of the legislative process.

The Private Seizure of Industrial Power

When we use the Sherman Act, we must understand
not only what it is designed to accomplish but also what
it is *not* designed to accomplish. It is not a piece of constructive economic legislation. It is not a regulatory
statute. It does not and cannot compel emergency adjustments that may be necessary in times of economic
crisis. It is not a constitutional prohibition of inconsistent legislation which Congress considers necessary to
relieve particular industries. It is aimed to prevent one
thing, and one thing only—the private seizure of power
over interstate commerce.

Of course there will always be some legislative exemptions from the Sherman Act. But the acquisition of
power over the market by public legislative processes
is not a serious danger in a democracy checked and balanced as ours is. Legislation never follows a consistent
logical pattern. Economic legislation, and indeed all
economic activity on the part of government, must be a
compromise between pressure groups. This is illustrated at every turn. For the past four years we have observed a struggle between budget balancing and the
necessities of (a) relief expenditures and (b) farm subsidies. The result has been a series of legislative battles
but no legislative policy. It can be described in terms

of a balance of conflicting pressures, but not as any consistent reasoned action on the part of anybody There was no weighing of the respective economic effects of adding to farm subsidies while cutting WPA subsidies. In fact, economic theories are always a confusion of inconsistencies. The contradictory legislation makes sense only to one who knows the strength of the various political pressures behind it. Of course, there are plenty of editorial writers who think that Senators should act as if they did not care whether they got elected or not. The trouble with this sort of preaching is that Senators who fail to get elected cannot vote on any legislation at all. This political fact cannot be removed by blaming anyone, and no amount of preaching can wipe it out. If you want a democratic government you might as well accept this as one of the incidents of that kind of government.

The same pressures that affect legislation affect the policies of our great political parties. As we noted in chapter III, one hundred Republican thinkers, under the leadership of Glenn Frank, gave birth to a platform which was supposed to crystallize the ideals of the opposition party. When we read that platform we were surprised to discover that every one of the New Deal objectives, which were so violently opposed only a few years ago, were accepted as necessary to our economy. There was endorsement of parity prices to farmers and of farm subsidies. Social security must not be cut off in the interests of economy but must actually be increased. There was approval in principle of regulation of our security market by the SEC, which only a few years ago was denounced as the chief obstacle to recovery. Even the enforcement of labor's right to collective bargaining was endorsed. And on top of all these recommended subsidies and new activities the platform insisted that the budget be balanced immediately.

It is no criticism of this platform to say that it is inconsistent. Political platforms cannot be consistent until political parties are dominated by one group only. The Republican party, at the time the platform was written, appealed for support to four organized groups. The first was the businessmen and bankers who wanted economy. The second was the farmers who wanted aid. The third was the "ham and eggers," who insisted on the state giving them security for their old age. The fourth was organized labor. It was more important to get the aid of all of these groups than to follow any consistent line. Thus, both parties today, in meeting their political problems, are endorsing practically the same general philosophy of the function of government.

So we see that a democracy is not only an organization of *legal* checks and balances, which play against each other and result in some form of compromise, but also an organization of *economic* checks and balances. Neither big business, nor the farmers, nor the "ham and eggers," nor organized labor, will get everything they want. All of them, if they are sufficiently organized, will get something to make their economic life more bearable. This is not planning, but it is democracy. It proceeds by experimentation. It is never static.

The Sherman Act is designed to force such compromises and special privileges as may be granted to special groups into the open, where they are subject to democratic criticism and democratic repeal. It does this by preventing private groups from seizing and capitalizing special privileges in secret ways which the democratic process cannot correct. In times of emergency the legislature, under pressure, will make all sorts of compromises with our ideal of free competitive enterprise. This was done under the NRA. Yet because the NRA was a public act, and not a growth of intrenched private combination, it was terminated by democratic checks and balances.

Today we face a crisis in military preparedness. No doubt certain privileges may be demanded by industries in the name of national defense which may be unwise. However, we can survive the legislative grants of power because what has been granted by the democratic process can be safeguarded and can be taken away by the same democratic process. The Sherman Act should be regarded not as a strait-jacket which prevents Congress from meeting emergencies, but as our front line of defense against the seizure of industrial power without the approval of Congress. It is the private seizure of industrial power that builds the kind of irresponsible organizations which can wreck a democracy. That power is subject to no election every four years. It is acquired in secret. Its operations are veiled in the mystery of meetings of boards of directors, dominated by single individuals and with interlocking lines of interest and control. It recognizes no public responsibility. It must not be allowed to get a foothold and then, after thousands of investors have invested their savings in the continuance of its illegitimate earnings, to present Congress with the problem of unscrambling the eggs. Laws do not in themselves have much effect on economic conduct. An enforcement organization which follows traditional procedures has enormous effect.

We repeat—nothing in the Sherman Act determines legislative policy. It simply provides a background necessary to make any legislative policy work in a democracy. For example, a few readers may be opposed to expenditures in preparation for war. Some readers will be opposed to government subsidies for peace time industries. The Sherman Act does not resolve such debates. Instead, it assumes that the debate will go on and be resolved by Congress. The advocate of antitrust enforcement should regard the Sherman Act as a balance wheel, whatever legislative program is passed in war emergencies as well as peace emergencies. If you are an old-fashioned, *laissez faire* economist, you need a free competitive market to get the benefit of the law of supply and demand. If you insist on high protective tariffs on goods from abroad, in order to develop home industries, you must have free trade at home to make these industries pass the fruits of their savings on to consumers. If you believe in farm subsidies, or subsidies to any other low-income group, you need a free market so that these very subsidies will not raise prices and defeat themselves. Even if some particular group obtains from Congress the right to fix prices, the rest of the market must be kept free, or else these very price-fixing privileges will not bring profits because they will grow like a snowball in each step from raw material to the consumer until they finally crush the goose that was expected to lay the golden egg. If you belong to either of the extremes, complete *laissez faire,* or $200 a month for old people, your plan is equally dependent upon the market's being free from private restraints of trade. And finally, if you belong to that forgotten, unorganized group made up of the great mass of our people who sell their raw materials or services in a closed market, you must break down the restraints which make the market closed or you will be crushed.

It has long been a tenet of the Socialist that the best road to Socialism lies in permitting the great corporations to destroy democracy by organizing an industrial empire which is beyond the control of the democratic process. Then, the Socialists argue, the state will be forced to take over industrial government, and an enlightened public opinion will throw kindly professors of Socialism and enlightened thinkers like Norman Thomas into positions of government power. The premise on which they operate is unquestionably correct. The state has always had to take over industrial cartels when they finally established control of the market because of the disparity of prices which that control created. The conclusion of the Socialists, however, that kind, tolerant people can control the state when that stage is reached is opposed to all political experience. Yet, paradoxically enough, an industrial democracy with a free competitive market is essential to allow expression for that Socialistic dissent. When an industrial democracy disappears, political dissent goes with it.

PROCEDURE TO PREVENT SEIZURE

If you control the market you can control political expression. Recently a businessman in a western state, whose business had been ruined by the aggressive tactics of a large organization, made a speech attacking that organization. He was called into his bank and told that he had better seek financing elsewhere. The bank did not wish to be in the position of encouraging those elements in the community opposed to business recovery. This particular businessman has been quiet ever since.

Industrial democracy dies only where no one recognizes the hidden symptons of the disease. We do not connect the loss of free markets with the destruction of political democracy. When people are caught in the power of some gang obstructing the market, whether it be small or large, they are not in a position to make a public protest. An official of a large company told me that he did not dare do anything else than follow the prices of his still larger competitor. I asked him what would happen if he did not follow these prices. He replied, "That is a question which I hope never to be able to answer from experience." Perhaps in this particular case the larger company would not have retaliated. Nevertheless, the mere fact that they dominated the market deprived the small man of all initiative. He had a family to support. He had to play safe.

The eternal problem of a democracy is to keep governing power in the hands of the people. Successful attacks on democratic institutions in this country have come from two sources: First, the political machine and, second, the industrial machine. Neither of these machines makes a frontal attack on democratic institutions. Both preach the formula of democracy while they seize their arbitrary powers. No greater shouter for democratic principles can be found than the old-fashioned political boss, and no firmer public supporter of rugged individualism exists than the large corporation which is dominating the market. Neither of these groups claim publicly that they want special privileges. If they did, they could not get them in secret.

We have gone a long way on the road to control our *sub rosa* political machines after toleration of their private seizure of power since Grant's administration. Of course, corrupt political machines still exist and probably will continue to exist. But the realization of the evil they do and the knowledge of the means of stopping them are so well established today that the power of the political machine is far more precarious than it used to be. Not soon again will the President of the United States be selected by a few politicians in a smoke-filled hotel room.

Our great problem today is the undermining of American democracy by private groups in big business, little business, and labor. In a smoke-filled room in one city, protective tariffs are passed to exclude all Southern lumber without the consumer having any knowlege of it. In another smoke-filled room the prices for necessities are fixed. In a third smoke-filled room the market is divided between a few powerful groups, and consumers are taxed to maintain profits on that division. The channels of trade in the distribution of every necessity are taxed by organizations which give no public account of the use of that power.

The simple remedy to destroy the *sub rosa* industrial machine is the same which is used to destroy the *sub rosa* political machine. It is nothing more or less than prosecutions in our courts of justice, case by case, of those who violate the law.

I repeat, the Sherman Act is not a legislative program. Its enforcement, however, is essential to allow legislative programs to work. It is the only instrument which we have or which we are likely to have for that purpose.

VI.

The Test is Efficiency and Service—
Not Size

THE pull against a balance wheel is always greatest when the balance wheel is most needed. Whenever huge government expenditures are contemplated, arguments against antitrust laws are taken out of the closet, dusted off, and made ready for instant use. We can observe this already in our present national defense crisis. The arguments for spending defense money in a closed market are the same as those for spending relief money in a closed market.

In the first place, there is the idea that the higher prices climb the more confidence business will have, and that business confidence is necessary to national unity. If prices rise higher, business can make more profits; if it can make more profits, it can pay more wages; if it can pay more wages, the farmers can sell more products; and, therefore, everyone will produce more.

It is an appealing idea. We heard a lot about it in 1929 when economists were saying that because we had reached a high level of prices on the stock market we

TEST IS EFFICIENCY AND SERVICE

were the most efficient country in the world. Now we know that argument was false with respect to our industrial organization in 1929. But the ideal of letting private organizations agree on what is fair competition and reasonable price policies is still put forth as a way to stimulate industrial efficiency in producing defense materials in 1940.

In the second place, there is the argument that distribution of goods by great private cartels is more efficient than distribution by competition. This is no new idea either among socialists or industrialists. Forty years ago the Civic Federation of Chicago, with the cooperation of the Governors of all our States, arranged a conference on "Trusts" in Chicago's Central Music Hall. It was a truly democratic conference. All shades of opinion were expressed freely and with vigor. An editor from New York, a Mr. George Gunton, expressed a point of view which has prevailed in some editorial sanctums ever since. He said:

If the raising of corn were in the hands of a few well-informed corporations, instead of thousands of uninformed farmers, the erratic ups and downs in corn farming would be largely avoided.[1]

No doubt Mr. Gunton believed in this statement. The dream of a regimented economy, controlled by a few so-called "wise business leaders," has always been an appealing one in this country. The competitive struggle always seems disorderly to that kind of dreamer. Under the influence of that kind of thinking the process of industrial centralization in America has

117

gone on for forty years, as Mr. Gunton would have wished it. However, the farmer knows today that the one thing centralization of industrial power has not done is to eliminate erratic ups and downs in our economic lives. Highly organized industry has accomplished marvels in technical research, organization, and capacity for greater production. It has, however, intensified instead of solved the problem of distribution in war as well as peace.

It is unnecessary to argue today against a planned political state in America so long as Europe is presenting us with a clinical example of the working of that great delusion. It is still necessary, however, to argue against the idea so plausibly expressed by Mr. Gunton —the notion that private groups can create prosperity for all and distribute goods more efficiently by regimenting industry and eliminating competition. For real competition, it is said, tears down capital structures. It hurts inventories. How can you have a profit system when you allow cutthroat competition which attacks profits? Businessmen lose confidence when the state steps in to protect competitors who refuse to put a floor under prices and thus break down the dream values of their accumulated inventories. An ideal capitalistic economy should be one in which everyone makes money. The only way for everyone to make money is to allow each group to organize against the ruinous competition of others. So runs the idea.

The best way to destroy such an illusion is to set out concrete examples of how it works. In the beginning of the development of the automobile industry, there were nearly 200 corporations building cars, employing labor, and struggling to survive. They had an association for mutual protection against ungentlemanly tactics by competitors. A non-conformist named Henry Ford appeared on the scene with the idea of making a cheaper car. He was refused membership in the association because, they told him, as Edsel Ford testified, that he was "a fly-by-night producer." [2] Let us reconstruct the conversation which might have taken place:

REPRESENTATIVE OF THE ASSOCIATION: "Mr. Ford, we are not going to let you make cars. In the first place, you have every appearance of a ruinous price-cutter. The industry is having a difficult struggle. We are making cars as efficiently as human ingenuity can make them. If you start a price war you will destroy the confidence of the splendid business leaders who now dominate the industry and who are all for one and one for all. You will take away their business initiative by striking at their profits. New people will not go into business under such circumstances. The ones already in business will be forced out. Companies will go bankrupt. Chaos will follow. We must protect the capital structures of our great country. We must operate to preserve the confidence and initiative of those now in the business, every one of whom is solid, substantial and respectable, and anxious to preserve a capitalistic system based on profits. It might be different if the companies in this field were making *unreasonable* profits, but they are not. There is plenty of competition of the right sort. We don't want your kind of competition because it is the wrong sort.

And, anyway, the 'tin lizzies' which you are about to make are a disgrace to the American highway. They are unsafe. They are a menace to health, safety, and good taste. We are interested in the health and safety of the American people and their standards of taste. We insist on maintaining, through the power of our organization, the orderly marketing of nice products by nice people.

Therefore, if you attempt to manufacture cars, the entire force of this association will be employed to destroy you."

HENRY FORD: "Isn't this going to be tough on the purchasers of cars?"

REPRESENTATIVE OF THE ASSOCIATION: "The consumer ought not to expect to buy goods which are sold at a loss. He ought to be willing to help keep up the industrial structure by paying the tribute necessary to give the men who control it enough confidence to carry on. We must protect the public from the temptation to buy from chiselers like you."

There is evidence that the above conversation might have taken place almost as described. Indeed, I have taken every idea expressed in it from a brief filed by the Ethyl Corporation in the Supreme Court of the United States [3] in 1940 during the present war in Europe to justify the attempt to put a floor under the price of 85 per cent of all motor fuel in the interests of health, safety, good taste, and the restraint of competition in gentlemanly ways.

The battle between Ford and the automobile association is now history. It was a long and bitter fight. Ford lost in the lower courts. He won in the Court of Appeals against this combination. He was allowed to make cars. It is true that this new competitive force did finally break the capital structure of existing companies, but it did not stop initiative in the industry. On the contrary, the necessities of that bitter competitive struggle so stimulated initiative in the automobile industry that it became the greatest industrial development of the era. A system of distribution of automobiles grew up under these forces which has made cars become so cheap that today beggars may (and do) ride.

Suppose Henry Ford had lost his fight against this association. In that case I think it would be safe to say that the average car would cost $5,000 while the members of the association protected each other from price wars. Today there is evidence that the "tin lizzie" of tomorrow is having a hard struggle.

In emphasizing the contribution of men like Henry Ford to our economy, I have no desire to endorse all or any of their ideas. The reader may not like Henry Ford's labor policy. Only a short time ago, the Department of Justice indicted the Ford Motor Company because the Department thought it had evidence that the Company was excluding independent companies from financing the purchasers of cars. But the way to solve the abuses of power of competitors who become successful is to employ the same means by which you protected them when they were struggling to achieve success. For free markets do not maintain themselves. The very essence of competition consists in getting the better of the other fellow. Great organizations start by being more efficient. They get into power. It is inevitable that they will use that power to protect themselves against the new crop of independent enterprises which may be pushing them to the wall in the competitive struggle.

THE BOTTLENECKS OF BUSINESS

A referee is always necessary in the competitive game as each new enterprise climbs to power. The maintenance of a free market is as much a matter of constant policing as is the flow of free traffic on a busy intersection. It does not stay orderly by trusting to the good intentions of the drivers or by preaching to them. It is a simple problem of policing, but a continuous one.

In order to overcome the idea that the antitrust laws are opposed to efficiency, we must educate the American consumer as to the real meaning of a free market in a machine age. Much has been written and spoken in the past based upon the idea that the destruction of size in business was the objective of antitrust enforcement. Competition has been identified with small units. The Head of the Antitrust Division has been referred to by the man on the street as a "trust-buster." Thus he has been made to appear as standing in the way of efficiency of mass production in a machine age.

This emphasis on the antitrust laws as a method of making little businesses out of big businesses regardless of the efficiency of distribution has been made more pointed by books that have been written on the supposed evils of bigness in itself. There has been a continuous debate for forty years on whether big organizations are good things or bad things. That debate is like arguing whether tall buildings are better than low ones, or big pieces of coal better than small ones. Such discussions have no meaning in the abstract since the answer depends on the purposes or functions the organizations are supposed to perform.

The confusion caused by the notion that the antitrust laws are an attack on size in itself has been one of the principal handicaps to public support of antitrust enforcement. The only force capable of giving us antitrust enforcement is an informed consumers' movement. And consumers never can be convinced that size in itself is an evil. They know that the automobile they ride in could not be produced except by a large organization. They remember the time when glasses and dishes and hammers and all the things that are now sold at the ten-cent store at low prices were luxuries. They know that this efficiency in distribution could not have been accomplished without mass production and mass distribution. Consumers are unwilling to lose the advantages of a machine age because of sentimental attachment to the ideal of little business. For forty years we have been preaching against Wall Street and the trusts, while every election showed that this protest was by minority groups. The American consumer does not hate big business and he should not be made to hate it.

Therefore, the only thing needed to obtain the cooperation of the great army of American consumers for antitrust enforcement is to show them how it can aid the distribution of the products they have to buy. They are not interested in economic principles. They are interested in the price of pork chops, bread, spectacles, drugs, and plumbing. To catch their imaginations you must talk in terms of concrete items in the family budget. Antitrust enforcement must come down from the blue sky of economic and legal theory and concern itself with these family budget items, one at a time. When this is done, anybody can understand the purpose of the Sherman Act, and the great body of American consumers can be mobilized in their own self-defense.

It is important, therefore, to emphasize that the fundamental objective of the antitrust laws is not to destroy the efficiency of mass production or distribution. Our ideal of a free market does not contemplate an inefficient market. It is not size in itself that we want to destroy, but the use of organized power to restrain trade unreasonably, without justification in terms of greater distribution of goods.

If we are to catch the imagination of the American consumers, on whose support the success or failure of the antitrust laws must depend, to get a different slogan than "trust-busting," the new slogan should be "the maintenance of free trade between the states." This means free markets in which unorganized groups may exchange their raw materials or their labor for manufactured goods without paying a tribute not justified by a service rendered. This new slogan takes the emphasis away from size and puts it upon service.

The farmer of America is helped and not injured by any great organization which makes possible a wider distribution of farm products at a lower cost because this enables the consumer to buy more farm products. The farmer is also helped and not injured by any large organization which distributes to consumers manufactured goods at a lower cost, because this creates more goods for which he can exchange his farm products and thus raises his standards of living. Labor is helped because more distribution means more work.

TEST IS EFFICIENCY AND SERVICE

Therefore, there is only one sensible test which we can apply to the privilege of organization, and that is this: Does it increase the efficiency of production or distribution and pass the savings on to consumers?

This test means that we should say to every business enterprise: "You may grow as big as you can provided that you can justify the extent of your organized power by showing that it contributes to the efficiency of mass production and distribution. We will protect you against organized groups of small business which attempt to prevent you from giving cheaper goods to the public. We will, on the other hand, attack you if you seek to maintain your system of distribution by using your organized power to prevent experimental developments by others either in production or in distribution or in price policies. Size in itself is not an evil, but it does give power to those who control it. That power must be constantly watched by an adequate enforcement organization to see that it does not destroy a free market."

This is the economic substance of the rule of reason * which the Supreme Court at an early day read into the Sherman Act. Without that rule of reason the Sherman Act would be unworkable in a machine age, because every combination between two men in business is in some measure a restraint of trade. Combination will be attacked only if it is unreasonable, and the limits of the

* If this statement were made legally accurate it would have to be elaborated at some length. As it stands it is an oversimplification which however is useful to express the economic purpose of the rule.

term "reasonable" must be sought in a case by case examination of the economic justification of particular enterprises in the light of their particular facts. You will not find the rule of reason expressed in these particular terms in any single decision by the Supreme Court of the United States. That is because no broad program of antitrust enforcement in the interest of the consumer was ever attempted by the government. Yet I am convinced that the decisions, read as a whole, lead to this interpretation. Indeed, I can think of no other sensible interpretation which can be made. Therefore, this is the formula which the Antitrust Division is prepared constantly to urge before the Court in the prosecution of pending lawsuits. It can become a great force in our economic life if consumers can be made to understand it.

It can become a great force, because consumers will be unable to stand the growing cartelization of industry in the United States much longer, particularly in the face of great defense expenditures. They have put up with it a long time, seeking to increase their incomes to meet the rising prices. But today, when great groups of farmers and laborers and unemployed are forced to turn to the government for incomes during their old age, a different type of support is being given to antitrust enforcement than ever before. It has compelled the Department of Justice to plan its activities with economic results as the objective rather than moral lessons. It has led Congress to double the staff for enforcement twice in the past two years. It is behind the present newspaper support for the pending attempt of the Antitrust Division to clear away the restraints of trade in building.

The market place of today in the United States is shot through with restraints of trade and economic toll bridges in the hands of private groups. They cause disparity of prices. They create the need for subsidies to balance that disparity and for special privileges to unorganized groups to offset those of long standing held by organizations which have too strong a hold on their special privileges to be deprived of them by a democratic government. This pyramiding of subsidies and special privileges cannot go on indefinitely without threatening our political institutions. Unless we can preserve our industrial democracy, our political democracy will disappear.

Typical Ways of Keeping from the Consumer the Savings of Mass Production

Two types of restraints of trade are instrumental in destroying a free market. One type protects inefficiency by eliminating standardized materials and the products of mass production. The building industry is burdened with many examples of this type. For years it has been impossible in Chicago to use ready-mixed concrete in the construction of a house. Every consumer has had to have it puddled on the building site in an expensive and obsolete way.

The other type of restraint is the development of more efficient processes which consist in the control of new methods by a few large combinations which dominate the market in such a way that the savings are not passed on to consumers. The tobacco industry is an example. By more efficient methods of production the great tobacco companies have lowered the cost of cigarettes. By advertising they have created such a demand for their product that cigarettes are today a necessity instead of a luxury. How have they passed on these savings in production and distribution? The retailers, today, are forced to sell cigarettes practically at a loss. Farmers receive, in some years, less money as the gross price of the entire tobacco crop of the United States than the major companies make in net profits after paying all their taxes and all their expenses. And finally, how has the consumer fared? There has been plenty of competition between these companies in everything but price. Since they cannot advertise price, they advertise hokum. "Not a cough in a carload," "the blindfold test," "every one of them toasted," and so on, are the slogans which cost millions of dollars. Don't blame the advertising companies, because what else is there to advertise when price competition is out of the window?

It seems to me that it is proper to say to these companies: "You are entitled to our thanks for your efficient methods of production. But you must still explain to us why it is necessary for you to dominate the market and preserve uniform prices on your cigarettes in order to maintain that efficiency. The government, by granting you the use of the corporate franchise, has given you what almost amounts to governmental power over a vast industry. If that power is not used to pass the savings of your efficiency on to consumers, what reason can you give for not being dissolved into smaller units which can introduce an element of competition into the picture?"

The antitrust laws are not aimed at limiting the profits of any individual. He may charge prices for anything which he owns without regard to whether they are reasonable or unreasonable. However, if he chooses to restrain trade by combining with others and to dominate an entire industry, he must justify that privilege of combination by showing that the restraint has some economic purpose. This is not a test of size— it is a test of economic service.

If it were possible for individuals to dominate our markets without combining, the antitrust law would not work because the law does not affect the activities of individuals. If an individual without the use of organized power gets control of a radium mine, there is no limit to the way in which he can restrict the distribution of this necessity. However, the power and the wealth of individuals are not real problems. It is impossible to dominate the industrial markets of America without using the privileges of combination which have been created by the government. It is these privileges and the use of organized power by groups which the antitrust laws curb. When this curb is intelligently applied, the great organizations of a machine age will help and not hurt those who have to exchange their services or their raw materials for the products of industry.

Of course there are other ways of distributing goods. An army does not need competitive forces in order to make food and ammunition available to all its soldiers.

But an army has to have a single unified command. If you want the democratic way, you can maintain it only by preserving a free market through the use of continuous governmental power against those who destroy it.

And this is the answer to the question: How can the antitrust laws be used to maintain a free market? They do not do it by destroying the efficiency of mass production and distribution. Indeed, a free market means that if Henry Ford has a more efficient method of transportation, he should be allowed to furnish it to the consumer even though he destroys a lot of little automobile companies. A free market does mean, however, that Henry Ford's combination should be dissolved or curbed the moment it is not giving consumers the savings which his more efficient methods are capable of producing. When this is allowed to happen, three things occur: labor is displaced by technological improvements, capital is lost in obsolete industries, and so the purchasing power falls. The consumer dollar does not go any further and so that purchasing power is not transferred in the interests of progress. When this happens in a large number of industries, people write books on technocracy and claim it is the technological efficiency which creates unemployment. Actually, the cause is not technological improvement in itself. It is because improvement has been thrown on a closed market which prevents the consumers from getting the advantage of it. In a free market, the displacement caused by even the most revolutionary invention would only be temporary because it is capable

TEST IS EFFICIENCY AND SERVICE

of freeing purchasing power to go into other channels.

It is the purpose of the antitrust laws to prevent the combinations which control technological inventions from using their power in this way. The rule of reason has the effect of preventing the antitrust laws from destroying the efficiency of those combinations that are actually serving, instead of exploiting, the consumer.

VII.

Procedure Under The Sherman Act—
How It Operates

THE Sherman Act affects the conduct of every business, every farm organization, and every labor union. Therefore, if it is to work, businessmen, farmers, and labor must understand it. This means that it must not be kept behind the veil of learned mystery. No highly technical piece of legal machinery, requiring expert interpretation by specialists, can be effective in breaking down the barriers of trade.

Nor can the Sherman Act be a catalog of specific rules. The problems of production and distribution differ with each product. The types of organization which are reasonable in each industry depend on how the industry has grown up in the past, as well as on the mechanical necessities of the present. This means that we must have a clearly defined general principle which is understandable to laymen and which is elastic enough to be applied to different industrial situations in a common-sense way.

In order to enforce an act which contains directions general enough so that they permit elasticity in the consideration of particular facts and circumstances, it is necessary that the procedure of enforcement be simple and easily understood. It should contain no technical traps. It should require no peculiar experts to put it into operation. With these broad requirements in mind, let us examine, first, the provisions of the antitrust laws, and, second, the legal procedure through which they are enforced.

The Substance of the Sherman Act

The Sherman Act itself is very short;* it may be explained in a few paragraphs. The first section declares *every combination in restraint of* interstate commerce to be illegal. The second section declares *monopolies* which affect interstate commerce to be illegal. These two sections cover different kinds of restraints. The first applies to combinations among separate concerns. This is the most common kind of antitrust violation. Such combinations are not "trusts," neither are they monopolies. For example, the District Medical Society of Washington and the American Medical Association were indicted for combining to destroy Group Health Association. There was no "trust" involved, though the case was erroneously referred to in the press as an attack on the *"medical trust."* There are very few so-called "trusts" among the restraints of trade which we found in the housing investigation. Indeed, actual monopolies in the United States are comparatively rare. The difference between an attempt to monopolize and an attempt

* For the text of the Act see Appendix I, page 299.

to restrain trade is, of course, only a difference in degree. Nevertheless, the Sherman Act treats the two problems separately in two sections. The effect of these two sections is to require every combination of separate businesses and also every acquisition of power by a single organization to justify itself under the rule of reason laid down by the courts, or under some specific legislative privilege.

The third section applies the Act specifically to the District of Columbia. Here, interstate commerce is not necessary. This section is the model which state antitrust acts should follow if consistent enforcement is to be obtained.

Violation of the first three sections is subject to criminal penalty. The fourth section gives the government the additional power to enforce the Act by civil proceedings, without penalty. The Supreme Court has held that civil proceedings and criminal proceedings may be used at the same time. In providing for civil as well as for criminal enforcement, the Act departs from the ordinary conception of the enforcement of criminal law. It is not usual to find civil and criminal proceedings used together. We look at criminal law as something which must be enforced regardless of consequences, because law enforcement is an end in itself. We think of civil proceedings as actions which may or may not be brought according to the judgment of the party to whom the remedy is granted. It is no one's *duty* to start a civil suit. Therefore, civil suits may be settled or compromised without causing the theoretical lack of respect for law which is supposed to follow discretion in the use of criminal proceedings. If a man committed burglary, for example, it would not be considered proper for the prosecuting attorney to settle the criminal case upon the payment of damages to the injured party. Therefore, in dealing with ordinary crimes, civil and criminal proceedings are not used concurrently.

An antitrust violation is not an ordinary crime. The Sherman Act is violated by respectable people. Violation is an economic offense, the seriousness of which is not related to the moral turpitude of the offender. It is for that reason that the Sherman Act is different from ordinary criminal law in expressly authorizing civil and criminal proceedings to go on at the same time. The criminal procedure puts a hazard on unreasonable business combinations by penalizing past conduct. The civil action gives the court of equity power to maintain competition in the future, or to reestablish it when it has been destroyed.

The fifth section consolidates the prosecution of a Sherman Act conspiracy in a single federal court by extending the court's power beyond the limits of the judicial district in which it sits. In this way persons all over the country who have conspired to restrain trade in a single district are brought into one proceeding.

The sixth section, providing for seizure and forfeiture of property transported in violation of law, is comparatively unimportant.

The seventh section gives to private parties injured by violations of the Sherman Act the right to recover triple damages, including attorney's fees. It is this section which puts a part of the power to enforce the Act in private hands.

That is all there is to the Act itself. Supplementing these provisions, the Clayton Act[1] was passed in 1914. The Department of Justice and the Federal Trade Commission have concurrent jurisdiction to enforce this Act, the Department by judicial proceedings and the Commission by administrative proceedings subject to court review. Administrative power was conferred upon the Commission upon the theory that this procedure is more adequate to deal with some of the business problems presented than the judicial process. It would be a digression to describe the Clayton Act in detail here, because all the important prosecutions by the Department of Justice are under the original Sherman Act.*

The Sherman Act has also been supplemented by many laws which grant special privileges to agriculture, labor, retail merchants, and others. The Agricultural Marketing Agreement Act[2] and the Miller-Tydings Act[3] are examples. The general purpose of such legislation is to put unorganized business in a position to bargain collectively with great corporate enterprises. Some of these Acts in effect serve to put a floor under prices for particular groups of industry or agriculture to provide for limited combinations in the interest of what

* The Federal Trade Commission Act, passed in 1914, is enforced exclusively by the Commission by administrative proceedings. Typical of the Commission's jurisdiction under this Act is its policing of false advertising and unfair methods of competition.

is called "fair competition" as opposed to "ruinous competition." When such privileges are granted, the function of the Sherman Act is to prevent their use for purposes not intended by Congress. It provides a balance wheel to keep legislative privilege within bounds.

I have set forth about all that anyone needs to know in regard to the antitrust laws themselves. Indeed, it is about all that even the most skilled lawyer needs to carry around in his head. The application of these general principles to specific industries can only be decided after study of the economic conditions in those industries. And so dependent is such a decision on knowledge of the facts that no lawyer has any advantage over a layman expert in the facts of the industry in guessing whether the courts will approve or disapprove a particular method of doing business. The Act can be as well understood by laymen as by lawyers. Indeed, the guess of legal experts who fumble around among the decisions and forget business results have usually proved to be wrong. No better general statement of the function of the Sherman Act can be found than the following by Professor Walton Hamilton of Yale, which appeared in *The New Republic* of April 15, 1940. He said:

The Sherman Act has by Mr. Chief Justice Hughes been likened to the Constitution. Its usefulness lies in the general character of its provisions. Reduce it to a catalog of specific taboos—then activities drift farther and farther from the law's veto; stresses and strains develop; ingenuity contrives lawful ways to forbidden fruit; a gulf yawns between offense and practice. Only as they are kept general can clauses remain flexible and relevant. The administration of Antitrust cannot escape the constant exercise of judgment. How to grant power and withhold discretion is an age-old enigma, just as likely to be solved as squaring the circle or making motion renew its own motion. The text of the Act may remain intact, yet Antitrust today cannot be Antitrust of the irresponsible twenties, of the far-off year of 1890, of the common law of a machineless England. In a national economy the right of the worker is set over against the right of the consumer to decent goods at a fair price. It was James Madison, the father of the Constitution—not Karl Marx—who taught that the function of policy is to obtain a just balance among the interests which make up the commonwealth.

It is obvious that we have here a general principle which subjects business to a hazard of prosecution which is somewhat indefinite. That hazard is no different from the one which accompanies the test of reasonable and due care in every branch of the law, whether it relates to reckless driving or to the duty of directors of a corporation toward their stockholders. It is the same kind of test that governs our fundamental conception of due process in constitutional law. Nevertheless, the impossibility of reducing antitrust laws to mathematical logic has been often urged against their enforcement. Similar argument, based on lack of legal precision in decrees directed at monopoly, was an important factor in stopping effective enforcement by logically-minded Germany until it drifted into direct price-fixing as a more precise substitute.

PROCEDURE UNDER THE SHERMAN ACT

In this country we have built up a tradition around the Sherman Act that such an argument is not likely to prevail, though, of course, it will be made over and over again in every antitrust proceeding. After fifty years of the Sherman Act, we have become accustomed to the lack of precision in the test which it applies. Our experience with the NRA has disillusioned us as to the wisdom of delegating to separate industries the power to make their own rules of reasonableness. We have always distrusted direct price-fixing as a cure for disparity of prices. And so, in spite of their lack of precision, we are again thrown back on the standards of the Sherman Act as the only practical curb on the uneconomic use of industrial combination. Actually, the uncertainty of antitrust prosecution is more imaginary than real. It is perfectly possible to develop a practical procedure which will eliminate most of that uncertainty.

The Procedure by which Antitrust Laws are Enforced

To obtain constructive results from an act aimed at eliminating an economic evil, procedure is all important. If it is simple, non-technical and understandable, the act will work. If it is not, the act will fail. Prior to the broad campaign of antitrust enforcement now under way, the machinery of enforcement was not well understood. No general plan of attack on the distribution of products in industry had been formulated because there never was enough money to put such a plan into operation. The hit-or-miss prosecution by the government, coupled by irresponsible, private litigation, added to the confusion.

It has been demonstrated, I think, today that antitrust procedure is capable of being used so that no *unnecessary* or onerous uncertainties or hazards are thrown across the path of the businessman, farmer, or laborer willing to subject his plans for combination or cooperative action to government examination. He does not even need a lawyer to make him safe. He does not even have to follow the advice of the government if he disagrees. All he needs to do is to work in the open.

Any layman can understand the process. The simplest way to explain it is to follow its application in a hypothetical case. Suppose three corporations, X, Y, and Z desire to enter into a marketing agreement which they believe will not unnecessarily restrict competition. Any one of a large number of factors may be the basis for their claim that the agreement is reasonable. For example, public health, national defense, economies in production, economies in distribution, the acquisition of bargaining power sufficient to put the three corporations on a level with others, the elimination of fraudulent or corrupt practices, all are relevant in such a situation. At this point they are compelled to consider whether their proposed agreement will run afoul of the Sherman Act.

There are two things which these three corporations may do. First, they may go ahead without consulting anyone. If they do this, however, it is important that they be sure of their ground. The agreement must be one which no reasonable person would question. It must be apparent to any reasonable man that it does not present dangers that in the future the operation of the agreement will unreasonably restrict the balance wheel of competition. If, under these circumstances, these three corporations proceed privately to put their agreement into effect, they are taking a chance on their economic judgment. If that judgment is wrong, they will be subject to criminal prosecution.

This is the plain intention of Congress in providing for criminal penalties, *i.e.* to put a hazard on private combination—to compel businessmen to move with caution. That intention has been short-circuited in the past through the operation of what has been commonly known as the consent decree. This term has no technical meaning. Every decree in every complicated case involving financial reorganization is reached at least partly through negotiation and consent. The term "consent decree" in antitrust cases got a special meaning because it came to represent a device which was nothing more or less than a process by which a criminal offense was condoned. It worked this way:*

The government, having procured evidence of violation of the antitrust laws, would either prosecute or threaten to prosecute the business involved. After the investigation was started, the defendants would be

---

* The description which follows does not represent any past policy of the Antitrust Division. However, it fitted the settlement of *some* cases, and thus created a public impression that the practice was common.

called in. If they felt they could not justify their conduct in open court, they would make a private agreement with the Department of Justice consenting that they be enjoined from repeating that illegal conduct. As a *quid pro quo* for this agreement the government would drop the criminal proceedings. In effect, this process abolished the penalties for violations of the antitrust laws. Further than that, it made the decrees themselves ineffective. They were necessarily long and complicated. They enjoined only the particular acts which were complained of. Therefore, after one of these long decrees had been entered, astute counsel for the defendants would evolve another scheme for the elimination of competition which could be plausibly argued not to come within the express prohibitions of the former decree. The government would attack again in an equity proceeding, since the suit was not on the civil side of the docket, and no hazards or penalties were involved. A second decree would be entered after protracted litigation, either by consent or after a hearing, enjoining the new practices. Whereupon, the astute counsel would think up something else and start the process all over again.

This use of the consent decree was nothing more or less than a form of unemployment relief for lawyers. Its absurdity can be understood by anyone. It flourished only because a cloud of mystery which hung over the Antitrust Act prevented the public from understanding what was going on.

Let me illustrate. The Aluminum Company of America in 1909, by virtue of aggressive activity in plain violation of the law, eliminated its largest competitor and set itself on the way of becoming one of our greatest monopolies. In 1912, in a civil suit,[4] it admitted it had done wrong and was enjoined from eliminating that particular competitor any more. But at the time of the 1912 decree, the competitor was gone. The decree could not and did not revive that competition. It was only a gesture to symbolize that the Sherman Act was still on the books while the Aluminum Company went merrily on its road to absolute monopoly. In addition to that, the fact that the civil process had been used was an advertisement to others that if they could combine fast enough, they were safe. In any event, there was no harm in trying because there was no penalty. Combinations in restraint of trade under this process were simply a race by the lawyers skilled in the arts of delaying litigation and a government which never had sufficient personnel to prosecute litigation vigorously or on a wide front. It was a duel in which one of the opponents was armed with a gun and the other with a pillow.

We should, however, be slow to blame the officials of the Department of Justice of the past who developed this consent decree method. It was the natural consequence of the failure of Congress to provide funds for enforcement. It is a hard, brutal fact that if a prosecuting officer has no men to try a case, he *must* settle it. That was the situation which confronted every Assistant Attorney General in charge of the Antitrust Division during the past forty years. There lies the real cause of the condonation of illegal business conduct.

Today this use of consent decrees has been definitely repudiated by the Department of Justice. If the Act is violated, criminal prosecution will follow.[5] It will not be compromised because of the cessation of the conduct complained of. (The consent decree has an entirely different function which will be explained later.) Therefore, if the three corporations in the hypothetical case we are discussing wish to combine without laying the plans before any public authority, they must be sure that both in present appearance and in future operation it will not be questioned by reasonable men.

I have said, however, that there are two things that persons desiring to combine may do, and the first has been described as going ahead without consulting anyone. But suppose that the X, Y, and Z corporations in the above case desire to protect themselves against the hazards of future criminal prosecution. If so, there is a plain and easy road for them to follow, and this is the second course I mean to describe. It simply consists in submitting all the facts to the Department of Justice in order to find out just what the risks of prosecution are. At this point it should be emphasized that the Antitrust Division has never been delegated quasi judicial power. It cannot make a decision which will have in court even *prima facie* bearing on what the law is. It has no authority to *approve* anyone's plans for combination. That power lies only in the courts.

However, there is one thing the Antitrust Division *can* do. It can tell businessmen whether it *intends* to prosecute or not. It can say to them, "We believe that your plan is so unreasonable that it is illegal on its face," or it can say, "We see no reason for prosecuting at present." This might appear at first blush to be an authority so limited that it will not help the X, Y, and Z corporations because the plan may work out in the future to be a restraint of trade, or because some future Attorney General may take a different view regarding the reasonableness of the plan. Yet, if we go a little further in the procedure we will find that the machinery of enforcement actually offers the businessman in such circumstances every reasonable protection.

In order to understand that procedure, let us look at the *Appalachian Coals* case.[6] In that case, the Supreme Court examined a plan for a marketing agency to serve a number of coal companies. The court said in effect that the agency was reasonable enough on its face. It went on to say, however, that perhaps in the future the agency might work in such a way as unreasonably to restrain trade. It, therefore, adopted the common sense course of directing that the case remain open, giving to the government the right to check up any time in the future and ask the court to stop the plan if it gave to the marketing agency an unreasonable power over prices.

It would not have been fair to allow a business to go ahead subject to criminal penalty if such plan openly proposed in good faith did not work out. However, that was not the result. The civil action contemplated by the Supreme Court to be applied in the future provided no penalty whatever. Therefore the decision in this case in a very simple way allowed the plan to have a chance. It subjected the businessmen to the kind of curb to which no one could object, *i.e.,* the power to stop them without penalty if their activities proved in practice to be contrary to the purposes of the law. Such a procedure gives a premium to the business concern which acts in the open—which does everything in its power to subject its ideas of what combinations are necessary and reasonable to public examination. It brings the activities of great industrial combinations out of the cellar where the most aggressive seekers after short-run profits have all the advantages. I believe that ninety per cent of all the violations of the antitrust laws which are now being prosecuted would never even have been considered by the violators if they had involved advance submission to a court.

If the corporations in the *Appalachian Coals* case had desired to work in secret and to try out their admittedly doubtful procedure (since the lower court held it to be illegal) without submitting it to anyone, it would not have been in the least unfair to have subjected them to criminal process if the plan did not work out. And as a matter of fact, as business experience has shown over and over again, the plan probably would have resulted in an unreasonable restraint of trade had it been put into effect without this kind of public examination.

It is this plain and simple principle of the *Appalachian Coals* case, rewarding the business that works in the open, which is the basis of the policy of the Department of Justice in differentiating between the civil and criminal process. Let us continue our hypothetical case and apply this principle to the prosecution policy of the Department.

Since the law has put a duty on corporations X, Y, and Z to proceed with caution, obviously the sensible course is to inform the Department of the agreement they propose to enter into. They should do this in plain and simple language giving all the facts. They do not need a lawyer to recite these facts. All they need is someone with the power of clear expression and the ability to analyze a business situation.

Let us suppose that such a statement is submitted to the Department. The Department then has two courses open:

1. *It may tell the corporations that the agreement is a violation of the antitrust laws on its face; and that, therefore, a criminal prosecution will follow if they carry it out.*

It may be that the lawyers in the Antitrust Division are so occupied with other cases that they cannot start immediate prosecution. However, by giving this warning, the X, Y, and Z corporations are put on notice that at some time in the future they may be called before the criminal bar. Under such circumstances, if they go ahead, they must be sure that the government is wrong. They have not lost their opportunity for a day in court. They have only been warned that they necessarily take a chance when they act against the decision of a responsible public official.

Such a difference of opinion between corporations X, Y, and Z and the Antitrust Division on any publicly proposed plan is actually very unlikely. Many of the cases being prosecuted today involve violations so flagrant that it is doubtful whether businessmen would have submitted them, in any event, for public examination. One cannot imagine, for example, any businessman in his right mind submitting as a serious plan the distribution system charged in the indictment in the plumbing industry, or indeed, in any other of our present indictments. In practically all antitrust cases the defendants deny the activities charged instead of attempting to justify them.

Therefore, the chances are ten to one that when the Antitrust Division examines the agreement proposed by corporations X, Y, and Z it will not appear to be clearly unreasonable on its face. As a mere matter of public relations, businessmen probably will not submit plans which have that appearance. The plans submitted will usually be ones that can at least be plausibly supported.

The test of the reasonableness of such plausible plans is found only in economic performance. No man can predict what will happen under a plan or agreement, plausible on its face, when it is thrown into a competitive situation. Therefore, the reasonableness of practically every plan which will be publicly submitted will depend upon how it operates in the future. This leads to the second course open to the government when a plan is submitted.

2. *The government will tell corporations X, Y, and Z that it is unable to state definitely whether the*

agreement in actual operation will unreasonably restrain trade.

In such a situation the three corporations may try out the agreement without fear of criminal penalty, following the principle of the *Appalachian Coals* case. The good faith of the defendants in laying their cards on the table is protection against the hazards of criminal prosecution. After submission of a scheme, business is entitled to experiment. If the experiment proves to be a failure, the only penalty will be that they will be told to stop, which is not a penalty at all. The worst that they would get would be an injunction. There is nothing more that they can reasonably ask in the way of protection against the uncertainties of the law, because they are not actually uncertainties of the law but they are the uncertainties of industrial development against which no business can be protected.

If corporations, X, Y, and Z, do not care to attempt this simple procedure, it should not lie in their mouths to complain if the government puts upon them the risk of criminal prosecution. This procedure is open to any group. It gives protection to a labor union as well as to business enterprise. I have yet to hear a reasonable objection to it. I quote an editorial in the *Washington Star* of April 17, 1940, to show that there is nothing about this procedure which prevents its being explained in ordinary newspaper language:

Aid for Labor

In offering to rule on union activities—contemplated or in operation—to determine if they violate the anti-trust

THE BOTTLENECKS OF BUSINESS

laws, and thereby give those responsible an opportunity to avert criminal prosecution, Assistant Attorney General Arnold has taken an effective step to refute the charge that labor is being treated unfairly in the current drive of the Justice Department on restraints in the building industry which has resulted in a number of indictments.

The offer was made to John P. Coyne, head of the Building Trades Department of the American Federation of Labor, which has objected vigorously to the Government using the Sherman Act against labor. From the tenor of Mr. Coyne's remarks on the subject before the International Union of Operating Engineers, it was favorably received.

The plan contemplates that the Justice Department be asked for an opinion as to legality whenever a union decides upon action that will restrain interstate commerce, even though it considers the restraint "reasonable." If the finding is adverse, the union, of course, will proceed at its own risk. If for any reason the department is unable to reach a conclusion, the union will be at liberty to act, and if it later is determined that its course is illegal, it will be subject only to civil instead of criminal proceedings.

The Government undoubtedly would be grateful to have labor take the fullest advantage of this plan, which would go far toward settling the trouble that has been stirred over the anti-trust campaign. The most apparent drawback is the fact that labor is claiming exemption from the Sherman Act, and might not on that account be willing to have any action measured by its provisions. The Supreme Court, however, soon is expected to decide if unions are subject to the act, and if this is determined to be the case, the Arnold proposal affords a means by which

150

labor can enjoy the fullest exercise of its rights, while at the same time guarding the public against abuses.

As the editorial points out, the procedure received a favorable reaction from the head of the Building Trades Department of the American Federation of Labor. The confusion about antitrust procedure in the past has been that a consistent prosecution policy has never been worked out. The precedents have been there to follow, but the prosecution policy has not been consistent enough to apply them. Today, in order to formulate a consistent prosecution policy, public statements are made giving the reasons for each important action taken by the Department. Out of such statements, which are considered as precedents for the Department to follow in the future, a consistent policy is being developed in the traditional American way— that is, case by case.

The specific Departmental precedent which gives authority for the procedure outlined above was publicly stated in the case against the Association of American Railroads. In 1934 this association had laid before the Department a plan to eliminate joint rates between railroads and motor carriers. The Department took no action when the plan was submitted. After I came into office, the situation was called to my attention by responsible complainants. I considered it a plain violation of the antitrust law. Nevertheless, in view of the previous action of the railways in laying their cards on the table, a civil prosecution was commenced instead of a criminal prosecution. The reasons were given in a public statement as follows:

THE BOTTLENECKS OF BUSINESS

The agreement which it is alleged contravenes the antitrust laws in this case consists of resolutions passed by the Association of American Railroads. The existence of these resolutions was revealed to the Department of Justice some time ago but due to limitation of personnel it has been impossible for the Department to investigate and take action. The agreement thus continued with the full knowledge of the Department. Moreover, the defendants in this action have cooperated fully with the Department in the investigation that preceded the filing of this case by providing it with complete information as to the conditions surrounding the agreements and other factors involved in the situation. In view of these circumstances and in view of the fact that a civil suit will adequately present the issue involved, the Department believes that a criminal action is inappropriate.

This procedure requires a consistent policy of criminal prosecution where business, or labor, or farmers do not see fit to submit in advance plans which skirt close to the edge of legality. A hazard of criminal prosecution must be put upon reckless business conduct or else the Sherman Act will have no deterrent effect whatever. It is for this reason that the occasional use of the civil process as a means of condoning past offenses has been definitely and finally repudiated.

There remains the exceptional case, where businessmen need protection, not only from criminal prosecution but also from civil prosecution. These are cases where large investments are necessary in order to make a proposed plan effective. It should certainly not be the purpose of the antitrust laws to prevent business

PROCEDURE UNDER THE SHERMAN ACT

expansion. The example of the Ford Motor Company
comes immediately to mind. No sane economist would
have wanted to stop such a development. Suppose,
therefore, that the plan of corporations X, Y, and Z requires expenditure of a million dollars which cannot
be borrowed if an injunction suit, even without any
penalty, is a possibility in the future. Such cases are
not frequent. However, when they are presented to
the Department, it is only reasonable that the businessmen involved be given more certainty than the mere
submission of the plan can offer. The Department itself cannot give that certainty because it has no judicial power. It must, therefore, take such a situation
directly into court. Here is a case for the proper use
of the consent decree.

It works in this way. Corporations A, B, and C in
such a case need judicial approval of their plan because
the department has not and should not have judicial
power. Therefore, the plan will be drawn up in the
form of a proposed decree to be submitted to a court.
Such a decree should contain every safeguard consistent with financial stability. It should be subject to
reexamination by the court at the earliest convenient
time, since no one is able to prophesy business conditions very far in advance. It should provide access to
the corporate books and records so that examination
of how the plan is working will be easy. This does not
involve any general principle that the government is
free to look at corporate books and records. It only
means that where a corporation desires to secure a continuing judicial approval, it should offer every con-

venience to the court to determine whether that judicial approval should be given or withheld.

So safeguarded, the decree will be presented to the court in a civil proceeding. Such decrees are ordinarily called "consent" decrees. However, the term is not accurate. The Department and the three corporations may agree that the whole decree is reasonable, or only part of it or they may agree on none of it. Nevertheless these three corporations should be entitled to their day in court if they think the Department is wrong. Therefore, the word "civil" decree is a more accurate description of this process than "consent" decree, even though many of these decrees may be entirely negotiated by consent.

When the case has reached this stage, the plan will be submitted to the federal court. This submission is public with an opportunity given for everyone to object. This includes competitors, consumers, municipalities, or anyone else.

For example, in the decree entered into in the Ford and Chrysler cases, the independent finance companies were heard at length. The court, after listening to them, adjourned the proceedings to enable them to explain the terms of the decree to a convention of the finance companies and then to make further objections. It was only after that full opportunity for hearing was given that the decree was signed. In the plan of reorganization submitted in the Columbia Gas and Electric case, not only were the competitors heard but also the representatives of municipalities which the gas companies involved were serving. People who appear to object to the decree may or may not be parties to the suit. If they are not parties, they appear *amicus curiae* (as a friend of the court) to fully inform the court of the effect of the decree on their interests. Such precautions are not necessary in the ordinary decree by consent in an equity suit. It is because antitrust decrees which curb the conduct of great enterprises have such a far-reaching effect that it is necessary to throw this protection around this process. It is also necessary because office settlements between the Department of Justice and business are subject to suspicion. It is just as important that the Department of Justice work in the open in the application of the antitrust laws as it is for business to work in the open. Neither one of them is entitled to any secrets in matters which so finally affect the public interest.

This policy has been often misrepresented in the public press by persons whose chief aim is to sabotage antitrust enforcement. A typical example of that kind of misrepresentation is set out below in an editorial from the *New York Mirror*, December 23, 1938:

"I Am the Law"

─Editorial─

"*CONSENT DECREE*" *is a mysterious legalistic term that describes a system by which ex-professor Thurman Arnold, as Assistant U. S. Attorney General, is building up a private little dictatorship over every form of Ameri-*

156

PROCEDURE UNDER THE SHERMAN ACT

can enterprise—extended this week to include jurisdiction over the entire medical profession.

● BACK TO THE BLUE EAGLE

The NRA, declared unconstitutional by the Supreme Court, has been revived in effect by Thurman Arnold. Here's how he works it:

FIRST—Arnold picks out the industry he wants to "regulate" under a code of "fair practice." Then under the antitrust laws, he threatens prosecution of various firms and their officers.

SECOND—Der Fuehrer Arnold lets it be known that if the victims will propose a "code" which not only promises to cease the alleged violations, but promises further self-regulation in the direction of what Arnold considers is proper, then the indictment will be dropped.

Arnold's department officially admits that the threat of an indictment is used to force changes that are not required by the law.

● MORE THAN THE LAW DEMANDS

The "code" of business practice coerced from a corporation must be constitutionally acceptable to a Federal Court, and economically acceptable to Arnold.

Under Arnold's system, the code "may contain positive provisions requiring definite rearrangements in an industry, the adoption of new techniques for carrying on business, and the doing of many affirmative acts which in and of themselves the law does NOT require."

THE THIRD STEP in Arnold's system of one-man coercion of industry is this:

If the "code" as proposed by the threatened or actually indicted firms is acceptable to Arnold, then the indictment

THE BOTTLENECKS OF BUSINESS

is dropped and the "code" is made binding upon the firms by a "consent decree," which shall last for four years.

● ALL BEHIND LOCKED DOORS

Unlike the codes that were drawn up under the NRA by open meetings of Labor, Management, and Government, the "codes" muscled through by Arnold are arrived at by a process of forced negotiation that is never submitted to the protective light of publicity that is one of the strongest guarantees of democratic government.

History has recorded too many examples of this unchanging rule: Where mystery begins, democracy ends.

From the Star Chamber to the "confession trials" of modern Red Russia, Justice has never survived secrecy.

Arnold will argue—accurately—that he does not "suggest" the terms of the "code" to any of the firms he cracks down on with this system. That does not alter the fact that he has the final say on what is "fair practice." By a process of rejection, he can steer any indicted firm or organization into his own conception of "fair practice."

If you want to see just how baffling Professor Arnold's conception is, try to understand his latest mystery book, "The Folklore of Capitalism."

Which should have as its subtitle—"Mein Kampf."

The above misrepresentation of the consent decree procedure is set out to be compared with the statements of fact in this chapter so that the reader will not be misled by the inevitable recurrence of this type of thing whenever litigation which is displeasing to special interests is started.

There is only one more use of the consent decree which needs to be explained, and then we are through.

PROCEDURE UNDER THE SHERMAN ACT

Suppose that the X, Y, and Z corporations, acting under the sporadic and indefinite prosecution policy of the past, had been indicted or were being investigated by a grand jury. Suppose that no moral turpitude was involved. This often happens. As I have shown above, antitrust violations are often morally excusable as defense tactics used out of necessity, because the government failed to enforce the law against others. Suppose that the X, Y, and Z corporations were defendants in this sort of case. In such a situation, enlightened business leadership might consider it advisable to enter into a decree that would eliminate the conditions in the entire industry which compelled these illegal practices. Suppose a voluntary plan to accomplish such a purpose were submitted. Suppose that by cleaning up the entire industry for the future the plan went further in the public interest than any criminal penalty could possibly go. In such a case, the Department would submit to the court the question of whether the prosecution should be dropped on condition that the plan was incorporated in a decree.

This is an entirely different thing from the old consent decree. No prosecution today will be dropped merely because the defendants have ceased the practices for which they are being prosecuted. A plan to be the basis of a *nolle prosse* of an indictment must give substantial advantages to the public, to consumers, and to competitors in maintaining reasonable business practices in the future which cannot be obtained by continuing the criminal prosecution. In addition to that, the court must be persuaded of this in an open hearing.

For example, in the Ford and Chrysler cases, a criminal proceeding was *nolle prossed* because the defendants not only agreed to stop the practices for which they had been indicted but also voluntarily submitted a plan of conducting the finance business voluntarily entered into that took care of most of the perplexing problems which had led to the violations of law in the past. It provided for the active support through advertising by the great motor companies of those independent financing companies which chose to adopt fair collection methods and fair interest rates. It was limited in time. It was subject to reexamination if it did not work. It obtained far more public benefits than could possibly have been secured through further prosecution.

This process puts it up to businessmen to correct the evils in their own industries. The Department under no circumstances tells them what to do. It simply puts a deterrent upon the violations of law and gives them the opportunity to work out a different method of accomplishing their lawful objects if they choose.

A simple case of where a decree might be submitted as a basis for dismissing a prosecution is found in the labor prosecutions on account of jurisdictional strikes where one legitimate labor union attacks the employer to get him to break his contract with the members of another union.

In this case the violation consists in stopping goods in interstate commerce in order to destroy a legitimate labor union. The employer who is willing to bargain collectively and to pay any reasonable wage, or provide for any reasonable hours or conditions, is helpless because if he employs members of one union the other will attack him.

If a union is indicted for such conduct, the prosecution will not be *nolle prossed* simply on the grounds that the strike has been stopped and the particular suit settled. However, suppose that the union involved agrees in a decree to set up arbitration machinery by which such strikes could be settled in the future and to abide by the results of arbitration. Perhaps some arbitration machinery may already exist but has failed because the union can refuse to obey it with impunity. If, however, the machinery, including the agreement to abide by the arbitration result, were incorporated in a decree, the union would have to obey the award or be guilty of contempt. Thus the possibility of a jurisdictional strike would be eliminated. The Antitrust Division has no interest in *how* such disputes are settled—that is, in which union finally wins. It is only concerned that goods be not stopped in interstate commerce by the effect of such useless labor battles between labor unions, or between unions and their employers. Such consent decrees would completely clean up the situation which created jurisdictional strikes in the building trades all over the United States. It is difficult to argue against such a solution. It goes much further than simply agreeing to stop the particular jurisdictional strike in question in a particular case, hence the Department would be justified in asking the court for permission to *nolle prosse* the case upon the submission of such a decree.

It is important that every step of this process should be public. The decree should be submitted to the court together with the reasons why the Antitrust Division considered that it justified a *nolle prosse*. Objectors should be heard as *amicus curiae* in the discretion of the court.

In using this procedure it is important that the Department should not tell defendants what they should do, but should leave to them entirely the proposal of constructive solutions. The Department's sole function is to enforce the law. But when businessmen, labor union, or others are compelled to stop illegal practices that have gone on for a long time in the past, they often are faced with a new situation which requires them to adopt new practices. Since they are familiar with the business, they are in the best position to determine what these new practices should be. If new combinations are necessary, which look reasonable in themselves but which may in the future result in unreasonable domination of the market, businessmen should be free to try out these new practices without incurring the hazards of criminal penalties. The use of the consent decree as a ground for *nolle prossing* a criminal prosecution gives a reward to businessmen who really desire to clean up their industry and to prevent situations arising in the future which would lead to violation of the law.

The power to *nolle prosse* a case is inherent in the office of every prosecutor. It is a power which is easy to abuse. The best protection against this abuse is to formulate a policy forcing the prosecutor to make public his reasons for a *nolle prosse*. The dangers of the use of *nolle prosse* lie first in condonation of offenses because of political pressures on the prosecutor, and second in the use of criminal prosecution as a club to enforce the prosecutor's ideas on business. These two dangers can be avoided only by subjecting the *nolle prosse* procedure to *public* examination. It is the secret use of the *nolle prosse* which has caused scandals in prosecutor's offices. The power to *nolle prosse* can never be taken away except by Congress. The greatest safeguard against the dangers inherent in the power to *nolle prosse* consists in laying the reasons for each action before the court in a public record.

It is customary for businessmen who seek to avoid being prosecuted to come to the office of the Antitrust Division and ask what it is that the Department of Justice wants them to do. The invariable answer of the Antitrust Division should be that it does not know, —that its function is simply to prosecute for past offenses. It should, however, not close the doors to constructive plans for the organization of business if those conducting it choose to offer them.

From the foregoing, it should be clear that the procedures under present law are simple, and that they offer ample protection to those persons or groups willing to operate in the open and submit their proposals to public scrutiny.

VIII.

The Clarification of Law Through
Public Enforcement

WHY has the Sherman Act failed to work in the past?
The answer to this question is that it has worked for
those who used it. The trouble has been that enforcement has been predominantly in private hands. Therefore, enforcement has been used only for private purposes.*

* When I submitted this statement to a well known economist I got the following comment. I quote verbatim.
"The first paragraph is too sweeping and gives the
wrong impression. It seems to say that triple damage
suits represent all the antitrust activities in the past.
You weaken your case by overstatement. As a matter
of fact, the public prosecutions under the Sherman
Act are quite imposing. The trouble is they are
spread over fifty years instead of ten.
"If I understand these pages, they give the impression of all private and little public enforcement in
the past. This, I believe, is wrong, both from the
point of view of fact and policy. You had better give
predecessors some credit for suits in the public interest as a matter of courtesy."
In spite of this criticism, I decided to let the paragraph stand
because I consider it as accurate as any broad generalization
can be.

CLARIFICATION OF LAW

Section 7 of the Sherman Act gives any private party the right to recover triple damages, including attorney's fees, for any violation of the Act which has injured him. The intention was to supplement public enforcement, but the result has been to overshadow public enforcement. The great majority of prosecutions since the passage of the Act have been controlled by private interests. The whole public purpose of the Act to maintain a free market for consumers has been obscured for reasons which are inherent in any system of private enforcement of a public law.

In a private suit the interests of the consumer cannot be presented to the court. The money which pays the costs and the lawyers' fees *must* come out of the corporate treasury of an organization interested only in more profits for itself. This is a perfectly legitimate interest. The manager of a business *must* be principally concerned with the profits of his company. He cannot be a philanthropist. His duty to his stockholders excludes the larger national interest. If he spends too much time trying to be a philanthropist, he will be a poor businessman, and his Board of Directors will discharge him. We need sharp businessmen to keep our wheels turning. But we must not put them in the impossible position of enforcing a public law designed to put limitations on their own organizations in the interest of consumers.

The interest of the consumer cannot be represented by persons under obligation to their stockholders and directors to get the maximum spread between costs and prices. But the vice of private enforcement is broader than this. Private enforcement of *any* public law will make of it an instrument detached from its real purpose. Private litigation is a tool which is always most effective in the most powerful hands. When privately paid police in Pennsylvania took over the responsibility of keeping law and order in industrial disputes, the system inevitably degenerated into the oppressive use of the policing power against those whom it was designed to protect. Private enforcement of a public law has always created distrust of the law itself. To the private enforcement of the antitrust law may be attributed nearly all of the misunderstandings of its purposes and function which now exist.

The only justification for private enforcement is the necessity of filling the gap when public enforcement has failed. Such gaps are incidents of every pioneer community. They result in various types of vigilante organizations. But vigilante organizations cannot continue without creating a lawless attitude on the part of those who are unable to maintain their own police force. Therefore, the best intentioned vigilante organization must sooner or later surrender its power to a public organization. Private policing can only be justified as a transitory necessity to meet an emergency situation.

In general, private enforcement has been a battleship without a rudder making sporadic raids against concentrated economic power but incapable of developing a consistent campaign. It has fired its heaviest guns against unorganized industry. For years the antitrust laws were an obstacle in the development of farm cooperatives and worried even consumer cooperatives.* Therefore farmers failed to see how enforcement would give them a free market in which to sell their products. Private enforcement of the antitrust law has been used to break legitimate strikes. Therefore organized labor has come to regard the Sherman Act as a special weapon against labor objectives. Highly organized industry has felt the teeth of the antitrust laws most keenly in so-called "strike suits" designed to collect booty from a board of directors which has made a misstep. And therefore business has come to regard the Sherman Act as a trap and a hazard which rivals may throw across the path of legitimate expansion. Finally, private enforcement in the hands of legitimate competitors in practical effect gave those who injured them the option of buying them out instead of breaking them.

A single example will show how this last process worked. The Bausch Machine Tool Company was being crushed by the Aluminum Company of America. It brought suit for triple damages against the Aluminum Company for violation of the Sherman Act. In that private suit it got a verdict against the Aluminum Company for about a million dollars.[1] The litigation was finally settled for cash and the Bausch Machine Tool Company disappeared. In other words, the Aluminum Company was forced to buy its competitor. This was fortunate for this private plaintiff, but it did

* There were few if any proceedings against farmers' cooperatives but many legal opinions. The worry was caused by legal opinions.

not accomplish the purpose of the Act, *to wit,* maintenance of a competitive market in aluminum.

Such instances as this have occurred over and over again in American industry. They have made it financially costly for organizations to control the market by robbing their competitors. But they have never touched the larger interests of consumers or the public.

Private prosecution also became an actual weapon in the hands of organizations strong enough to finance lawsuits against those who were not sufficiently astute or who could not afford to use this method of protectection. Let me illustrate by another specific example.

Under the outrageous system of block-booking of the motion picture cartel, independent theaters were at the mercy of the major producers. A large producing company sent its agents into a certain territory and demanded of the independent theaters an increase in payments for the company's pictures ranging from 35 per cent to 45 per cent. The independent theaters protested that such an increase would be ruinous. They had no real choice, however, but to accept the increase, because the supply of pictures was under a cartel control which also controlled competing theaters. Since the producers had their own theater outlets in the same territory, they were under no pressure to meet the independents even half-way.

The salesmen assured the independent theaters that during the next year they were going to get certain new pictures of tremendous popular appeal. They described the pictures and named the actors. Finally the independents stuck their heads in the noose and signed on the dotted line.

When the time came for delivery, none of the great pictures was forthcoming. There were delays. The exhibitors were paying the increased price without getting the feature pictures. One picture that had been "sold" in advance under these representations was "Lost Horizon." It was tremendously popular. But instead of furnishing it to the theater under the system of block-booking, it was exhibited specially in "road shows" at high prices until the cream was all skimmed off. Only then could the independent theaters obtain it as part of their contracts.

The independent theaters protested. They said it had been represented to them that certain specific pictures with well-known actors would be given to them in exchange for the increased payments. They demanded performance of these representations. At this point legal representatives of the producers called on the independents. They pointed out certain fine print in the contracts which said no representations of sales agents would be binding on the company. They told them about the Statute of Frauds which prevents oral representations from being used to vary the terms of a written contract.

Deprived of a legal remedy the independent theaters organized a boycott against the producing company to prevent the use of such tactics. At this point the producing company instituted a private suit against the independent theaters for combining through the boycott to restrain trade in violation of the Sherman Act.

THE BOTTLENECKS OF BUSINESS

Thus was the Act used by a powerful private company to enforce its own monopolistic price control over film.

Sherman Act enforcement should function as an umpire in the competitive game. However, the umpire can never be in the pay of one of the competing teams and still remain an umpire.

The reason why public enforcement could never operate effectively is a very simple one. From the time of the enactment of the Sherman Act until the last two years, we have never given the Department of Justice an adequate staff. For forty years we have been just about ready to enforce the law. We have written books; we have passed supplemental legislation; we have preached; we have defined; we have built a great system of legal metaphysics; and we have denounced. Indeed, we have done everything except to get an organization together and do an actual practical job of policing.

Let me illustrate this by the era of Theodore Roosevelt when trust-busting was supposed to be at its height. To read the history of that time is to get the impression that antitrust enforcement was one of the principal activities of government. Yet in fact there was very little enforcement activity. How many employees were engaged in enforcing the Sherman Act? You will be surprised when I answer that the personnel of the Antitrust Division during that famous crusade consisted of only five lawyers and four stenographers. Follow the enforcement organization of the antitrust laws during the intervening years—years of the greatest industrial growth and economic power which any government has ever known. From 1914 to 1923 there aver-

CLARIFICATION OF LAW

aged only 18 lawyers in the Antitrust Division. When this Roosevelt administration came into office in 1933 there were only 15 lawyers. This small group was supposed to police the enforcement of a law covering the industrial activity of a nation of 130,000,000 people. At the same time these lawyers had to handle all legal proceedings connected with 31 other major acts of Congress. Compare this with other government activities of narrower scope. The Maritime Commission has a personnel of 1,200; the new Civil Aeronautics Authority has 2,800 though the function of neither of these agencies approaches in extent that of the enforcement of the antitrust laws. A closer illustration is that of the Securities and Exchange Commission. It has eight regional offices and a personnel of over 1,200. If you were to leave all existing securities statutes on the books and cut the personnel of the Securities and Exchange Commission to the size of the Antitrust Division, its enforcement program which is so widely applauded today would be completely wrecked. You cannot keep order in a nation with a corporal's guard.

This small organization charged with antitrust enforcement has never been able to bring enough cases to give consistent application of the Sherman Act to new and changing business conditions. This inability has prevented any consistent body of precedents from being developed to spell out the broad purposes of the Act. Such a line of precedents can come only from a consistent prosecution policy argued before the court in cases selected and presented by a public agency for the purpose of explaining and defining that policy. The helter-skelter selection of cases by private interests for private ends furnishes no opportunity for the interest of the government or the consumer to be presented or argued. The result has been that the judicial interpretation of the Act in the last 40 years has not only lacked precision, it has also lacked any direction whatever. No one has been able to explain along the lines of any consistent theory what cases under the antitrust laws mean.

The effect of these scattered and inconsistent precedents has been to make the antitrust laws full of legal ambushes and traps. Small business could not afford to litigate in an area of confusion where almost any result might be expected from a lower court. It could not afford to pay for the interminable trials necessary to present a case in which sixteen different theories of defense are possible. No public prosecution policy existed to provide landmarks necessary to keep the Sherman Act to its original direction.

In this confused situation, opinions by astute legal counsel backed by huge defense funds had the effect of decisions in court because the appeal from them to the expensive process of litigation was beyond the power of consumers and beyond the means of small business. These legal opinions moved the Act from case to case, as a man moves from tree to tree in a forest, until they had it headed in the opposite direction. These were the fruits of the failure of government to provide enough personnel to formulate a publicly-stated prosecution policy.

The devices used to divert the Sherman Act from

CLARIFICATION OF LAW

its purpose were many. The methods were always the same, *to wit,* to use some legal privilege such as a patent, or the right to organize a trade association, or the use of the corporate faction as a sort of barbed-wire entanglement to prevent the Act from reaching an unquestioned combination in restraint of trade.

No better example of this can be found than in the organization of the glass container industry where legal opinions ground out in private law offices, backed by threatened litigation over patent privileges, created a cartel with dictatorial powers over the distribution of a necessity. The terrorizing effect of these legal shock troops was testified to by a small glass manufacturer who gave in when he saw descending on his city what he called "a train load of attorneys and experts."

It may be useful to spell out in detail how the glass container cartel used oppressively for its own ends the legal confusion which existed in that area where the doctrines of patent law and the Sherman Act overlapped.

Glass containers are a necessity everybody has to buy. They include milk bottles, fruit jars for the house, and all the glass jars in which food is sold by grocery stores. A small group of people in Hartford, Connecticut, operating under the name of Hartford-Empire Company, got control of most of the patents on machinery and processes for making glass containers. They do not manufacture anything, but they do decide whom they will let make fruit jars and other glass containers, how many they can produce, and where they can locate their plants. By the skillful use of its patents Hartford-

THE BOTTLENECKS OF BUSINESS

Empire determined who could go into business and who must keep out. It determined who could manufacture bottles, what type of bottles they could manufacture, and in what quantities. It determined in what areas they could do business. To use the language of one of their memoranda, one of their purposes was "to fence in their competitors" and "to block the development of machines which might be constructed by others." It exercised its power by threats, backed by the showing of its great resources. When ingenious use of their own patents was not sufficient, they combined with others.

The Corning Glass Company was making "specialty" glassware—kitchen dishes which would resist heat, light bulbs, thermometers, and glass scientific instruments. The Hartford-Empire Company was in a position to compete. To eliminate this competition, Corning and Hartford-Empire got together and divided the field between themselves. Corning got a monopoly position in specialty ware, and gave Hartford-Empire a monopoly in glass containers. Both got the power to stop everyone else from making glassware.

But this was not all. Owens-Illinois Glass Company also owned patents connected with the manufacture of bottles. It was the largest glass company in the world. Hartford-Empire Company and Owens-Illinois Company got together and agreed that Hartford-Empire should do all the licensing under its patents—in other words, Hartford should decide who should make glass containers and who should not make them. In return

174

CLARIFICATION OF LAW

Owens-Illinois got half the profits from Hartford-Empire.

The final result is that three companies produce 78 per cent of all the milk bottles in the United States. The other 22 per cent are manufactured by seven other companies, but they are so scattered and so restricted by the Hartford-Empire Company that they offer no competition to the larger three companies.

The following examination of Mr. H. Goodwin Smith before the Temporary National Economic Committee[2] illustrates the supervisory power exercised by the Hartford-Empire Company and how it determines who can produce glass containers, what kind, and how much.

THE CHAIRMAN: I am trying to develop the conclusions which we must all reach after having listened to your testimony. Your company has received from the Government of the United States certain patents which may or may not be granted, according to the position that Congress may take with respect to matters of public policy, so that you are the beneficiary of a grant of power from the Government of the United States, that is from all the people?

MR. SMITH: Quite true.

THE CHAIRMAN: And as the result of that grant, your company now, through its control of patents, dominates this particular industry?

MR. SMITH: That is right, if you leave out the suction.

THE CHAIRMAN: And you do not sell your patents, you do not sell the machines that are made under them, you follow a policy of leasing only. No person may buy a machine outright, and no person or company may use a machine except under the condition that you lay down?

MR. SMITH: Correct.

THE CHAIRMAN: So you follow as a policy the program of strictly examining the power of every licensee to produce?

MR. SMITH: Correct.

THE CHAIRMAN: And you define that power?

MR. SMITH: Correct.

*   *   *   *

DR. LUBIN: May I ask a question of Mr. Smith? You may not be in a position to answer it, but I would be interested if you could. If I were a person with the necessary capital and reputation and I wanted to go into the production of milk bottles, and assuming for the sake of argument that at the time I came to you and asked for a license the milk-bottle production was more or less on a par with the market situation—in other words, you didn't have that large over-capacity that you now have, would you give me a license in preference to somebody who already owned a license who wanted to expand his production?

MR. SMITH: That is a pretty tough question. We certainly would receive with great seriousness your application. Whether we would give it to you or not would depend on probably 10 or 15 other different reasons. I just can't tell you. I can get up a set of reasons some time. I can't tell you now.

And here is how that dictatorial power over a necessity was maintained by threats of ruinous litigation in the absence of a public prosecution to protect the consumer's interest in competitive production.

Out in Texas a small concern was manufacturing

CLARIFICATION OF LAW

bottles for the local market. I quote from the testimony of the President of the concern:[8]

> we had three to five visits from various representatives of the Hartford-Empire Co. They sent us copies of their patents to explain just where we were infringing upon their patents. This went on for some time. In fact, we did not have the money to engage in any extended litigation with them, and, frankly, we tried every means possible to delay the thing and carry it along, to keep them away from us and out of court as long as possible, for I realized that we couldn't pay $100 or $150 a day to stay in the Federal Court. Of course, they realized that too.

* * * *

> I discussed this with Mr. Goodwin Smith, and I guess with five or six others. They had a generous supply of attorneys. I will say this, that I tried to alter the scheme. My partner, Mr. Knape, had been up there a few months before, and it is a sort of variation of my understanding of the third degree to spend 1 hour in this room and 1 hour in the next room, and when he got back he was a nervous wreck, so I insisted I talk to all of them at one time and I have my health.

* * * *

Needless to say, no more milk bottles are being manufactured in Texas.

The Knox Glass Associates in Pennsylvania used to make milk bottles. Hartford-Empire claimed that Knox machinery infringed some of its patents. Although its counsel believed it had a 50-50 chance to defeat these claims, the Knox Company decided not to resist. Mr.

THE BOTTLENECKS OF BUSINESS

R. R. Underwood, president of the Knox Company, testified as follows:[4]

Q. Did the greater resources of Hartford have anything to do with your making that decision not to take up the 50-50 fight?

A. I would say that that has always been an influence in the life of our company, patent wise.

Q. You felt that they could continue the fight longer than you could?

A. That's right.

Q. And that resources and persistence and an army of experts and counsel are as important in a patent fight as they are in any other kind of war?

A. That's right. My file indicates that.

Another example, The Amsler Morton Company had been manufacturing glass machinery ever since 1915. In 1934 it was told to stop or to sell out for what it considered an adequate price. Litigation commenced. Its customers were circularized advising them of the dangers of buying from the company. An infringement suit was begun against a customer named Swindell. I quote from the testimony of the treasurer of Amsler Morton: [5]

Q. Can you tell me how much the Swindell litigation cost your company?

A. Well, it was tremendous for a small concern.

Q. How much was it?

A. It amounted to close to $50,000 and that doesn't take into consideration the expense of our organization.

*   *   *   *

Q. I would like to ask you this: You told us, I believe, that you have sold only one lehr so far this year?

178

A. That is correct.

Q. That you sold no lehrs last year. What would you say the value of the glass—manufacturing machinery business is now? That is, your business.

A. I will give you a comparison. In '28 we were doing $800,000 worth of business and last year we had $18,000 worth of business in the glass industry—quite a drop.

Another example will show the manner in which the Hartford-Empire Company's patent toll bridge backed by threatened private litigation was used to keep new concerns from entering the glass industry. Mr. George Day found that Detroit breweries were having difficulty in obtaining an ample supply of beer bottles. He also learned that a location 20 miles south of Detroit was well adapted to the manufacture of beer bottles, because of the ready availability of the necessary raw material ingredients and fuel. Moreover, Mr. Day was successful in raising sufficient capital to enable him to go into the business of manufacturing bottles. The Hartford-Empire Company urged him not to enter the field, but he was not to be discouraged. He therefore asked them for a license. Now follows this testimony:[6]

Q. And they said they wouldn't refuse you a license, but when you left the meeting you didn't have a license?

A. That is true. However, they made a suggestion that they would not care to grant us a license direct but we could go out and buy up a couple of broken-down glass factories who have a license and we could obtain it that way.

Q. What did you say in reply to that?

THE BOTTLENECKS OF BUSINESS

A. Of course, that is expensive. We didn't have the money to buy a plant and move it to Detroit.

* * * *

Q. And you have never at any time received a license from Hartford-Empire?

A. Never.

Q. Is this group in Detroit still interested in starting a glass factory?

A. They are still interested.

Q. Is the capital still available?

A. It is still available. I had a visit to my office yesterday of the same group of men who are interested in forming that company.

The government has at last stepped in. Proceedings are pending against the Hartford-Empire and its confederates.[7] New competitors will now receive protection—but it is too late to help the ones who have been destroyed by private litigation.

The Hartford-Empire is not an isolated case. A more current example is found in the recent investigation of the beryllium industry. An individual interested in the manufacture of beryllium recently stated before the Temporary National Economic Committee:[8]

. . . we had spent considerable money and a few years' work; if we continued the development we might find after five or ten years a lot of overhanging patents, owned by Siemens which would be held against us and we would be told some day "Well, you can't operate any more," or "You can't make beryllium copper and heat treat it, or you can't use beryllium copper alloys for certain specific pur-

CLARIFICATION OF LAW

poses, or you can't heat treat beryllium nickel, and so forth."

As in the dyestuffs industry the patents were held as a means of preventing a business in this country.

Finally, in order to go into the beryllium business, this individual was forced to agree to restrict his activities to America, barring himself completely from doing business in the European market. Beryllium is an important war material.

This sort of thing can be accomplished by other devices than patents. Often the cloak is protection for efficiency or health. The trade association, an admirable movement in this country, may be illegitimately used to establish a tight system of control and ruin the independence of its members. Let us illustrate by another example.

There were about 350 manufacturers of corrugated paper boxes located all over the country. During the time of the depression they naturally succumbed to the desire to bolster up their prices against a falling market. A prominent New York firm of efficiency engineers took advantage of this situation. It sent missionaries to all the firms and organized the majority of them into fourteen regional offices in the interests of efficiency and put its personnel in charge of the associations. Then on top of the fourteen regional offices was imposed a national association, also controlled by the employees of the firm of efficiency engineers. The manufacturers who wanted to remain independent were forced into the association by all sorts of pressures.

Then the association began to take control of the price policies of the manufacturers. It gave them legal advice and accounting service. The lawyer in the small town lost his business. So did the small town accountant. All control became centralized in New York. Thus, without investing a cent, this firm of efficiency engineers became the real owners of the entire container industry. Their profits were enormous while many members of the association were losing money. It was something like the holding company device excepting it didn't require the purchase of any stock. This firm is now under indictment, but prior to that time through the weight of its expert advice it had convinced those who joined their organization that the plan was legal.[9]

Such are the fruits of turning over antitrust enforcement to skilled lawyers hired by private industrial concerns. Briefly summarized, this system puts a premium upon ingenuity in using the recognized legitimate legal privilege to avoid the Act. Antitrust law becomes written not by courts with the interests of consumers in mind but in great corporation law offices. Their ideas of the law become reflected throughout the industry. And thus it happened that industries like plumbing and glass and oil found confidence to fly in the face of every objective the antitrust laws were intended to reach, backed by the elaborate legal opinion of the supposed great experts in the meaning of the Sherman Act. Such, I repeat, are the fruits of turning over the enforcement of this great public law to private organizations.

Congress cannot keep up with this process. It centers

its attention not upon the organization itself but on the device which is used. When holding companies become a scandal a special law is devised to destroy them. But this special law will have the united opposition of thousands of investors whose savings have become dependent upon the capitalization of a restraint of trade. You do not stop unreasonable restraints of trade by waiting until the illegal use of some otherwise legitimate device has become a matter of public knowledge. It is too late then. The combinations are already formed. Investors have put their savings into them. They cannot be destroyed without enormous dislocation. And while you are destroying them the industrial empire builders are busy using new methods which, in the absence of a public prosecution policy, they cloak with the trappings of legality.

Under the ingenious and illegitimate uses of otherwise legitimate devices, restraints of trade developed into the following definite types:

1. The monopoly. Curiously enough this is the rarest type of all. Perhaps the existing organizations which come nearest to being monopolies are the Aluminum Company of America and the United Shoe Machinery Company.

2. The control of the supply by a few large concerns which decline to compete in price, but instead try to get the greatest share of the market without dropping their prices. An example of this is found in the oil industry where a few large companies dominated the market.

3. The control of the system of distribution in such a way that all new supplies must pay tribute to that system. The plumbing industry is an example of that. In this in-

dustry, an indictment brought in Cleveland charges that a combination of manufacturers, jobbers, master plumbers and journeymen plumbers have conspired to adhere to a system of distribution, wasteful and expensive, because it involves five steps from the manufacturer to the consumer. The indictment charges that through this bottleneck of distribution control must flow not only over manufactured plumbing but the manufactured parts which go into plumbing. This system requires an elaborate organization with a labor union as its front line of defense to prevent those who attempt to use more efficient systems of distribution from putting their plumbing into a modern house.

4. The Chinese bandit system of restraint in unorganized industry. This is found in such things as the distribution of food or fuel. In New York City the cumulative toll on the necessities of life levied by a lot of little groups because no public agency watches them is enormous.

At the end of 1938 the Antitrust Division, for the first time in history, had a large enough organization to develop a public prosecution policy. In this situation the task which confronted the Antitrust Division was to develop a publicly-stated prosecution policy that would destroy the atmosphere of legality which protected so many of the restraints of trade flourishing everywhere. In the report of the Antitrust Division for 1938 there was announced a policy for the clarification of the antitrust laws, which I quote here:[10]

An important part of our task is to facilitate compliance with the laws by helping conscientious businessmen to understand them. Forty years of sporadic enforcement of

CLARIFICATION OF LAW

the antitrust laws have created a situation under which the application of the law is confused in almost every concrete industrial situation. This is one of the outstanding difficulties of antitrust enforcement at present.

The lack of definition of the boundaries of the law has created a vicious circle which runs as follows. It is not fair to enforce the antitrust laws against businessmen in cases where their application is not clear. At the same time the application never becomes clear because the cases are not brought before the court. The solution to this dilemma lies in understanding the true function of litigation. It should not be regarded as a moral assault upon wicked individuals. It is an orderly means by which general provisions for economic adjustment are made concrete through localization and application to the conditions of a particular industry.

The necessity of the case method of development and clarification is in accordance with our judicial tradition. It has peculiar utility with respect to the Sherman Antitrust Act because in every new case it is necessary to seek the judgment of the court on at least one of two questions. The first is this—Does a particular type of organization go beyond the necessities of efficient mass production and become an instrument of arbitrary price control? The second question is—Does a particular combination among organizations tend toward the creation of orderly marketing conditions which facilitate the distribution of goods, or is it an instrument to maintain rigid prices? The answer to these questions for the benefit of American industry can only be obtained by presenting factual situations to the courts in a sufficient number of cases to cover our industrial problems. The laws will never be clarified before they are enforced—they will only become clarified afterwards. Not only judicial policy but prosecution policy must be developed by precedent and on publicly stated grounds if it is to clarify the law. Indeed, prosecution policy in a sense takes in a larger area than judicial policy. It must consider economic factors which cannot be stated in the narrow issues of a case drafted according to the necessary requirements of legal strategy. Businessmen are entitled to know what kinds of situations will lead to prosecution, because prosecution itself is a most important business hazard regardless of whether the Government succeeds in proving its case.

a. The Function of Public Statements of Prosecution Policy.—In consequence, on May 18, 1938, the policy was adopted of publishing explanatory statements in connection with each important step taken in the administration of the antitrust laws. These statements are intended cumulatively to formulate a consistent antitrust policy through the development of a body of explicit departmental precedents. It is hoped that a dual effect will thereby be achieved: to furnish a guide to businessmen; and to enable successive administrations to adhere to a consistent though evolving policy.

The result of that program has been the clarification of the Act in a single year by brushing aside the cumulative, inconsistent attitude which developed through the NRA period. Let us examine the development of antitrust law in the last year.

In 1939 public enforcement was paralyzed in the lower courts because of five unsettled questions:

1. Agricultural products had been declared exempt from the Sherman Act by a lower court.[11] The reason given was that agricultural legislation, permitting farmers to put a floor under prices under the super-

CLARIFICATION OF LAW

vision of the Secretary of Agriculture, was so inconsistent with the purposes of the Sherman Act that it constituted a complete repeal of the Act with respect to agriculture.

This decision not only effectively prevented prosecutions for restraints of trade with respect to food products, but it also threw into confusion each situation where Congress passed special legislation for the benefit of particular organized groups such as labor, small retailers, or the like. The only principle that will work with respect to such special legislation is that Congress and the courts shall share equally the responsibility of declaring what combinations are reasonably necessary and therefore are not to be prosecuted as restraints of trade. Where such combinations are permitted by a special act, they must not use that special privilege of organization beyond the purposes for which it was granted. If they do so use it, they violate the Sherman Act. The Sherman Act is the economic common law on which these special privileges are superimposed. It is not repealed by the grant of special privileges. Such privileges make enforcement all the more necessary to prevent them from being unreasonably used.

However, in 1939 this principle was not established; the policing of restraints of trade in food products was impossible; enforcement in other situations where special legislation had been passed was undermined.

2. In 1939 a lower court had held that the medical profession was exempt from the Sherman Act, and therefore could boycott new and experimental methods to distribute medical care, such as Group Health As-

THE BOTTLENECKS OF BUSINESS

sociation in the District of Columbia.[12] The principle
of this exemption was that doctors are professional men
not engaged in trade or commerce, and it went further
than the medical profession. It threw a cloud over any
restraint of trade imposed by any group which could
call itself professional. It raised doubt about attacking
restraints of trade in spectacles because optometrists
were learned. If doctors were exempt because professional, why were not engineers exempt also, even
though they worked on boilers? Indeed, there were no
limits to this broad exemption because realtors, mor-
ticians, and statisticians would all claim that they were
learned.

3. In 1939 patent lawyers thought that a dominant
group could license the use of a patented product in
such a way as to control both production and price.
The Ethyl Corporation through its patent controlled
the price of 85 per cent of gasoline used as motor fuel.
This kind of control was asserted in many industries
where machinery was used to make a product. Here
power was claimed so broad as to prevent the effective
enforcement of the Sherman Act. It was an open question what the Supreme Court would do about it.

4. During the NRA days the theory had grown up
that a combination in any industry could remove distress selling on the ground it was a competitive evil.
Distress selling in turn meant selling below such prices
as the majority of the industry thought were fair. Under this theory it was admitted that prices could not
be fixed. However, it was claimed that a floor could
be put under them by an organization buying distress

188

products and withdrawing them from the competitive market.

This theory in effect substituted a vague idea of fair competition for real competition. It permitted price fixing in order to stabilize the capital structure of any industry—a criterion so vague that it was a substantial handicap in prosecuting any price-fixing combinations.

5. In 1939, owing to the sporadic prosecution policy of the past quarter century, labor considered it was exempt from the antitrust laws, and on the other hand employers thought that the cases went so far as to apply the antitrust laws to every type of disorder or illegal conduct which occurred in legitimate strikes. During that year the Antitrust Division developed a prosecution policy with respect to labor which is set out in Chapter XI of this book. It filed with the Supreme Court in the *Apex* case not a brief but a statement of what that policy *was* to inform the Court how the law was actually being administered by an enforcing agency of the government which had the responsibility of making the best guess it could in the welter of conflicting opinions.

In 1940 every one of these sources of confusion in the enforcement of the Act in the lower courts by a series of sweeping decisions has been eliminated. These were the key situations which prevented public enforcement, yet the law had not been settled after half a century of private enforcement. Under a plan of public enforcement all these key situations were presented to the court during a single year.

In *United States* v. *Borden Company*[13] the United

States Supreme Court decided that agricultural products were not exempt from the Sherman Act and laid down the broad general principle that the Act is not repealed because Congress grants special legislative privileges to particular groups. In *United States v. American Medical Ass'n.*[14] the principle was laid down by the Court of Appeals of the District of Columbia that learned professions have no exemption from the Sherman Act on the claim that they are not engaged in trade. In *Ethyl Gasoline Corporation v. United States*[15] the United States Supreme Court decided that one patent cannot be used to wash the hands of another in such a way as to permit the patentee to dominate resale prices and methods of marketing products after the patentee has sold them. In *United States v. Socony-Vacuum Oil Co.* the United States Supreme Court decided that price fixing could not be justified under the plausible excuse that it was being used to prevent competition which actually lowered prices.

And finally, in the *Apex* case [16] the court said that labor when it interfered with competitors had no exemption unless that exemption could be justified by a legitimate use of the right of collective bargaining for a labor purpose.

These cases spelled out the attitude of the court on a broad front. They gave the Antitrust Division an instrument to maintain a free market which it never had before under the confusion in which the hodgepodge of private suits had left us.

IX.

Antitrust Enforcement for the Benefit of the Consumer

IT IS the function of a prosecuting agency not only to clarify the law but to develop the most effective method of using the procedure which has been given it. The tools which the Antitrust Division has at hand are the grand jury and the suit in equity. They may be concurrently used. The problem is to get the most effective results from that procedure.

The most effective antitrust enforcement consists in prosecuting simultaneously all of the restraints which hamper the production and distribution of a product from raw material to consumer. The reason for this is obvious. Combinations exist at every stage of the industrial process. Businessmen caught in a closed market are unable, by themselves, to change the general pattern of distribution in their industry. They have to violate the law in order to survive against aggressive combinations which attack them. If, therefore, we pursue single corporations or individuals, and leave others alone or prosecute them at a later time, we simply give an advantage to the violators who do not happen to be prosecuted. Also, very little advantage is given to the consumer if only some of the restraints in the total distribution process are wiped away. We must take up at one time all the combinations in an industry which affect the final consumer's product if we are to get a free market for its distribution. In the past, with a limited staff, this method of covering a product was impossible. Today it is still impossible to make the broad investigations of food, fuel, housing and other necessities which should be carried on. However, the organization has grown large enough so that in a few single instances we have been able to show the advantages of the broader type of enforcement just described over the old method of pursuing separate complaints.

The first prosecution to be conducted on the principle that all restraints in a given industrial situation should be attacked simultaneously was the Chicago milk case. There we found a combination of farmers, large dairy companies, a labor union, and members of the Board of Health, was forcing upon the poor a luxury system of distribution. This system consisted in leaving quart bottles at their doorsteps. It was enforced by boycotting distribution of milk by stores. The system was also used to create a milk shed around Chicago shaped like a sausage. Farmers two hundred miles away, who were within this privately-controlled milk shed, could get their milk into Chicago. Farmers, who were much closer to Chicago, were unable to sell their milk in the city limits. The indictment charged that this trade barrier was maintained by the use of an inspec-

ANTITRUST ENFORCEMENT

tion law by the Board of Health. Farmers who were not in the favored group found it impossible to get their farms inspected.

The favored group of farmers wanted higher prices for their milk and were willing to exclude other farmers to get it. The dairy companies wanted to maintain a luxury system of distribution, consisting of leaving milk in quart bottles on the doorsteps of the poor, by boycotting the cheaper methods of store deliveries. The union wanted to keep up the guaranteed minimum wage of $40 a week for milk wagon drivers, which in fact gave them an income of from $65 to $100 a week. All this expense was loaded on the consumers.

It worked this way: A students' cooperative boarding house at the University of Chicago tried to buy milk of an independent who did not subscribe to the system of leaving milk only in quart bottles at doorsteps, and therefore gave them milk cheaper. The labor union warned the students to stop buying from the independent. They paid no attention to the warning and food deliveries were stopped. They carried their food —then the garbage collections were stopped and the students gave in. The government charged results like this were due to a conspiracy between the Pure Milk Association, the Milk Wagon Drivers' Union, all the big dairy companies, and members of the Board of Health.

At the beginning of this proceeding, milk was selling at 13 cents a quart in Chicago, delivered at the doorstep. It could not be purchased cheaper without some risk. When the indictment was handed down milk

193

dropped precipitously in price. The farmers claimed that they were bearing the whole burden of a fall in prices. Thereupon the Secretary of Agriculture, acting under the authority of agricultural legislation, put a floor under farm prices by means of a marketing order. The judge of the lower court dismissed the indictment on the theory that the farm legislation was inconsistent with the antitrust laws. Milk then rose to 13 cents.

The Supreme Court of the United States reversed the lower court and reinstated the indictment. The effect was magical. The stores were now free to sell milk at competitive prices and, therefore, milk dropped to 8½ cents store delivery. Because of these cheaper prices 50 per cent of the milk is distributed through competitive grocery stores. The low-income groups thus had 4½ cents more to buy other farm products than they had before the indictment was sustained.* The boycott of store deliveries had amounted to a sales tax on a necessity paid by the lowest income group in the city in order to support a luxury system of distribution which they could not afford. By eliminating these restraints of trade, consumers of Chicago were saved about $10,000,000 a year.† Labor as a class benefited because it no longer had to pay this sales tax imposed by a private group. Farmers as a class were benefited because the low income consumer had $10,-

* Since I am using this as an illustration, I have complicated the paragraph by breaking the savings down into differences of prices between store deliveries and bottle deliveries.

† At a 4¢ drop, the saving would be $14,000,000, and at a 2¢ drop, the saving would be $7,000,000, etc. The actual saving was somewhere between these two figures.

000,000 more with which to buy other food products. The milk farmer still maintained a floor under his prices because of special legislation. However, this was done by an orderly process under public control and the question of whether this legislation was wise or unwise is a subject for public debate and not for the deliberations of private conspiracies.

Had any one of these groups been indicted and the others let alone, the uneconomic system of distribution would not have been affected as a whole. The Department, however, by including in its indictment all of the groups who had participated in the conspiracy, obtained a free, competitive market for milk distribution without disturbing the floor which the Department of Agriculture put under farm prices by a marketing order. It substantially reduced the price of milk for low-income groups by almost one-third. It saved low-income consumers $10,000,000 a year, liberating that money so it could go into other articles of diet. It saved substantial sums on the cost of relief.

Restraints of trade in milk are very similar to those in the distribution of food, generally, in large cities. The milk prosecutions furnish a pattern which underlies the prosecution policy with respect to food distribution generally.

The best example of the results which follow from taking up one industry at a time, from the raw material to the consumer, is found in the building prosecutions. We have already described in some detail restraints of trade in building.

Let us examine the methods by which the antitrust

laws attack such a situation. Building was the first investigation to be taken up with a view to prosecution on a nationwide scale. It was done in this way. The United States was divided into ten districts. Men were sent into each of these districts to get leads. Due to the lack of an adequate enforcement organization in each state, actual grand jury proceedings had to be limited to eleven cities. However, in these eleven cities every restraint of trade which affected the building of a house was investigated.

At the same time, nationwide investigations and prosecutions were carried on to eliminate restraints which were not local in character. Typical of these was the plumbing investigation which disclosed a situation where the large plumbing manufacturers controlled the distribution of plumbing through nationwide organizations combining with local organizations.

In the broadest sense this building investigation was an undertaking for the benefit of consumers. It went much further than the protection merely of a single group of businessmen. Out of our experience in this building investigation came several discoveries which make it useful as a pattern for an extension of the same type of activity to the problem of the distribution of other products to the ultimate consumer.

We discovered that vigorous investigation brings results beyond the actual cases that are prosecuted. These results spring from a realization by those engaged in the industry that an actual hazard exists if they violate the law. In investigating the building trades we were not dealing primarily with the criminal class of our population. We were dealing with ordinary law-abiding citizens who were caught in a vicious system which they were incapable of overturning without the aid of the government. The presence in a city of an organization engaged in antitrust investigational work gave to those law-abiding elements in an industry an assurance that they would not be forced into illegal practices through the necessity of protecting themselves against the unlawful aggressions of others, or through fear of retaliation. The presence of our investigators, therefore, in and of itself, was sufficient to stop many illegal practices. In one city, for example, since our investigation began, lumber prices have dropped 18 per cent and sand and gravel prices have declined 22 per cent. The low bid on a large electrical contract which was readvertised was 21 per cent under the previous low bid.

A second discovery was that an honest effort to prosecute impartially every unreasonable restraint affecting building costs, whether it comes from manufacturers, distributors, contractors, or labor, led to an understanding of the Sherman Act. It took the Sherman Act out of the realm of abstract law and made it a practical protection for the consumer.

As an example of this, we cite a portion of an editorial from the *Pittsburgh Press* of November 14, 1939, entitled, "Don't Drop This Great Work." The editorial says in part:

Thus far only an investigation of electrical costs—which

resulted in 58 indictments—has been completed, and the jurors are now studying heating and ventilating phases.

Yet despite the fact that the investigation is far from complete, there has already been a sharp drop in building costs which had allegedly been kept up through collusion between unions and contractors, bid-rigging and similar practices. On the Municipal Hospital, for instance, the low bid for electrical work submitted after the investigation had gotten under way was $33,000 under a low bid submitted before it started. Sand and gravel prices have dropped from $2.45 to $1.65 a ton since the inquiry began, and similar reductions have occurred in some other cases.

We believe that the savings in Pittsburgh alone would be sufficient to pay the entire costs of the national investigation. Few efforts undertaken by the Federal Government promise such important results at such low cost.

We sincerely believe that the elimination of racketeering, artificial restraints, collusion, bid-rigging, and similar restraints on building would result in such reductions in construction costs as to lead to the long-expected and long-delayed building boom, which has been nationally acknowledged as the surest way to induce economic recovery. The Pittsburgh district, we are convinced, would receive more benefit from elimination of unwarranted building costs than from any other single economic development. Work would be created for thousands of craftsmen, the real estate market would be stimulated, and all forms of business would profit directly or indirectly.

As another example of the support this sort of prosecution gets, we cite a column which has appeared in about 600 newspapers:

ANTITRUST ENFORCEMENT

BUILDING COSTS ARE REDUCED BY U. S. ANTI-TRUST INQUIRY

By Bruce Catton
Washington Correspondent

Washington, Nov. 25.—The anti-trust investigation of the building industry has barely scratched the surface so far, but it is already bringing about substantial cash savings to the consuming public.

This is made evident by a brief examination of results achieved in just one of the cities where the investigation is being conducted—Pittsburgh.

What has happened in Pittsburgh so far seems to bear out the theory of the man behind the investigation, Assistant Attorney General Thurman Arnold, that the success of this campaign will depend not on the number of indictments obtained but on the effect which a mere knowledge that an investigation is being made will have on organizations and individuals in the trade.

Knowledge of Inquiry Brings Change

One of the most illuminating aspects of the Pittsburgh situation is the effect the investigation there has had on electrical contracting.

Last May the Pittsburgh city engineer drew up an estimate of the cost of the electrical work in a new municipal hospital being built with PWA funds. His figure was $105,000; the city advertised for bids, opened them, and found that the lowest figure bid was $154,000. Specifications were revised and the city re-advertised. Lowest bid was $148,000, which was rejected.

The third set of bids brought a low offer of $152,000.

199

THE BOTTLENECKS OF BUSINESS

About that time the Department of Justice's investigating "team" of eight men reached Pittsburgh and went to work. This team advised rejection of these latest bids, and got busy with its investigation, which was widely publicized. On Nov. 3 a federal jury indicted 12 electrical contractors, a trade association and 45 individuals charging a conspiracy to defraud through collusive bidding. A few days later the city got a new set of bids for this hospital electrical work—with a low, this time of $117,000.

Identical Bidding Practice Stopped

That is only part of the picture.

The Pittsburgh Housing Authority is about to construct a new project known as Terrace Village. It advertised for bids for the excavating work. The bids came in after the papers had been full of the anti-trust investigation—and the lowest one was $200,000 under the engineer's estimate.

Not long ago the city opened bids for the purchase of sand and gravel. For the first time in years, the sand and gravel bids it got were not identical—and the quoted prices dropped from the hitherto prevailing level of $2.25 a ton to $1.65 to $1.80. This means a saving of $17,000 on sand and gravel for the first quarter of 1940.

That saving more than equals the expense of the Pittsburgh investigation to date.

Small Force Does Job

Eight Department of Justice men were sent to Pittsburgh from Washington. Their salaries for the period of the investigation total $4833. Their travel and living expenses to date come to $1700 more.

They have spent $720 on the hire of three stenographers, miscellaneous expenses have amounted to $500, and court reporting cost $3,000. In all, then, the investigation in Pittsburgh has cost $10,753—which is less than two-thirds of the sum that Pittsburgh will save on its first-quarter sand and gravel purchases alone.

To say that the country-wide investigation has barely scratched the surface is not to exaggerate. Indictments have been returned so far in five cities—Pittsburgh, Cleveland, St. Louis, Washington and New York.

In none of these cases is the investigation nearly completed. In many other cities it has hardly begun. In Chicago, for instance, only the preliminary lines have been drawn for what the Department of Justice confidently believes will be one of the most sensational and far-reaching parts of the entire program.

A third discovery was that a staff in the field, equipped to investigate thoroughly the complaints in a given locality, obtains an amazing amount of voluntary assistance from groups who otherwise might not have taken the initiative to complain. A display of activity invariably causes businessmen and consumers who have been the victims of improper practices to take heart and offer their active cooperation. In one large city, for example, there were a number of bid depositories operating in a way which we considered to be restraint of trade. The members of these depositories were interviewed by our investigators. In a short time every one of them informed us that he was ceasing the practice we were investigating. This was done before we had developed any case against them. They told us they were doing it because they believed that if other unlawful restraints were cleared away from the building industry they would be better off without these depositories. Although it would be unfair to announce publicly the names of the individuals concerned or the city where this happened, I think I can safely say that this is typical of what is happening in many places.

I am using the building investigation as a pattern for activity in all fields where prices are behaving unreasonably.

A fourth discovery is that these benefits will not be permanent, in building or any other industry, if the staff is withdrawn. If we were to withdraw our investigators from any locality where we have already accomplished beneficial results, it is almost certain that within a year the old abuses would reappear. 'As we have often asserted, the problem is similar to that of controlling traffic. There must be a traffic policeman on a crowded corner. If the policeman is there the law will be obeyed. If we have an adequate staff in the field to receive and investigate complaints, we will get the complaints and the investigations will accomplish beneficial results. If the men are not there, nothing will happen and the consumers will get discouraged and the law will be ignored.

The problem of enforcement, therefore, requires two things:

1. An adequate prosecuting group sufficient to break

up the organizations imposing restraints, which can be withdrawn after the prosecutions are over; and

2. One or two men assigned permanently in each state to preserve the gains by hearing complaints and keeping in close contact with the situation.

A large permanent staff in the field is not necessary. One or two men located in the larger cities to receive complaints and make investigations would be sufficient, if the public knows that we have men in reserve who can be called out in the event a local situation gets out of control. The men permanently allocated to each state could act as a clearing house for consumer information and complaints. With such an organization we could change what is now an unorganized protest into an intelligently organized enforcement movement. With various existing consumer groups, such as farmers, consumer associations, trade associations, women's clubs, state and federal officials, retailers, manufacturers, wholesalers, and unemployed persons disseminating information gathered by the resident field staff, profiteering would become unprofitable.

Antitrust enforcement consists in taking up a large number of concrete cases. The cumulative effect of a large number of these cases is tremendous. There is no better device for this kind of prevention than the grand jury investigation.

These are real investigations and not mere machinery for obtaining indictments. They are aimed at uncovering all of the restraints of trade which affect the distribution of a product from the raw material to the consumer; therefore hundreds of people are called. Everyone in the industry begins to realize that there is a hazard against reckless business aggression. Of course there is never time to uncover evidence on every possible complaint, but this is not necessary. The mere summoning of witnesses before a grand jury is enough to drive the lesson home to everyone in the industry. Businessmen are perfectly willing to conform to any standard that is reasonably enforced. That willingness is illustrated by the fact that whenever there is an active investigation in any city businessmen come into the Department to submit their plans for combination to avoid any risk of future criminal prosecutions. The mere public submission of these plans automatically eliminates most of the kinds of restraints of trade which the Department finds growing up in unpatrolled industries.

It takes the shock of indictments to clean up a bad situation in the distribution of a product. But after that shock is over, it takes only slight supervision to keep the market free.

For example, in Los Angeles a grand jury in the building industry was held for months. Hundreds were called who were not indicted. At the end of the grand jury, the newspapers got out the following extra edition:

ANTITRUST ENFORCEMENT

EXTRA

U. S. INDICTS 171 IN
L. A. BUILDING PROBE

Conspiracy to Fix Prices
Is Charged to 50 Groups

In a sweeping action today the Federal
Grand Jury brought its four-month probe of
Southern California's hundred million dollar
construction industry to a dramatic climax
by voting indictments against eight business
trade associations, four labor unions, 38
corporations and 171 individuals.

All the indictments charged conspiracy
or overt acts in violation of the federal antitrust laws, with particular emphasis on
price-fixing in construction of homes, office
buildings and other structures.

That was all that was needed to free the building industry in Los Angeles. After such an investigation all
that is needed to keep the market free is that complaints
be effectively called to the attention of the appropriate
organization.

Scattered prosecution will not achieve results like
this. The expense of prosecuting all of the restraints
simultaneously is only a small fraction of the expense
of handling them in separate investigations. The effect
is cumulative. It spreads not only throughout the building industries, but also the distribution of other products in the same city. Consumers become organized,

THE BOTTLENECKS OF BUSINESS

educated, and able to enforce the act themselves by
public information and pressure.

Cooperation with State and Municipal Authorities

The ripples of antitrust enforcement on a broad
scale spread in other directions. They create a public
demand for state and municipal enforcement of local
anti-monopoly laws or marketing regulations. The Federal government cannot do the whole job. Its power is
limited to restraints of interstate commerce. State antitrust laws exist practically everywhere but they have
been a dead letter. Many lawyers are not even aware
of them. Prosecuting attorneys do not understand them
and avoid them. But when consumers wake up to the
dramatic intervention of the Federal government,
apathy by state and municipal officials becomes impossible. This was illustrated when the Antitrust Division
first announced that it would prosecute labor unions
for an illegitimate activity. The Antitrust Division was
not concerned with extortion or the various abuses of
power by labor leaders against their own members. Indeed, it was not concerned with labor activities, except
in the building trades, because of its policy to take up
the distribution of a product rather than pursue individual offenders. Nevertheless, all over the country
there was an awakening on the part of the rank and file
of labor and on the part of the public to what a few
corrupt labor machines were doing to them. Westbrook
Pegler dramatized the issue. Prosecuting officers were
forced to take up cases against labor leaders which

ANTITRUST ENFORCEMENT

would never have been brought had not the rank and file of labor suddenly realized that some relief was possible. The ripples spread in all directions. The A. F. of L. itself was forced under pressure to clean house.

What this meant was that men within the A. F. of L. and the building trades, particularly those who had preached in vain against the aggressive tactics of some of their colleagues, got a new hearing and a new respect. A few prosecutions in the building industry had more effect on cleaning up union abuses than anything that had happened in ten years. The effect was out of all proportion to the money spent. Out of 1180 people indicted, only 50 were connected with labor unions. Yet these few cases started the union to clearing house.

We have not yet enlisted the cooperation of state and municipal officials in many cities but the beginning has been made. Mayor LaGuardia in New York had attempted to get cheap milk to the poor of his city by distributing milk in trucks among the pushcarts of the East Side. A few organizations had forced these trucks off the streets. Restraints of trade in the distribution of milk and other foods were matters of concern to the Mayor. He asked for the cooperation of the Antitrust Division. This was the first time in the history of the Department of Justice that the antitrust law had acted jointly with a municipal government to free local markets. A public announcement was made. Other mayors have written to express their interest in similar cooperation between federal and local governments.

THE BOTTLENECKS OF BUSINESS

Judicial Delays Cause Expense but do not Hamper Enforcement

Nothing moves slower than a contested antitrust proceeding. They have been so rare that the judges do not understand them. Inconsistent language in various cases permits lawyers to confuse the issue. The number of lawyers who are ordinarily retained for the defendants is in itself an element of confusion and delay. In the *Madison Oil* case there were 101 defense lawyers who had leased an entire hotel during the trial. Multiplicity of counsel is common in every large antitrust suit. It results in divided advice and endless motions, objections and arguments. The production of testimony is usually unduly long. For example, the *Aluminum* case is now in its third year of actual production of evidence at the trial. These cumbersome trial records and these delays are in part a result of the numerous different theories of defense which arise out of the confusion of the past. Actually an antitrust suit presents a very simple issue. Usually the issue is one of fact, *to wit,* the existence of a conspiracy and its effect on interstate commerce. Such facts are usually proved by circumstantial evidence by voluminous exhibits from the files. As the law becomes clarified, prosecutions have begun to move more rapidly. More defendants are pleading guilty or *nolo contendere* than ever before. More civil decrees are being entered. Nevertheless, when any antitrust prosecution is commenced there remains the probability that it will take years before it is finished.

ANTITRUST ENFORCEMENT

In spite of these delays, however, no handicap is put on actual enforcement by the slowness of legal procedure. Indeed, paradoxically enough, slow legal procedure of antitrust cases seems actually to aid in antitrust enforcement The reason for that is that the pendency of a criminal proceeding puts such a real hazard on the continuance of the practices which are complained of, that the defendants invariably stop their illegal activities after indictment is filed.

For example, in the trial in which General Motors was convicted of coercing independent finance companies, they denied the fact of coercion. When the case was presented, it was found that there had not been a single instance of coercion since presentation of evidence to the grand jury nearly four years before. The evidence on which the government obtained its conviction related solely to activities before the grand jury had been called. In other words, the mere calling of the grand jury had ended the coercion.

Again when the Teamsters' Union in Washington was prosecuted for tying up construction by a jurisdictional strike, the strike was settled within three days after the indictment. In that case the court directed a verdict of acquittal on the curious ground that the union had no criminal intent in calling its jurisdictional strike. This was a disappointment to the attorneys for the government. However, the strike which had been called off after the indictment was never resumed.

Our experience shows that the first thing a defendant guilty of violating the antitrust laws does is to stop the practices which are charged against him. The next thing he does is to deny these practices in order to disprove them at the trial. An astonishingly large number of respectable businessmen will strip their files of incriminating documents. This may make the government's case hard to prove, but it does not alter the fact that the fear of the consequences which led to the stripping of the files has also led to the stopping of the illegal activities. Indeed, it has been the unvarying experience of the Antitrust Division that a pending prosecution has the same effect in breaking up restraints of trade as a conviction—that even the acquittal makes the defendants draw a breath of relief and resolve never to undergo such an expensive hazard again.

Of course, I am not referring to cases where defendants persist in a practice because they desire to get a final decision on the law. But in most of the antitrust cases the main issue is a question of fact. In such cases the longer the proceeding pends the stricter is the actual enforcement. Therefore, delays in antitrust procedure, failure to get them to trial, and long appeals are not a real handicap on enforcement. They are regrettable; they are expensive, but that very expense is an element which makes violation hazardous. Ordinarily the expense of defending an antitrust suit is greater than any possible fine.

The fact that it is a tremendous burden on any business to defend an antitrust prosecution puts a heavy responsibility on the government in two ways:

1. To make its prosecution policy clear so that no

businessman will be entrapped into pursuing a
course which leads him to this expense.
2. Not to obtain indictments without the most search-
ing investigation.

As evidence that the government feels keenly that
the bringing of its cases in itself is a financial hazard
which should not carelessly be imposed on business, we
point to the fact that in the last two years the Antitrust
Division has finally lost only one antitrust proceeding.
Antitrust cases are hard to prove and it is not likely
that any such average can be continued in the future.
We cite it here only to show that we are aware that
prosecution itself is a real punishment and there ought
to be safeguard against careless use.

It is not a difficult task to maintain a free market.
It does not require nearly the number of policemen
that are necessary to keep traffic flowing freely. There
is, therefore, no excuse for American democracy dying
at the top because of economic toll bridges, provided
the American consumer is awake to the problem and
insists on an organization adequate to maintain free
trade between the states. We do not have that organization now. However, for the first time in the history of
the United States, we have made a start. We have
marched half way up the hill. We can already see the
view. We desire to go the rest of the way. Whether we
do or not depends on whether an adequate organization
is provided.

I am aware of the drive for balancing the budget.
Therefore, I want explicitly to point out that the Anti-

trust Division is not an expense but a revenue to the government. Here is the difference in expense between enforcement and non-enforcement. From 1929 to 1936 the Antitrust Division spent about $300,000 a year. That small organization, occupied with the 31 acts which are related to the antitrust problem, collected $73,000 in fines during that period. Last year the Antitrust Division was given $1,300,000. Six months of that year have gone by and approximately half of that appropriation has been spent—about $700,000. We have already collected $2,400,000 in cases handled by the Division and we have a potential of $5,000,000 more. Of course, we are not running the Division to collect fines, but the differences between the two types of enforcement as a narrow budget balancing matter are strikingly illustrated by these figures. If you don't want antitrust enforcement you can always get non-enforcement by paying lip service to the principles and cutting down appropriations, but your excuse can never be economy because the Antitrust Division pays revenue into the Treasury instead of taking it away.

Therefore, I put the question frankly to the consumers of this country. Do you want to maintain a free market for the distribution of your products? Do you want free trade between the sovereign States of this country?

If you do you must provide an adequate force to patrol the road.

X.

Bottlenecks Between the Farm
and the Table

AT NO place in our economic system is there more
need to break down restraints of trade than in our food
distribution. The distribution of food is the fundamental aim of every economy. Our investigation of
milk in Chicago showed that the per capita distribution was not sufficient for health requirements according to the advice of competent physicians. It also
showed that five-sixths of the milk produced near Chicago was being withheld from the citizens of Chicago.
Figures, for whose accuracy I cannot vouch, indicated
that Hitler was distributing in Berlin slightly more
milk per capita than low income groups got in Chicago.
Hitler's trouble was lack of supply. Our trouble was
an artificial excess of supply coupled with a noncompetitive distribution.

Milk gives us a picture of the problem of food distribution in a nutshell.

Of course I recognize that some of the problems of
milk distribution arise from fixing prices to the farmer.
I recognize also that farmers cannot stand (or will

not) the deflation of suddenly establishing an absolutely competitive market. I am not now discussing the wisdom of our agricultural legislation. I do, however, point out that the sudden liquidation of an entire group in the interests of free trade is never a political possibility. During a period of adjustment legislative means of maintaining parity to farmers cannot be avoided. However this very necessity makes it all the more essential that the channels of distribution be cleared. Only if they are cleared is there any chance of the farmer being able to swim in a free market at a later time without these inflated governmental waterwings.

Restricted diets have already extended beyond the very poor. As I write this the following story by Ida Jean Kain appears in the *Washington Post* of June 24, 1940:

Planning well-balanced health-giving meals on a highly restricted budget practically amounts to an art. One ingenious student, Ora-Blanche Burright, worked out a 90-day experiment of three meals a day at a total cost of 29 cents per day, including the cost of cooking and refrigeration:

Breakfast

Orange juice
Farina—whole milk
Scrambled egg
Toast
Glass of milk

BOTTLENECKS BETWEEN FARM AND TABLE

Luncheon

Tomato soup
New cooked cabbage
Bread and butter
Stewed prunes
Cocoa

Dinner

Split peas, buttered turnips
Carrot and lettuce salad
Hot corn bread, butter
Raisin cookie
Tea

You will note that this college student is going without meat in a country where the market is such that farmers are going without other necessities because they cannot get them in exchange for their beef.

Every reader knows of a family which likes to think of itself as within the middle class, whose children are struggling through college under conditions in which every cent counts. When we talk in terms of a diet of 29 cents a day, two and three and four cents' savings on each item of food means a difference between nutrition and malnutrition.

The elimination of restraints of trade in food distribution depend upon awakening the consumers to a consciousness of what can be done for them. In the last Congress, the Antitrust Division asked for a million dollars, an infinitesimal sum when compared with the present defense appropriation, to conduct grand juries to break down these petty exactions in food on a nationwide scale. This was denied, in part because it was requested at a time when budget balancing was at its height, but principally because there was no public understanding of the problem. In the absence of these funds the Antitrust Division must proceed on an extremely limited scale. The first task of limited operations against food restraints must be to show the consumer a way to break the log jams between the farm and the table. An organization is not going to be provided with funds to free the channels of trade in food until the public has some idea of what such an organization can do.

Therefore the Antitrust Division has undertaken by a preliminary survey to outline the campaign which it would like to undertake and to put into operation at least in one and perhaps two cities when men become available. The building investigation offers us our model. The success of those proceedings in ten cities, we think, has demonstrated that a broad grand jury investigation of all the restraints of trade which affect the distribution of a product can produce extraordinary economic results. To date that investigation has cost less than $300,000.00.

The survey of the problem set out in this chapter lies in the realm of hope and not in the realm of accomplishment. Nevertheless, we think the survey itself is one of the most important functions that the Antitrust Division can perform today because it may be used as a springboard for more effective proceedings in the future. This idea is nowhere more aptly expressed than in the following limerick:

BOTTLENECKS BETWEEN FARM AND TABLE

> There was a young lady from Q
> Who found a dead mouse in her stew.
> Said the waiter, "Don't shout,
> And wave it about,
> Or the others will want a mouse too."

As this is written, the food investigation of the Anti-trust Division is still in the shouting and waving-it-about stage.

Let us start our shouting with the farmer. We have already pointed out that the farmer's share of the consumer dollar has dropped from fifty per cent to thirty-eight per cent. Part of this loss is in the toll taken by organized groups who process and distribute food. A farmer gets thirty cents for his potatoes and the consumer pays a dollar. The farmer sells his milk for from three to five cents a quart and the consumer pays from twelve to fourteen cents. The fruit that nets the farmer twenty to thirty cents costs the consumer a dollar. The meat which the farmer sells for five or six cents a pound costs the consumer twenty to forty cents at retail. Poultry for which the farmer gets ten cents costs the consumer thirty cents.

Something is wrong with this picture in an age when mechanical efficiency should be bringing distribution costs down. And certainly something is wrong with the diet of the fifty or sixty per cent of our families with annual incomes of only a thousand dollars a year. Meat is becoming a luxury. The consumption of bread has declined since 1929. The farmer is unorganized. The distributors are organized in various ways—some big and some little. The mere recital of the figures on the

217

spread between the farm and the table is some indication that the test of reasonableness of the combination distributing food, *to wit*—efficiency passed on to consumers—is not being met.

Let us take a concrete case of how at least one type of combination operates. An important fertilizer company in the East, whose activities are under scrutiny by a grand jury at the present time, told the Federal Trade Commission a few years ago that

The way we conduct our operations is this. Through our agents we buy and furnish the farmer with his potato seed, furnish him the fertilizer, and furnish him his barrels. We allow him a certain amount of expenses for harvesting the crop of potatoes. The crop is turned over to us and we market it. We deduct from the net proceeds all that is owed us, *assuming that there is enough to pay,* and if there is anything left we keep one-fourth of it and give the farmer three-fourths.

You see farming is as simple as that. *If there is anything left* after the distributors get through they will give the farmer a *part* of it.

This "anything left idea" is the curse of farming as a business. This is no new idea, of course, but it is now being accepted as a commonplace. It has been accepted that of course the retailer must have his normal margin in selling farm and food products. Of course commission merchants must have ten per cent, even if they have to combine to put a floor under prices to get it. Food brokers must have twenty dollars a car or they can't pay their office help. And truckers, to be sure, will combine to let the products rot on the local or terminal platforms unless their pay is certain. Even the railroads, strangely enough, seem to expect their freight bills regularly. All these services are organized. Each group is in a position to charge all the traffic will bear, and each gets its toll as a prior lien on the farmer's products before he comes in for anything at all. And so the farmer is also forced to combine to raise his own prices and thus raise the entire food price structure. And so the government must appropriate money to keep this entire structure from collapsing.

Today the levies which the traffic is forced to bear all along the line between the farmer and the consumer are being increased because a number of new economic toll bridges are being erected at various stages of the distribution process, and they are in private hands with self-acquired power to determine the amount of the toll. These long series of distribution charges are not determined by competitive forces. At almost every stage they are based upon deliberate agreements in restraint of trade, entered into with a view to what the traffic will bear.

There is no question but that local dealers frequently get together and fix the prices they will pay for farm products. It is also commonplace knowledge that the men who handle and transport these products often have agreements on minimum rates. The handlers at the terminal markets are notorious for their trade restraints. There is now a major lawsuit in progress in New York City involving practices at terminal markets.

There are also a multitude of petty rackets that begin with the pennies and add up to the dollars. Years ago, for example, when poultry was shipped in crates by freight cars, the crates were large and required two men to handle them. Then, at a later time, it was decided that it took four men instead of two to handle these crates although smaller crates were often being used. Probably one man could have handled the smaller crates, but four men's wages were paid for it.

Even religion has got mixed into the problem. A large percentage of the poultry products in the large cities must be ceremonially butchered. It is a matter of record that many of these ceremonial butchers have been indicted for engaging in restraints of trade along with other groups in the industry. It is a healthy condition, of course, that no group is exempt from the prohibitions of the Sherman Antitrust Act and that a generally worthy purpose does not create immunity for those who engage in unreasonable restrictive practices.

Those of you who have some knowledge of the marketing of farm products may think that the degree of control over their prices and distribution has been exaggerated in my statement. But the files of the Department of Justice reveal many amazing devices for rigging the prices that consumers must pay for farm products. Take cheese, for example. Cheese is bought and sold all over the United States, and it might, therefore, seem that it would be beyond the range of price-fixing techniques.

As is generally known, the Department of Agriculture compiles and reports the prices of cheese for all of the principal markets of the United States. Quotations on cheese are available for New York, Pittsburgh, Cleveland, Chicago, St. Louis, Denver, Dallas, Seattle, San Francisco, and Los Angeles. But what do these prices mean? It is not so generally known that on Friday afternoon of each week a few men interested in cheese go to Plymouth, Wisconsin, only a few miles from Madison. After a good lunch, they meet for a few minutes at the Plymouth Cheese Exchange. After friendly conversation the secretary of the Exchange gets up at the blackboard, unless the procedure has been changed very recently, and calls for offerings of cheese. There is then a few seconds of shouting not understood by the laymen, whereupon the secretary writes offering prices on the board for a few lots of cheese. After a ceremonious interval, the secretary calls for bids, whereupon Babel breaks out again for a few seconds following which the secretary writes on the board that Borden bids 15 cents for Swift's lot, Swift bids 15 cents for Kraft's offering, Kraft bids 15 cents for Armour's offering, and so on for a few thousand pounds of cheese. Word then goes out on the wires to all parts of the United States that the price of cheese on the Plymouth Exchange is 15 cents per pound. Now comes the significant part of this whole transaction. This price, determined in such a gentlemanly manner at Plymouth, becomes the basic settlement price for the whole week for millions and millions of pounds of cheese bought and sold throughout the United States. Therefore, New York, Chicago, St. Louis, Denver, Dallas, Seattle, San Francisco, and Los Angeles cheese quotations mean little or nothing. They are merely calculated, allowing differences in quality and transportation, from the base price at Plymouth.

If this hocus-pocus were limited to cheese the farmer and the consumer might survive. As a matter of fact, the same situation applies in a greater or less degree to a multitude of farm products. Quite often it takes the form of sales being made on the basis of the cryptic phrase "price arrival." This means that everything from spinach to roosters is sold on the basis of "quotations" on the day of arrival at terminal markets. How thin this market may be is illustrated by the fact that for many products, a market reporter goes down about 9:00 o'clock and talks a few minutes with dealers in various lines. Whereupon, at 10:00 o'clock, with great formality and solemnity, a printed circular announces that the price of spinach is 40 cents per basket. This price then becomes the settlement price for all arrivals during the day for the spinach world—merely a modification of the Plymouth Exchange procedure but with much less formality.

At this point in the analysis of the distribution problem we encounter on many sides a note of pessimism. How can you expect, says the pessimist, to remedy these obvious evils by lawsuits. The restraints are so many, the cumulative effect so great, the amount involved in many of the particular ones so small—how can they all be broken up with the kind of limited enforcement organization available?

Since our experience in the building industry, we face this pessimism with a confident hope. A year ago

BOTTLENECKS BETWEEN FARM AND TABLE

the pessimist was saying that we couldn't do anything about reducing the cost of building because a building is made up of brick, lime, lath, lumber, steel, glass, plumbing fixtures, a heating plant, a slate roof, a brass knocker on the door, and a lot of labor which gets higher and higher daily wages with less and less yearly income.

In the particular cities where we have had grand jury investigation in the building industry we are beginning to see that a little reduction on plumbing and heating, on the brick and carpentry work, and on the roofing and the siding, begins to add up into a pleasing total. Gradually it is beginning to dawn upon even the pessimist that if a six thousand dollar house can be cut to five thousand dollars by breaking up numerous trade barriers, a thousand dollars is saved the consumer which can be spent for food and other things.

In the long run, something of this order of saving can be done by breaking the log jams between the farmer and the food consumer. Suppose we, by breaking the log jams, save the consumer a little on bread, beef, pork, bacon, ham, poultry, eggs, butter, cheese, cream, potatoes, onions, spinach, peaches, grapes, oranges, grapefruit, and so on down the line with hundreds of side items, such as the soap for washing the dishes. This total mounts up into real money. But most important of all, it is real money to the lowest income group, and that saves relief money to the government. It is the poor on the East side that really suffer. Prices in high-class groceries are less important than prices among the pushcarts. As Mr. Dooley once said,

"The root of the currency problem is the fact that the people who need money the worst don't have any."

We, of course, shall not forget the obvious fact that the farmer is likewise one of the most important of the consumer groups. If we can break up the toll bridges between him and the consumer we shall have the strange case of having our cake and eating it too. The campaign promises of hopeful candidates to get "higher prices for what the farmer sells and lower prices for what he buys," may after all take on some meaning instead of being merely texts for political speeches to be forgotten or excused on grounds of impossibility of performance.

The Antitrust Division is preparing, therefore, to attack the restraints in the distribution of food along the same lines that it attacked restraints in the building industry. Mr. Corwin Edwards, an economist whose efficient work in planning the building investigation for the Antitrust Division has been outstanding, was asked to make a preliminary survey of the restraints of trade in food in our large cities. He has prepared a memorandum which I am printing in part, in spite of some repetition of material already presented, because I think it is the best preliminary survey of the practical problem facing the consumer that is now available.

BOTTLENECKS BETWEEN FARM AND TABLE

June 13, 1940

MEMORANDUM FOR ASSISTANT ATTORNEY GENERAL ANTITRUST DIVISION

Re: *The General Outlines of the Food Investigation*

1. *The need for the food investigation.*

Public action about food prices is needed chiefly because a large part of the American people cannot afford an adequate diet at present prices. The annual cost of various diets for an average American family has been calculated by the Bureau of Home Economics and the actual amounts spent by American families for food in 1936 have been studied both by that bureau and by the Bureau of Labor Statistics. These studies show that for most of the American people an adequate diet is an aspiration—not a reality.

Fourteen per cent of the families studied spent too little upon food to obtain even a restricted diet, that is, a diet which contains the irreducible minimum food requirements but is not adequate except for a limited period. An additional 27½ per cent spent too little to obtain an adequate diet at a minimum cost, that is, a diet which meets physiological needs if food is chosen with care, but which provides little variety and little margin of safety in vitamins and minerals. The first of these groups was able to spend only $466 per family for food, clothing, shelter and all other family needs and the second was able to spend only from $500 to $1,000 per family. Eighty-seven and one-half per cent of the families studied, that is, those spending for all purposes less than $2,500 a year, could not obtain with the amount spent for their food an adequate diet at a moderate cost, that is, a diet which provides greater variety, better balance, and more vitamins and minerals.*

This situation was apparently worse in 1936 than during the prosperous 20's, but even in 1939, the 2,700,000 non-farm families with incomes of $1,000 a year or less spent on the average only enough for a restricted diet and 4,700,000 additional non-farm families with incomes of between $1,000 and $1,500 a year spent on the average only enough to buy an adequate diet at a minimum cost. More than seven million families, in other words, were finding it so hard to get enough to eat that they had little or no margin of safety in diet, and more than a third of them were on a diet which could not keep them permanently healthy.

Such a situation inevitably involves the wholesale malnutrition of the American people. Sixteen per cent of the school children in the Borough of Manhattan in 1929 were definitely undernourished. In 1932 the proportion had risen to 29 per cent.

To correct such a condition must be a major object of governmental policy at any time. It is all the more urgent now that the entire resources of the nation are being surveyed from the point of view of national defense. Nothing can be more fundamental to the protection of the United States than the health of its people. This fact was forced upon the country in 1917 and 1918 when 29½ per cent of the men examined during the draft were found to be partly or totally disqualified for military service.

* This estimate is made by reducing the required annual expenditure in 1929, as compared by the Bureau of Home Economics, by an amount equal to the decline in the Bureau of Labor Statistics Index for Wholesale Food Prices between 1929 and 1936. The resulting annual expenditure requirements were then compared with the average expenditures for food as summarized in the National Resources Committee report on Consumers' Expenditures in the United States, p. 23.

BOTTLENECKS BETWEEN FARM AND TABLE

The food investigation is also necessary because of the plight of the American farmer. In a report upon agricultural income in 1937, the Federal Trade Commission recorded with dismay its belief that the survival of independent farming by farmers who own their own farms and maintain an American standard of living is in jeopardy. It called attention to the fact that nearly one farm in four was foreclosed between 1930 and 1936, that there was a net migration of more than seven million people from the farm to the city between 1920 and 1935, and that the total value of farm land and buildings in 1935 was about two billion dollars less than in 1910 although the total land area devoted to farming had increased by more than 9 per cent. These evidences of distress are directly related to the fact that between 1913 and 1920 the American farmer received from 52 to 60 cents out of every dollar spent on food by the consumer whereas in 1938 and 1939 he received from 40 to 41 cents out of each such dollar.

Most farm prices are so low that government aid to farmers has become a part of the program of both major political parties, and yet food prices to the consumer are so high as to threaten the national health. It is imperative to find out why the processing and distribution of food cost so much and why they have been taking a growing share of the nation's food expenditures.

2. The scope of the food investigation.

Neither the American consumer nor the American farmer would obtain much help from a few sporadic prosecutions of isolated groups processing or distributing food. There have been such prosecutions in the past. Indeed, from the passage of the antitrust laws until last September about 23 per cent of all cases which the government

227

brought under those laws dealt with food products. Most of these cases accomplished little because they attacked isolated restraints by a few groups without proceeding at the same time against related restraints by other groups. Thus they could have no more than a limited local effect either upon the diet of the American people or upon the income of the American farmer.

During the last year the Department of Justice has tested its belief that effective enforcement of the antitrust laws requires a systematic nationwide attack upon the entire body of restraints which affect the final cost of a product. It has carried on such a campaign in the field of housing with very significant results. The same technique will be used in the case of food.

This means that restraints upon all major food products will be examined at every level from the original producer to the final distributor and that simultaneous prosecution of unlawful practices will be undertaken at all levels of the industry in important centers of population throughout the country. The speed with which the program can get under way will depend upon whether new funds and personnel become available or whether we must wait upon the release of personnel from the housing investigation and from other cases now being investigated and tried.

3. *The practices to be investigated.*

In general the investigation will deal with attempts to create monopolies and with restraints of trade which seek to fix prices, exclude competitors, or maintain wasteful practices in food processing and food distribution. The food industries have presented to the casual observer a deceptive appearance of competition because they handle farm products which are usually intensely competitive at the farm. Most farm crops are produced by many farmers scattered throughout the nation and unable, without direct government aid, to control their output or their prices. By contrast, however, many lines of food processing and distribution are under the effective control of a few large enterprises, and within the last generation the growth of some of these concerns in size and power has been unmatched in other American industries. Again, farm prices fluctuate widely and many retail foods reflect these changes, so that the rigid prices which often go with price-fixing are less apparent in the food industries than elsewhere. Nevertheless, the processors' and distributors' margins which are added to the farm price appear to be for some types of food more rigid than the prices of other industries which admittedly suffer from monopolies and restraints of trade.

Let us consider a few of the instances in which a concentrated group of food processors or distributors dominate the national market. The Federal Trade Commission found in 1937 that three tobacco manufacturers buy more than 46 per cent of the total crop; that three flour milling companies buy more than one-fourth of the nation's wheat crop and more than 38 per cent of the wheat which is commercially sold; that three meat packers buy more than 40 per cent of the cattle and calves and more than 25 per cent of the hogs produced throughout the country; and that twelve milk and milk products companies buy more than 13 per cent of the total commercial milk production.

Although these percentages are impressive they understate the power of large processors and distributors. An even greater concentration appears in the manufacture or distribution of certain food products. Three tobacco companies sell more than 80 per cent of the cigarettes and 64

THE BOTTLENECKS OF BUSINESS

per cent of the smoking tobacco; three meat packers sell more than 55 per cent of the beef carcasses and cuts, 83 per cent of the veal carcasses and cuts, 25 per cent of the pork carcasses and cuts, 36 per cent of the cured and processed pork products, 23 per cent of the lard, and 56 per cent of the hides produced in the United States. Three flour millers sell 29 per cent of all the flour produced; three milk companies sell 44 per cent of the canned milk, 42 per cent of the cheese, and 16 per cent of the butter produced in the country. If the sales of these products by three great meat packers are added, the six companies sell 51 per cent, 79 per cent and 33 per cent of canned milk, cheese, and butter, respectively. Three canners process 67 per cent of the plums, 56 per cent of the asparagus, 52 per cent of the dried beans, 47 per cent of the spinach, 32 per cent of the prunes, 32 per cent of the pears, and 30 per cent of the peaches produced for canning.

The actual dominance of large enterprises in some of these fields is much greater than the percentages indicate. In many cases the big company has concentrated its control in the large centers of population. In major cities, from two to five milk companies frequently distribute all the milk. The great meat packers, the great bread bakers, and the great flour millers occupy the outstanding position in the nationwide distribution of their products whereas the small concerns which produce and sell the rest of the supply operate for the most part in small local markets where sharp local competition by the large concerns could readily destroy them.

Since the combinations which restrain trade in the food industries stand between the original producer on the farm and the ultimate consumer, they are essentially middlemen, whether they merely distribute a product or also process it. Their power is expressed both in the way they buy and in the way they sell. On the one hand they increase the unbalance of the American economic system by driving farm prices down and thus nullify in part the Government's effort to bring farm incomes back to parity. On the other hand, they impair the American standard of living by raising food prices to the consumer.

The unlawful practices which have such results differ widely from one group to another. They are illustrated by cases which have recently led to legal proceedings by the Antitrust Division or the Federal Trade Commission. Within the last five years the Federal Trade Commission has found and issued orders against price-fixing by a trade association of rice producers in California, an association of bean jobbers in Michigan, an association of dealers in seafood in the District of Columbia, wholesalers of confectionery in New York state, distributors of candy and tobacco products in the areas around Wilkes-Barre, Pennsylvania, and Binghamton, New York, distillers and local distributors who attempted to fix liquor prices in the District of Columbia, and manufacturers of butter tubs, wooden crates, paper food dishes, and veneer containers. Complaints in which the Commission charges price-fixing activities are now pending against the largest cheese manufacturers, the principal importers of dates, the Cup and Container Institute, Inc., The Milk & Ice Cream Can Institute, United States Maltsters Association, liquor wholesalers in California, ice manufacturers in the District of Columbia, and the Milwaukee Jewish Kosher Delicatessen Association. Other recent orders by the Commission have required that the National Biscuit Company shall cease giving jobbers special discounts to agree not to deal with rival biscuit manufacturers, that a large New York milk

THE BOTTLENECKS OF BUSINESS

pasteurizer shall stop coercing milk producers into a boycott of cooperative associations, that the California Pack-
ing Corporation and the Alaska Packers Association shall
stop coercing shippers into the use of shipping terminals
owned by the latter, that the Fall River Wholesale Grocers'
Association shall cease boycotting manufacturers who sell
direct to retailers, and that leading distributors of candy
through vending machines shall cease coercing candy manufacturers to cut off supplies from rival vending machine
companies. Cases are pending in which the Commission
charges that bakers in Minneapolis, Des Moines, Sioux
City, Omaha, and Council Bluffs attempted to restrict business to a group of approved dealers by cutting off supplies
of bakery products from their would-be competitors, and
that the Good Humor Corporation of America and the
Popsicle Corporation of the United States have sought to
misuse patents in such a way as to fix prices upon frozen
stick confections and to prevent rival companies from making such confections.

During the same period the Antitrust Division has secured convictions in criminal cases charging a conspiracy
to monopolize commerce in artichokes in the New York
metropolitan area, a combination to fix prices of confectionery and to boycott manufacturers who sold to concerns
not observing the fixed prices, a conspiracy to fix prices
upon fresh-water fish, and a conspiracy to fix prices paid
for fish by wholesalers.

In other cases during this period the Department secured permanent injunctions against activities of the Sugar
Institute designed to maintain uniform prices, and against
local 807 of the Teamsters' Union which had exacted a fee
from interstate truckers before allowing them to deliver
their merchandise in the New York area. Cases now pend-

ing include the prosecution of the principal dairy companies in the Chicago area for fixing prices and shutting out cheaper methods of distribution, an indictment of the Dairymen's Association of the Territory of Hawaii for an effort to fix prices and to exclude competitors by special price cuts in their markets, an indictment of the Wine, Liquor & Distillery Workers' Union for a boycott designed to prevent the sale in New York City of wine bottled in California, and indictments of two locals of the Teamsters' Union for efforts to exact fees or require the hiring of duplicate local drivers in the interstate delivery of butter, eggs, dairy products, and fresh fruits and vegetables.

*   *   *   *

Although twenty-six food cases are now being investigated by the Antitrust Division, the complaints we have received are so numerous that it has not yet been possible to make even a preliminary survey of most of them. The restraints upon milk in many major cities are said to be as restrictive as in Chicago. In some places public authorities have cooperated to keep milk prices high not only by discriminatory inspection such as is charged in Chicago, but by directly handicapping distant milk sheds or by directly prohibiting economies in distribution. Rhode Island, for example, permits the sale of milk from sources beyond the regular milk shed only if it is first colored red. The city of Boston prohibits the sale of milk in paper containers, although the use of such containers would make it possible to lower the price to the consumer.

Closely related to the restraints upon milk, it is charged, are a series of restraints upon various milk products. The price of natural cheese is arbitrarily fixed once per week in a few isolated transactions on the Wisconsin Cheese Ex-

233

change. The production and price of process cheese are controlled by the abuse of certain minor patents held by one of the large companies. Patent control is also used to establish certain restraints upon ice cream and ice cream handling equipment. The production of evaporated and condensed milk is concentrated in the hands of two or three companies. Through the control of cold storage warehouses the milk companies and the large packers exercise a growing influence upon the markets for poultry, butter, and eggs.

In general, the great dairy companies have a much firmer control over the markets for cheese, evaporated milk and ice cream than over the market for fluid milk, since in this latter market their dominance in the larger centers of population is always threatened by the possibility that farm cooperatives will distribute milk directly, or that more distant dairy country may be admitted to the milk shed. The exploitation of these different degrees of power has set up in the United States a price system for milk under which the farmer receives much less for the milk to be used in manufacture than for the milk to be hauled and sold as fluid. This price structure is the exact reverse of that which is socially desirable, for it means that the American public is limited in the most important use of milk for beverage purposes, in spite of the fact that there is a great potential market expressing a great dietary need for fluid milk at lower prices. The luxury milk products, instead of paying the higher prices, command the lower ones.

Bread and bakery products also have to carry the burden of restraint. The Federal Trade Commission reported three years ago that grain brokers also act as traders for their own pocket, to the sacrifice of the interest of the shippers; that the rules for delivery of grain facilitate squeezing the market and that the warehousing of grain is now even more subject to abuse by companies which own elevators than when the Commission first called attention to the matter many years ago. Past investigations have repeatedly revealed attempts by flour manufacturers to limit output and fix minimum prices. In 1926 the great national baking companies were prevented from merging only by Government action, and it is said that they still constitute a community of interest. Their policies are supplemented by price-fixing agreements among various local and regional bakers associations. In consequence, the price of bread often remains fixed when the price of flour goes down, and is sometimes arbitrarily increased when the price of flour rises, but by an amount which is more than sufficient to cover the increased cost.

The markets for fish are likewise shot through with restraints. For some varieties, there is formal agreement at the beginning of the season between a fishermen's association and the principal canners either to establish the opening price or to establish a price which shall prevail throughout the year. Large canners extend their control by acting as brokers for smaller concerns which are ostensibly their competitors. In some regions, a few dealers in fresh fish dominate the market by their strategic control of fish piers, fish icing companies, or similar market facilities.

In the canning of fruits and vegetables, the importance of restraints varies with the crop. Products which grow only in limited areas are often dominated by one or two large canners who buy more than half the total crop. There is similar nationwide dominance over some varieties of canned food, for example, soup, infant's food, or cranberries. In some cases the canners agree upon the price they will pay to the grower. Patents held by large food companies enable them to control the food canned by certain processes. All canners are dependent upon two large can manufacturers for their containers. The prices set by these can manufacturers are so high that from a third to four-tenths of the retail price of a can of vegetables represents the cost of the can.

The restraints upon fresh fruits and vegetables consist in exploiting a disorganized market. Many of these crops are grown in specialized regions and must be put on the market in a period of a few weeks during which they ripen. The truck farmers who produce some of these highly concentrated crops have apparently been reduced to a status very like peonage. They are financed by brokers and commission men, and in return must not only pay interest as high as 30 to 40 per cent but must market their crop when and where and for whatever price their creditor chooses. Through such financial control a few large middlemen in the principal terminal markets can dominate the marketing of the crop.

The perishable nature of fresh fruits and vegetables has become the basis for a series of wasteful and extortionate practices in their handling at terminal markets. In the largest cities these markets are often very badly located at points which are unduly congested and unduly remote both from railway terminals and from wholesale food establishments. Efforts to shift these markets to more economical locations are systematically opposed by local real estate interests which benefit by the present location, by local truckers interested in the maximum amount of haulage, and sometimes by railroads which are relatively nearer the present location than their rivals. In many of these markets trucking monopolies have been established and no truck owned by a wholesaler or an independent trucker is allowed to take delivery direct from the railway car, nor is any interstate trucker allowed to make delivery direct to his customer. Instead, either all the produce must be loaded on a truck belonging to the ring and then reloaded from that truck to the customer's truck, or else a fee must be paid for the unneeded and unused services of an extra driver or extra loaders. Similar wasteful distributive practices are often encountered in the handling of live poultry.

In the manufacture and distribution of ice, localized price-fixing monopolies are notorious. Local monopolies are established by price wars against independents and by violence against the drivers of their trucks. Independent plants are bought out or leased and shut down. Territories are allocated among manufacturers and dealers who have joined the conspiracy, and prices are then set at unreasonably high levels. Attracted by the high prices, new independents frequently build new plants in the hope that they will be bought out at a good price, and thus the ice industry, which is seasonal at best, is saddled with the high cost of an unwarranted excess productive capacity.

Restraints less important but equally flagrant are found among the producers and distributors of many specialized types of food. One or two buyers control the entire marketing machinery for certain varieties of nuts. Some large processors require their customers to boycott cooperatives by refusing to supply their product to any buyer who buys from a cooperative.

Restraints appear also among the wholesale and retail grocers who distribute most food products. It is charged that certain large chain stores threaten to boycott producers who do not use their subsidiary commission companies, and thereby establish control over the supplies which reach the independent distributors. It is also charged that chain stores engage in local price cutting in an effort to destroy independents and establish local monopolies which subsequently become the basis for higher prices. Independent retail grocers in many states have attempted to establish minimum prices through the enactment of state laws which forbid the sale of commodities at retail below cost. In some cases, under the cloak of these laws, independent grocers have arbitrarily fixed the level of so-called costs and have used their arbitrary computations as a basis for unlawful price-fixing.

The gain to the American farmer and the American consumer through the elimination of restraints upon food processing and food distribution cannot be estimated in advance. It can, however, be illustrated from the Chicago milk case, which is still being prosecuted. When the Antitrust Division found that milk producers, milk distributors, the milk wagon drivers' union, and even officials of the municipal board of health had organized a conspiracy to fix the purchase and resale prices of milk, to exclude independent distributors from the market, and to hinder sale of milk by stores in competition with the more expensive door-to-door delivery, it secured an indictment. Thereupon, the price of milk in Chicago stores, which had been from ten to twelve cents a quart, fell to eight or nine cents, and the price delivered in bottles was forced down to eleven cents. When a demurrer to our indictment was sustained, the price began to climb, store milk recovering to eleven cents and delivered milk to thirteen. When, on appeal, the Supreme Court upheld the indictment, the price in stores fell again to eight and a half cents, though the price delivered in bottles did not fall. More than half the milk in Chicago is now bought from stores, and the annual saving to store customers is at least three or four million dollars.

CORWIN D. EDWARDS,
Economic Consultant.

The Antitrust Division is convinced that economic results can be achieved by the coordinated grand jury investigations of food distribution in all our principal cities. It is the lack of personnel that is the principal difficulty. We are handicapped because an organization cannot be set up in separate states to investigate and clear complaints. In my opinion there is no excuse for not cleaning the Augean stables of food distribution. There is no reason, particularly in time of national emergency, for allowing inefficient spreads in price between the farm and the table because of the refusal to spend for antitrust enforcement sums which are infinitesimally small when compared to the vast expenditures necessary for national defense.

XI.

Labor—
Restraints of Trade Among the
Under-Dogs

THE labor movement in this country has lagged behind countries like Sweden or even England. It has presented the picture of constant battle rather than peace-time expansion. The need of fighting tactics on the part of labor to obtain the right to organize has given unions a fighting leadership that has gained many victories in Congress. The most important victory is undoubtedly the public recognition of the right of collective bargaining and its enforcement by the National Labor Relations Board. As this is written the enforcement of collective bargaining has survived the attacks of three years, and my guess is that it is destined to remain a fundamental principle of the labor legislation of the future.

Yet it must be obvious to anyone that government protection of the right of collective bargaining is not working smoothly. Four years after the passage of the Wagner Labor Relations Act the industrialists are still

LABOR—RESTRAINTS OF TRADE

unreconciled. The press is bitter. The Act is under constant attack and constant threat of amendment. It has not achieved that measure of public acceptance without which no legislation can work practically. For these reasons the National Labor Relations Board, which enforces the Act finds itself so hampered by investigations and other types of guerilla warfare that its whole efficiency is undermined.

The question, therefore, arises why, in a country where everyone recognizes that collective bargaining is an inalienable right of labor and where legislation enforcing it has survived every legal attack, it is today so difficult to enforce the Wagner Act without bitterness and conflict.

The answer, I believe, lies in the failure of government to confine organized labor to legitimate labor objectives. The right of collective bargaining is being enforced in favor of labor organizations which are using that right for illegitimate purposes, against the interests of consumers, against the interests of efficiency, and against the interests of labor itself. Industrialists found themselves forced to deal with unions many of which are nothing more than corrupt political machines that use the right of collective bargaining against the interests of the rank and file of laborers. Many unions are interested in restricting output, in building trade barriers between states, and even in discriminating against working men themselves for the advantage of a few. Many of these unions are undemocratic in organization and their leaders maintain themselves in power by coercion. Such type of organization inevitably leads to corruption on a large scale. Corruption in unions has become notorious.

The corruption itself was, I think, an incident of allowing a legitimate organization to be used for illegitimate purposes. The bitterness against enforcement of collective bargaining is due in large part to the fact that it was superimposed on a situation where collective bargaining was being used for purposes that could not be justified. Industrialists felt that they were being compelled to deal with labor leaders who they knew were not interested in the legitimate objectives of labor. When they tried to organize more reasonable groups they were penalized by the National Labor Relations Board.

I hold no brief for company unions. However, if we are going to outlaw them, we must give industry some protection against the kind of banditry which always springs up in organizations that are not confined by outside pressures to their legitimate sphere of action.

Let me give you an example. The Anheuser-Busch Brewing Company has always been fair to organized labor. It attempted to construct a million-dollar addition to its brewery in St. Louis. The whole project was stopped because "Big Bill" Hutcheson, president of the carpenters' union, got into a dispute over whether carpenters or mill hands should do a small portion of the job.[1] The company was helpless. It was willing to pay any reasonable wages or insure any reasonable working conditions. It had entered into a contract with a recognized union. But it could not build its building. Construction was stopped in the middle of the winter when the men needed the work most. It was stopped against the vote of the Central Trades Council composed of labor unions of St. Louis. Such is often the plight of the well-meaning friend of labor who finds himself a victim of the use of collective bargaining by a labor dictator to destroy another union.

And how about the consumer? Let me give another example. In the city of Chicago, Carrozzo,[2] another labor dictator, prevented the use of ready-mixed concrete. The obsolete puddle-method had to be used, or buildings would not go up. Consumers all knew of this outrageous extortion, yet they were helpless.

Another example—a contractor was building a long row of houses. Teamsters drove up with bathroom fixtures which they left on the curb in front of each house. The contractor asked the teamsters to help carry the fixtures in. They answered that it was against the union rules for them to work behind the curb and drove off. He asked the plumbers and carpenters to give him a hand. They said it was against their rules too. He got some unskilled workers who were picking up around the premises to lend him a hand. Then everyone on the job picked up his tools and walked off in protest.

The contractor finally went to a union business agent. Money changed hands. Everyone started to work again. But the bitterness and resentment of that contractor have made him a foe of organized labor for the rest of his life. No legislation is going to change that attitude. And when that attitude is multiplied in the hearts of thousands, labor legislation is not going to work.

One more illustration from small business. A small hatter in Washington was struggling to survive against heavy competition. He took pride in his shop. After a struggle between pride and thrift he put his savings into a new coat of paint for his shelves and walls. He got it done by a C.I.O. union. Immediately the A. F. of L. union put a picket line in front of his store. He began to lose business. The union told him that before the picket line would be removed he would have to have the painting done all over again with A. F. of L. labor. This is a true story, and similar things happen and will continue to happen all over the country so long as small groups are permitted to use the privileges of collective bargaining for illegal purposes.

How about free trade between the states? We find labor unions insisting on the right to erect protective tariffs by boycotting goods from other states, acting in combination with local firms. We find them enforcing expensive systems of distribution on low income groups.

And what has this sort of practice done to the labor movement as a whole? Today the labor movement is in complete confusion. It presents a confused picture of labor unions fighting among themselves and thus incurring the hostility of those who might be their friends. The rank and file of labor has no enthusiasm for the kind of Chinese banditry which now exists. It is not doing them any good nor is it doing the labor movement any good.

LABOR—RESTRAINTS OF TRADE

This condition is not the fault of labor nor is it peculiar to labor. It is simply the kind of thing which happens when organizations are allowed to grow up and no curb is put upon the illegitimate use of their organized power. Under such circumstances, small selfish groups get themselves in a strategic position; the rank and file have no one to whom they can appeal to get the selfish groups out; democratic processes do not operate because there is no power to hold free elections. The whole labor movement suffers from the depredation of a few political gangs whom labor itself cannot remove. This is no different from what happens in industry when no curb is put upon the illegitimate use of organized power. It is silly to blame labor for the failure of the government to protect the rank and file from the aggressive tactics of a few selfish groups.

The public generally indulges in both praise and blame. It cannot analyze the real causes why the Wagner Labor Relations Act has failed to promote labor peace. It therefore blames the Act. The key to the situation lies in confining the labor movement to its legitimate purposes. Labor unions so restricted need the protection of the National Labor Relations Board. But when that board compels employers to deal exclusively with labor unions dominated by political gangs the result is bitter reaction agains the board itself.

Do not get the impression that these gangs come from out of the rank and file of labor. Often they are the spearhead of some industrial combination which uses them to enforce price-fixing or to maintain some uneconomic system of distribution. The president of a great moving picture producing company gave the notorious Bioff, a convicted panderer in control of the I.A.T.S.E., $100,000 in cash.[3] Plumbing, building, food, milk, indeed every field of distribution to the ultimate consumer offers examples of the same kind of tactics.

The remedy is not to condemn labor. Labor should not be blamed for the failure of the government to protect its organizations from being improperly used by aggressive men who seize power. There has been no free election in the carpenters' union for eleven years, none in the hodcarriers' union for twenty-nine years. I could go on indefinitely citing other unions that have not had elections for years. The same faces appear year after year in labor councils, surviving every sort of charge of corruption and incompetence. The same people continue in power because labor cannot shake them off. The Department of Justice has thousands of letters from the rank and file telling of these conditions, but warning that if the writers' names are used retaliation will be swift and sure. The answer is not to blame labor but to free it.

The Sherman Act is the only instrument capable of preventing the illegitimate use of organized power. For fifty years its application to labor was confined principally to a series of private suits. Public prosecutions of unions were sporadically brought, but there was no publicly-stated prosecution policy. There was no attempt by the government to bring a series of cases which would not interfere with labor's legitimate activities, as many private suits had done. The absence of a public prosecution policy had made the Sherman

Act seem to organized labor to be a weapon against it in the hands of its enemies. Private groups originally used the Sherman Act to hamper legitimate strikes with the weapon of injunction. After the weapon of injunction was taken away by the Norris-LaGuardia Act, private suits for triple damages were substituted. As this is written there are pending against the Teamsters' Union in New England alone suits for over $990,000. Total damages sought against labor unions today in private suits pending under the Sherman Act probably run around $10,000,000. These suits have the potential power of crippling the entire labor movement. Even if labor wins the cost of defense is staggering. Labor has a right to complain of such private enforcement.

Enforcement of law in private hands in the nature of things cannot be fair enforcement. Its excuse and its reason for existence is the failure of the State to provide officers charged with public responsibility to perform that necessary function. The only remedy for the evils of private policing is to substitute policing by public officers not responsible to private interests.

In making the statement of its prosecution policy with respect to labor unions, the Department of Justice necessarily had to work within the limits of the law as interpreted by the Supreme Court of the United States. It was compelled to forecast what could be honestly presented to the Court within the four corners of those decisions. In some prior decisions the question whether a labor union had violated the Sherman Act appeared to depend on "intent" to violate the law. Such a test is impossible to apply. The conception of the "intent" of a large organization is a pure fiction. Therefore, the test that the Department urged the courts to adopt was this: that the question of whether the privilege of collective bargaining has been illegally used depends upon the objective for which it is used. If that objective is legitimate, then there is no *unreasonable* restraint of trade. This does not mean that there may not be a violation of some other law by a legitimate combination. There may be assault, murder, trespass or anything else. But the Sherman Act is not designed to take the place of state and municipal government. It must not be used as a vortex into which are whirled all forms of law enforcement. Both as a theoretical and as a practical matter, local policing of violence, trespass, appropriation of property, etc., should be left to local police.

With the test of objectives in mind it became necessary to spell out, case by case, what are the legitimate objectives of labor unions. The courts have the final word. But the Department of Justice, in fairness to those who seek to know what its initial action will be, should announce the kind of activities on the part of labor organizations which it intends to prosecute. This announcement should be based on actual cases before the Department. Therefore, on November 20, 1939, in the following public letter to the Central Labor Union of Indianapolis, the Department defined its prosecution policy with respect to the restraints of trade which were before it, principally in the building industry:

LABOR—RESTRAINTS OF TRADE

November 20, 1939
Dear Sir:

I reply to your letter inquiring about the application of the antitrust laws to labor unions. I make this reply public because numerous other inquiries similar to yours indicate widespread public interest in the question.

The antitrust laws should not be used as an instrument to police strikes or adjudicate labor controversies. The right of collective bargaining by labor unions is recognized by the antitrust laws to be a reasonable exercise of collective power. Therefore, we wish to make it clear that it is only such boycotts, strikes or coercion by labor unions as have no reasonable connection with wages, hours, health, safety, the speed-up system, or the establishment and maintenance of the right of collective bargaining which will be prosecuted.

The kind of activity which will be prosecuted may be illustrated by a practice frequently found in the building industry. Suppose a labor union, acting in combination with other unions who dominate building construction in a city, succeeds by threats of strikes or boycotts in preventing the use of economical and standardized building material in order to compel persons in need of low-cost housing to hire unnecessary labor.

Here is a situation with no reasonable connection with wages, hours, health, safety, or the right of collective bargaining. The union may not act as a private police force to perpetuate unnecessarily costly and uneconomic practices in the housing industry. Progressive unions have frequently denounced this "make work" system as not to the long-run advantage of labor. Such unions have found it possible to protect the interests of labor in the maintenance of wages and employment during periods of technological progress without attempting to stop that progress.

Preventing improved methods of production—as distinguished from protecting labor from abuses connected with their introduction—is, of course, not the only labor activity which goes beyond any legitimate labor purpose. We cite the example to emphasize the fact that union practices may become illegal where they have no reasonable connection with such legitimate objectives as wages, hours, safety, health, undue speeding up or the right of collective bargaining.

We have no choice in this matter. Such practices go beyond even the dissenting opinions of the Supreme Court of the United States, which recognize a broader scope for the legitimate activities of labor unions than the majority opinions. In our anxiety to be fair to labor we are not subjecting to criminal prosecution practices which can be justified even under the dissenting opinions of the United States Supreme Court.

In the present building investigation a large number of legitimate activities of labor unions have been brought to our attention by complaint. We have been asked to proceed against unions because they maintain high rates of wages, because they strike to increase wages, and because they attempt to establish the closed shop. We have consistently disregarded all such requests.

Refusals by unions to work upon goods made in non-union shops have also been brought repeatedly to our attention. In the past courts have held that such secondary boycotts are violations of the antitrust laws. In the *Duplex* and *Bedford Cut Stone* cases a minority of the Supreme Court presented the argument against this view. In view of this unsettled conflict of opinion among judges of the high-

LABOR—RESTRAINTS OF TRADE

est Court as to the reasonableness of such activities we have instructed the attorneys in the building investigation not to institute criminal prosecutions in such cases.

The types of unreasonable restraint against which we have recently proceeded or are now proceeding illustrate concretely the practices which in our opinion are unquestionable violations of the Sherman Act, supported by no responsible judicial authority whatever.

1. Unreasonable restraints designed to prevent the use of cheaper material, improved equipment, or more efficient methods. An example is the effort to prevent the installation of factory-glazed windows or factory-painted kitchen cabinets.

2. Unreasonable restraints designed to compel the hiring of useless and unnecessary labor. An example is the requirement that on each truck entering a city there be a member of the local Teamsters' Union in addition to the driver who is already on the truck. Such unreasonable restraints must be distinguished from reasonable requirements that a minimum amount of labor be hired in the interests of safety and health or of avoidance of undue speeding of the work.

3. Unreasonable restraints designed to enforce systems of graft and extortion. When a racketeer, masquerading as a labor leader, interferes with the commerce of those who will not pay him to leave them alone, the practice is obviously unlawful.

4. Unreasonable restraints designed to enforce illegally fixed prices. An example of this activity is found in the Chicago Milk case where a labor union is charged with combining with distributors and producers to prevent milk being brought into Chicago by persons who refuse to maintain illegal and fixed prices.

THE BOTTLENECKS OF BUSINESS

5. Unreasonable restraints designed to destroy an established and legitimate system of collective bargaining. Jurisdictional strikes have been condemned by the A. F. of L. itself. Their purpose is to make war on another union by attacking employers who deal with that union. There is no way the victim of such an attack may avoid it except by exposing himself to the same attack by the other union. Restraints of trade for such a purpose are unreasonable whether undertaken by a union or by an employer restraining trade or by a combination of any employer and a union, because they represent an effort to destroy the collective bargaining relationships of a union with an employer.

The principle applicable to unions is the same as that applicable to other groups specially protected by law. Investors may combine into a corporation, farmers into a cooperative, and labor into a union. The Antitrust Division has the duty to prevent the use of such legal rights of association in an illegal way for purposes far different from those contemplated in the statutes.

Unions stand to gain by the vigorous performance of this duty. In the past most labor cases under the Sherman Act have arisen through private suits instituted without public responsibility and often conducted as a part of a struggle to destroy a union or to avoid dealing with it. Organized labor suffers when the selection of labor cases under the Sherman Act and the presentation of argument in such cases is left in the hands of those who may be hostile to organized labor itself. By contrast, enforcement of the law by officials with a public duty to be fair, consistent, and constructive involves an equal care to protect legitimate union activities and to prevent unlawful ones. In such enforcement, labor and the public will necessarily be in-

252

formed as to the boundary between lawful and unlawful union actions; and by virtue of such information the harassment of unions by unjust private suits will become more difficult.

Sincerely,
THURMAN ARNOLD,
Assistant Attorney General.

Since the publication of the Department's policy, the *Apex Hosiery Co.* case[4] has been decided by the Supreme Court. It appears to sustain the Department's position in all its pending suits. The *Apex* case leaves much for future decision. It looks at least this far:

1. In a strike for a closed shop the use of organized power by labor is not a violation of the Antitrust law unless third parties are brought into the suit by boycott or otherwise. Where competitors are restrained labor has no exemption from the Sherman Act.

2. If a union is striking for a legitimate objective the court intimates that the secondary boycott or sympathetic strike may be used provided the objective of the union is legitimate. No decision is made on this point but the road is left open for an application of the test laid down by the Department in the statement quoted above.

A dissenting opinion was written by Chief Justice Hughes, in which Mr. Justice McReynolds and Mr. Justice Roberts concurred. This decision lays down the test urged by the Department of Justice.

The policy stated in the letter was immediately at-

tacked by two groups,—first, labor organizations themselves, and second, the type of liberal who could not
see any kind of fault in an organization which had once
enlisted his sympathy. They used the identical arguments which had heretofore been used by large corporations. In the first place, the Act was too vague to be
enforced. In the second place the hope of the labor
movement lay in the government letting alone the enlightened leaders who had the labor movement in
charge. The speeches of those who wanted labor let
alone under the Sherman Act were similar to those
arguing that big business should be let alone.

Then there were the fixers who rushed to Washington, who recognized the need for lip service to the law,
but who insisted that it be lip service only. They
wanted only the continuance of the comfortable ways
of the past. One labor leader made a proposition. He
said, "I understand your position. You have got to enforce the law. We don't mind an occasional prosecution. We have been prosecuted in the past. But this
idea of calling hundreds of union men before grand
juries all over the country in the building trades is destroying our leadership—it's demoralizing our unions."

What he meant was that the little groups in tight
control were being asked questions by the rank and file.
He meant that the democratic process was emerging
in the labor movement.

The great advantage of the publicly-stated prosecution policy of the Antitrust Division is that it will be a
protection to the right of labor to organize with democratic control within the unions. Labor unions are

endangered by employers, by other unions, and by combinations of other unions and employers, even after certification by the National Labor Relations Board. In such cases prosecution under the Sherman Act is an important protection to labor.

And finally, the Sherman Act can protect the labor movement from enemies within its ranks whom it has no power to control, who bring it into disrepute and thus give ammunition to labor-baiters. Without the intervention of the Sherman Act, it is possible for selfish men within a labor union to work themselves into positions of autocratic power and terrorize the members of that union into helpless submission to activities the purpose of which is only personal power. This tendency is not peculiar to labor. It can be found with equal frequency in organized business. To penalize such activities in business is not an attack on business but a defense of business. To penalize such activities in labor organizations is equally a defense of labor. If they are not penalized, such aggressive tactics will win, just as unrestricted force always wins. I know of no protection against such influence within labor unions that is as effective as the Sherman Act.

Of course every group, labor, business and agriculture, when faced with the necessity of reconciling its activities to the Sherman Act, always protests at first. I am convinced that the recent alarm of labor over the antitrust laws will change to confidence in those laws when the protection which those laws give to labor in their legitimate objectives is once understood. After fifty years of non-enforcement, it is natural that business, labor, and agriculture should give voice to alarm and seek special exemptions. The first reaction of every group whose activities are under investigation is to urge that the Department of Justice ignore the law. This is a normal reaction to all forms of law enforcement, and it should be understood and received without resentment by every prosecutor. It is harmless because it always dies down quickly in the face of fair and impartial prosecution. As an example of this I cite the fact that after the Supreme Court of the United States had sustained an indictment against an agricultural association, which the Antitrust Division was prosecuting under the Sherman Act, the powerful and influential American Farm Bureau Federation sent us a resolution approving our prosecution policy with respect not only to industry and labor but to agriculture.

The reasons which give rise to resolutions such as this are that no one who takes thought for a moment believes that there is any long-run advantage in getting some individual official to ignore any law which it is his duty to enforce. If any group wishes the Sherman Act repealed or amended the place to urge it is in Congress. That is the only body which can give them any relief. Honest and impartial prosecution is a positive aid in amending an inequitable law, because it shows up and clarifies its inequities. *Sub rosa* non-enforcement of the law simply prevents its clarification and results in unknown hazards in the future.

I do not believe that the rank and file of labor desires to see labor organizations used for purposes which have no relation to wages, hours, health, the speed-up system, or the right of collective bargaining. Indeed, the use of organization for such purposes has been the principal basis for attacks on labor by its enemies. Those who desire to prejudice labor in the minds of the public are constantly citing the occasional case of the employer prevented from using more efficient methods being held up by a jurisdictional strike, or the utilization of labor unions by labor leaders to conspire with employers for their own personal gain or aggrandizement. The rank and file of labor is at present powerless to stop these practices. A fair antitrust policy will do two things for them:

1. It will prevent their exploitation by small groups who do not have the interests of labor at heart, and
2. It will develop case by case the freedom of labor to organize for legitimate labor disputes. This freedom has been seriously handicapped by leaving the enforcement of the antitrust laws against labor to private groups with no responsibility as has been done in the past. The Antitrust Division will utilize its labor prosecutions to take the yoke off the back of labor by ridding it of the control of those who betray its own fundamental interests. The resulting sound trade unions will draw the teeth of labor-baiters.

A recent decree entered in Chicago as a result of a labor prosecution illustrates how antitrust prosecutions can promote effective and responsible labor leadership. Local unions affiliated with the Bricklayers, Masons and Plasterers Union of America were indicted in Chicago, St. Louis, and Detroit for restraining the sale of tile. They were charged with participation in a conspiracy to control the system of distribution of tile. They excluded the products of manufacturers and also excluded contractors who did not conform to the purposes of the conspiracy. The manufacturers and contractors were also indicted for entering into this agreement. In addition to the indictments, there were complaints against these unions from many other sections of the country. The international union was not indicted. It was led by two men, Harry C. Bates and Richard Gray, who showed every desire to cooperate with the Department of Justice in cleaning up the situation on a nationwide scale. Under their constructive leadership, the international union, though not a party to any proceedings pending, voluntarily became bound by the decree.[5] Under this decree it assumed responsibility to force local unions to discontinue illegal practices. It thus made it possible to clear complaints and to enforce the law with the cooperation of the international union in a single court, the United States District Court at Chicago. It probably would have taken years to clean up on a nationwide scale such restraints had not the international union become a party to the decree.

This type of action, possible under the antitrust laws through the case by case method of treatment, does not require the setting up of government boards and commissions. Nor does it involve government administration of codes for running private business. Instead what happened was very simple: the pressure of the indictment for violation of law forced a reorganization by the defendants of their business and labor practices, and the international labor union, not a party to the particular charges, came in and undertook a very important function, not only with respect to the union indicted but with respect to all its unions everywhere. In this way, through prosecution in a single city, further litigation in many other cities has been avoided and results have been accomplished on a national scale.

The whole decree, of course, was approved by the United States District Court and violation of its terms by the international union, as well as by the other defendants, would constitute contempt.

This is an example of the kind of constructive results that can be attained for labor by applying the antitrust laws to a situation labor is powerless to solve itself.

XII.

The Rise of a Consumer Movement

IF THE American consumer can be made to understand what the antitrust laws can do for him, the next few years of the Sherman Act will be an era of constructive achievement.

Who are the American consumers? They are that vast group composed of about 85 per cent of our population whose income is not quite sufficient to live on what we consider a reasonable standard in a machine age. They are the people who have to think of prices, who must drive their automobiles less if the price of gasoline goes up, who get a real advantage in diet when the price of milk drops from 13½¢ to 8½¢, as it did recently in Chicago. These things make comparatively little difference to the 2 per cent of families with incomes of $5,000.00 or more a year. Such families get the necessities of life regardless of prices. To them differences in price levels mean only a difference in luxuries. But it is on the 87 per cent of the families who are getting $2,500 a year or less that our whole system of distribution depends. These are the consumers of America whose voice has been too long unheard.

It is one thing to point out the need for a consumer

RISE OF CONSUMER MOVEMENT

movement as a balance wheel to preserve free markets. It is an entirely different thing actually to start one. It is important, therefore, to ask ourselves the following questions: Under what circumstances do consumers' movements grow? Why have they been so ineffective as a balance wheel in the past forty years of American economy? What present hope is there for such a movement today?

In boom times, when people see the chance to increase their incomes, consumer movements never get under way. It is considered niggardly to be concerned with prices when there is an economic frontier to be explored. The glittering success stories of large enterprises, their control of publicity, and their undoubted achievements in efficiency of mass production were sufficient in the past to prevent effective action by consumers. Consumers did not get stirred up by mere size of industrial organizations, and they were prone to think of the antitrust laws as being aimed simply at size.

As independent enterprises disappear, however, the opportunities for building up independent incomes disappear with them. More and more people get in a position where their exclusive interests lie on the consumer side of the market. Prices become psychologically more and more important. The consumers' protest is always most effective when it is apparent that the business institutions on which they rely are incapable either of distributing goods or giving more jobs at higher pay. That is exactly the situation today.

These attitudes explain the history of the Sherman

261

THE BOTTLENECKS OF BUSINESS

Act. Independent businessmen and farmers were strong enough to get the Act passed. They were not strong enough to compel sufficient appropriation for its enforcement. This much and no more did the movement against personal devils like Wall Street and the trusts accomplish. It kept alive the ideal of free and independent enterprise. It did not, however, emphasize practical economic results such as the maintenance of free markets for the most efficient enterprise. There was no organized consumer consciousness of the effect of prices on the distribution of goods. Antitrust enforcement became a series of crusades theoretically on behalf of small business instead of greater distribution. The slogan was not "free trade between the states," but "trust-busting."

This sporadic antitrust policy of the last half century had many incidental results. In the first place, it kept the government out of regulatory schemes. When regulation was proposed, it could often be defeated on the ground that the real remedy was to enforce the Sherman Act. It did not prevent concentration of economic power. Indeed, there is evidence that this kind of enforcement of the Sherman Act actually encouraged corporate mergers. The law prevented two corporations from agreeing on prices. But after a merger, this particular hazard against a concerted price policy disappeared because they had become one big individual, with all the constitutional rights of an individual.

Throughout this period of corporate mergers and sporadic enforcement there was no real consumers' movement—no public consciousness of what the Sherman Act could do for consumers. The Act was never used to clear the entire market in which a product was sold from all the restraints of trade, big and little, which impeded the flow of that product to the consumer.

Since the consumers' interest was not emphasized, such enforcement efforts as existed were directed at the punishment of offenses rather than the achievement of economic objectives. Indeed, in very few antitrust prosecutions was any practical economic objective defined or argued with respect to the distribution of any particular product. In this way the moral aspects of the offense, and that will-o'-the-wisp, corporate intent, became more important considerations than economic results. Antitrust enforcement, not being geared to the idea of consumers' interests, became a hunt for offenders instead of an effort to test the validity of organized power by its performance in aiding or preventing the flow of goods in commerce. The result was that although the economic ideal of a free competitive market as the cornerstone of our economy was kept alive, no adequate enforcement staff was ever provided to make that ideal a reality. Such, broadly speaking, was the state of the Sherman Act from 1890 down to the great depression.

Then followed the NRA—representing the antithesis of the Sherman Act. During the NRA period the consumers' movement completely disappeared. Indeed, any consumer who wanted to buy at the lowest cut-rate price possible in a deflated market was regarded as a contributor to public delinquency. And the chiseling

THE BOTTLENECKS OF BUSINESS

competitor who chose to sell at such prices was an actual criminal.

The NRA cannot be understood apart from the period of financial collapse which produced it. In such times the interest of people as consumers is completely submerged in their interest as investors. They see their own savings being swept away—or else the savings of the employer who pays them. No consumers' movement could make headway against the fear of such rapid deflation. Everyone began to parade in honor of the blue eagle, a bird devoted to keeping businessmen from destroying each other as they were whirled around the descending spiral of financial collapse. All that was left of the consumers' point of view were a few phrases in the National Recovery Act recognizing that the antitrust laws were still on the statute books. A few consumers' committees were formed and forgotten in the course of the administration of the Act. The entire staff of the Antitrust Division was occupied in defending the constitutionality of efforts to put a floor under prices. The Sherman Act was regarded as obsolete.

The job which the NRA accomplished was the stabilizing of financial structures. It succeeded, partly through positive action, mostly through moral effect. Foreclosures and bankruptcies finally stopped. Banks got on their feet. Insurance companies ceased to worry about the book value of their reserves. During the performance of that task the NRA got public support. When that job was done, the work of the NRA was ended. From then on it lost public support, and when the Supreme Court finally executed it in the *Schechter*

264

case[1] there were very few mourners at the funeral. Indeed, so unpopular had the Act become that its opponents refused to recognize the essential function which it had served during a time of crisis.

The *Schechter* case was decided just at the time that consumers were becoming conscious of what the elimination of competition was doing to prices. Under the NRA, the idea of competition had been very subtly changed. We were still to have competition—lots of it—but it was to be "fair" competition, that is, competition with a floor under prices. Real competitors were called chiselers. (A chiseler may be defined as one who puts a frozen price on the block and applies a chisel to it.) Competition which lowered prices was known as "cutthroat" or "ruinous" competition, which impaired investments and destroyed orderly distribution. A standard of competition on some vague notion as gentlemanly conduct had been set up. In answer the court said that the power to set up such new standards of fair competition was not one which could be delegated to anybody. In the words of Chief Justice Hughes:[2]

Debate apparently convinced the sponsors of the legislation that the words "unfair competition," in the light of their meaning at common law, were too narrow. We have said that the substituted phrase has a broader meaning, that it does not admit of precise definition, its scope being left to judicial determination as controversies arise. * * * What are "unfair methods of competition" are thus to be determined in particular instances, upon evidence, in the

light of particular competitive conditions and of what is
found to be a specific and substantial public interest. * * *

*   *   *   *

The Government urges that the codes will "consist of
rules of competition deemed fair for each industry by
representative members of that industry—by the persons most vitally concerned and most familiar with its
problems." * * * Could trade or industrial associations or
groups be constituted legislative bodies for that purpose
because such associations or groups are familiar with the
problems of their enterprises? And, could an effort of that
sort be made valid by such a preface of generalities as to
permissible aims as we find in section 1 of Title I? The
answer is obvious. Such a delegation of legislative power is
unknown to our law and is utterly inconsistent with the
constitutional prerogatives and duties of Congress.

The decision of the Court was unanimous. The opinion of the time put the late Justice Cardozo on the side
of the Administration in a Court that was rapidly becoming a political issue. But even Justice Cardozo said:[3]

* * * If that conception shall prevail, anything that
Congress may do within the limits of the commerce clause
for the betterment of business may be done by the President upon the recommendation of a trade association by
calling it a code. This is delegation running riot. No such
plentitude of power is susceptible of transfer. * * *

The *Schechter* case ended the attempts to legalize a
system of eliminating competitors whose prices destroyed established inventory values. It was popular
because when the fear of financial collapse had disap-

peared, when the necessity of keeping up book values in order to prevent savings from being swept away was no longer apparent, consumers began to wake up. They began to be interested in prices. It became more and more clear to them that they would be able to buy at the greatest advantage in a free market. They wanted their pants pressed at the lowest price they could get. They wanted to trade in their old automobiles for as much money as dealers competing against each other would give them.

These demands were clothed in the high-sounding phrases of individualism and opposition to dictatorial power. The power behind the movement, however, was not the magic of these phrases, as the Republicans found out to their cost in the bitter campaign of 1936. The force which destroyed the popularity of the NRA was the growing interest of consumers who wanted to buy in a free competitive market. They were not worried about bureaucracy. They did not feel angry with the Administration for having passed the NRA, because they still remembered how they had all felt when they paraded in its honor during the period of financial collapse. Therefore, the attempts of the opposition in 1936 to capitalize on that supposed indignation against bureaucracy proved to be mistaken politics. The voters did feel, however, that the time for taking this particular medicine had gone by. That is the reason the *Schechter* decision was popular and yet could not be utilized in 1936 as a weapon against the Administration that was responsible for the NRA.

When the NRA disappeared a period of confusion

THE BOTTLENECKS OF BUSINESS

was inevitable. Businessmen interpreted the *Schechter* case as a decision compelling a *laissez faire* policy on the part of government. It was not understood (as it should have been) to be a guidepost pointing to the necessity for maintaining free markets for the distribution of goods, but was erroneously thought to be the beginning of the end of government "interference" with business. Thus, following the *Schechter* case, all federal legislation designed to use the power of the national government to solve national problems was attacked. The Supreme Court was made to look like a protector of the independent power of feudalistic business organizations. Groups like the Liberty League, completely misinterpreting the spirit of the times, began to write a new constitution in the interests of special privilege. The Wagner Labor Relations Act, all farm legislation, even the Social Security Act, appeared to be in danger of the Supreme Court of the United States.

Out of this confusion came the famous Court fight. Those who demanded more liberal justices on the Court felt that this action was necessary to save for the federal government the power to pass legislation to protect unorganized groups who were becoming helpless in the battle between industrial giants.

Since this book is intended to promote understanding of the necessity of free trade within the borders of the United States, I do not wish here to raise the old issue of the Court fight, the bitterness of which has not yet died down. During the battle I was an ardent supporter of the Administration. The fight is now over.

268

Perhaps it is fortunate that neither side was forced to capitulate and that men can still argue the question of who actually won. The Supreme Court is our only symbol of national unity and of fundamental principle above political and economic pressures. Nations need that sort of symbol. The court is not a directing force; it is an inspirational force. The slowness with which the court moved, the fact that its decisions were theoretically limited to narrow issues, gave to those high judicial opinions the elasticity of the old Delphic oracle. It was a slow process, but it was so much a part of our most revered government tradition that there was no escape from it. And it had this great practical utility: It served to get the public accustomed to new ideas in times of change, without abandoning all our old ones.

Specifically with reference to the maintenance of free competitive markets, the judicial process enabled us to avoid the threatened destruction of the Sherman Act by broad, sweeping emergency legislation, without in the end denying the power of the national government to enact more specific remedies where Congress found that they were needed. It is easy to devise in a vacuum systems of government which work more smoothly than ours. Yet the fact remains that other nations, without this powerful brake of the judicial process, have seen their industrial democracies swept away by cartels organized under emergency conditions to save capital structures from too violent deflation.

The very slowness with which the Court moved during our period of crisis had its practical utility. Had the

THE BOTTLENECKS OF BUSINESS

Supreme Court acted promptly, had the *Schechter* case been presented at the same time as the *Nebbia* case [4] (which sustained state government price-fixing of milk), my guess is that the *Schechter* opinion would not have had a majority. In any event, had the NRA been struck down at that time, the public enthusiasm which led men to parade for the blue eagle might have swept the decision aside. The opinion, however, came at a time when the NRA had performed its functions as a financial stabilizer and consumers were getting tired of it. True, the *Schechter* case started the pendulum of governmental power swinging toward a *laissez faire* which would not work. But there were enough political pressures in this country toward social security, fair treatment of labor, and in aid for the unorganized farmer so that the pendulum could not swing too far back. The *Schechter* case remains as a bulwark for a free market and not as a limitation on governmental power where the facts show that power is needed.

Today, for whatever reasons the former partisans in the Court fight care to give, the Supreme Court has struck a balance. The ideal of a free competitive market is still the basis for our economic structure. The Sherman Act is still our economic common law, or as Mr. Justice Hughes put it "a charter of economic freedom." [5] Departures by Congress from that standard may be made, but they must be specific enough to be justified by the facts of particular situations. And the privileges which Congress may give to use organized power to restrain trade must be reasonably used for the pur-

RISE OF CONSUMER MOVEMENT

poses for which they were intended. Broad general legislation which impairs a competitive market is still forbidden.

Whether you think that the court was forced into this position by liberal leaders who became tired of reactionary opinions by aging justices, or whether you think the court maintained our economic freedom against left-wing ideas embodied in radical legislation, depends upon your point of view. Both positions may be supported plausibly. The truth lies somewhere in between. Of course, there were left-wing ideas, and of course there were reactionaries. In times of change extremists always drown out tolerant discussion. The court does not operate in a vacuum. Like every government institution in a democracy, the fundamental basis for the court's authority is public acceptance of its ideas. It must, therefore, fumble its way to a balance between the extreme views of important economic groups before we can achieve judicial peace. The point I am making here is that the balance has been struck, (not *how* it was struck) and today we do have judicial peace again.

The problem of turning this judicial balance into an economic balance is still before us. The only government instrument which appears to be effective in maintaining a free market and in acting as a balance wheel against the special privileges granted by Congress to particular groups is the Sherman Act. The reason why it is the only effective instrument is found in our form of government. In a vacuum it can be plausibly maintained that an intelligent use of the taxing and spend-

THE BOTTLENECKS OF BUSINESS

ing powers is a better instrument than the clumsy process of criminal indictment to eliminate the economic toll bridges which are built by private groups across the channels of trade. Yet it is becoming quite clear that our government is unable to use these two powers for practical objectives.

The reason for this is the political impossibility of delegating to the Executive branch enough discretion to use taxing or spending to regulate business. It invokes too much centralized power to be congenial to American thinking. Therefore there can be no nice adjustment of these powers to particular industrial problems in the light of their separate facts. The Corporate Surplus Tax was intended, for example, to curb monopoly power. It was found to be too inelastic in its application. It became so unpopular that not even the full force of an administration which had control of Congress could keep it in existence. The use of the taxing and spending powers has been a battleground between partisan political groups and will continue to be.

On the other hand, the idea of indicting criminally for the economic offense of putting unreasonable restrictions on trade is backed by an ancient tradition and unquestioned public acceptance. Look at the history of the Act and see how it has held the allegiance of the major political parties for fifty years. At the end of Grover Cleveland's first administration there was growing discontent, particularly in the West, over the power of industrial combinations. They were then called the trusts, and the name has stuck ever since.

Cleveland came out with the slogan that the protective tariff was the mother of trusts. The Republicans countered with the appealing idea that America could have her protective tariff and break up the trusts at the same time. The Republicans promised an antitrust law and that promise was one of the important factors in electing Harrison.

In 1890 the Republican Party fulfilled its promise with the Sherman Act. The great mass of American consumers were uninterested; it was a gesture to a group which was distinctly in the minority. Hence it was comparatively easy to emasculate the Sherman Act after it was passed by the narrow definition of interstate commerce in the *Knight* case.[6] No one seemed to mind. Yet the tradition had started to roll like a snowball, and during the fifty years the Act has been on our books we have never wavered in our allegiance either to the ideal or to the use of the criminal process in enforcing its principle.

Since 1900 every Democratic and every Republican platform has contained pledges of enforcement. Indeed, the Republican platform of 1936 contains almost an exact copy of the plank in the Democratic platform of 1932 by which these pledges were continued. Big business has struggled to avoid it; minority groups have claimed exemption; critics have denounced the Act as a failure; inconsistent legislation has been passed. Yet in spite of all this the Sherman Act has survived as part of our vital economic beliefs. Every time we have swung away from it, we have been compelled to swing back. We have ignored the Act at times, but no political group has ever been allowed by the American people to forget it for very long.

We have been passing through a period where the case by case method of reaching economic solutions was psychologically difficult because men were too much interested in broad ideas. The objection to the enforcement of the Sherman Act as a practical solution of our problems was always that we needed a more fundamental cure. Thus the radical Utopia of planning was set up against the conservative Utopia of *laissez faire,* and common sense was the first casualty in the ensuing struggle.

Today the pendulum is swinging against broad general solutions. That swing is illustrated by the impossibility of maintaining a crusading spirit in the new agencies of government which are under fire. It is also, unfortunately, expressing itself in reactionary legislation—in red hunts against dissenting groups which still have faith in sweeping government change. This may be regrettable, but it is one of the natural reactions of political organization. However, relief from the necessity of presenting some fundamental cure has had a compensating advantage. We can now get down to the tiresome job of handling smaller and more concrete problems in the light of their particular facts. And in such a situation the method of the Sherman Act comes into its own.

Its method is practical because, as I have said, it takes up one industry at a time. There are two ways of filling a hundred bottles, of different shapes and sizes, with water. One is to put them in the center of the room and throw water at them with a dipper. The other way is to hold one bottle at a time under a faucet. The latter is the case by case method with which enforcement of the antitrust laws should approach American business problems. It is effective because American industries are different. You cannot solve the problems of the distribution of steel by the same kind of organization necessary for the effective distribution of motion pictures. You cannot find out how reasonably to govern the use of patents on glass food-containers by studying the distribution of nitrogen by the Allied Chemical Company. Each of these organizations should be compelled to use its powers and privileges to pass the savings of mass production on to the consumers, but the activities which are reasonable in one case may not be reasonable in another. The test is performance,* and that test can only be applied case by case.

The combination of its ancient tradition and its present practical utility finally forced the attention of the government to the Sherman Act in 1938. It had been neglected for a long time. However, we had just gone through a violent deflation in 1937. During that time men had been forced out of employment faster than ever before. The action of the United States Steel Company, which discharged 55,000 men in three months, was typical. We, in the Administration, did not like to call it a depression, and hence we always

* Some powers are considered so dangerous in themselves as not to be permitted regardless of performance. Any form of price-fixing is in this category.

referred to it as the recession of 1937, but this was a euphemism.

It was particularly noteworthy that the recession occurred after the Administration had actually succeeded in balancing the national budget in the very real sense that the government was taking in more money than it was spending, and thus destroying credit instead of creating it. This budget balancing had occurred under pressure of conservative economists who had been worried about inflation and who had almost a unanimous press behind them. However, the deflation was so severe that spending had to be taken up again. And shortly thereafter came the President's monopoly message of 1938, which included an immediate additional appropriation to the Antitrust Division of $200,000, giving it more funds than it had ever had before in its history. The Antitrust Division was doubled in size during that year. The next year it was doubled a second time. Tracing the growth of personnel in this Division, we find that at the beginning of the Administration it included 18 men. By 1938, when the writer took office, it had grown to 50 men. This growth has not been for the purposes of antitrust enforcement but due to the enormous mass of litigation forced on the Antitrust Division by the various recovery acts. In 1938, after litigation over the recovery acts had practically ceased, the Division was increased to 100 men—today it has approximately 200. There are more cases pending than ever before. There is more interest than there ever was before. Complaints, which are an index of the public interest, have quadrupled in the last three years. In addition to that, there is a growing public support of the work of the Antitrust Division. Newspaper comment two years ago was invariably hostile. Today that hostility has changed to active support from all quarters. In the entire history of the Sherman Act there has never been such support for its enforcement. It is important to diagnose the reason for this.

The reason, I am convinced, is found in an awakening consciousness of the consumers of America of the importance of prices and price policies. The 75 per cent of the families with incomes of $1500 or less are no longer hopeful that any sudden business turn will bring them prosperity. The hope of the unemployed is only to get jobs of any kind at any wages. Even labor organizations are compelled to fight these pressures from unorganized labor and to adopt policies of exclusion of their unemployed brethren.

The hope of the farmers is to exchange their goods for the manufactured products they need, rather than to "make more money." There is an awareness that the real problem is distribution, rather than money income, and that distribution means fair exchange in a free market.

The present dependence of agriculture and labor on government subsidies and relief has increased that awareness—because nobody likes subsidies. Everyone hopes they are temporary. Therefore, even the subsidized groups want their subsidies spent in a free market, since only by establishing such a market is there hope that subsidies may no longer be required. Groups which are forced to bring political pressure to get their subsidies, against the criticism of the respectable press, become intensely interested in price policies. They become consumer-minded.

There is another factor of importance in this consumer movement for a free trade within the borders of the United States. It is the realization that our economic frontier has disappeared and that our population curve is flattening out.

The idea used to be firmly fixed in the minds of every local chamber of commerce in every American city, small and large, that the town was bound to grow and thus create expanding opportunities for income. Merchants' inventories, schools, and every sort of local commercial activity were based on this faith. I recall a wooden sign, fronting the railroad on the way to Denver. It was nearly a block long, and carried the legend in black letters ten feet high:

WATCH NUN GROW

Today Nun appears the worse for wear and the sign is being used for kindling.

An article by the discerning columnist Frank Waldrop in the *Washington Times-Herald* for March 27, completes the picture. I quote:

MR. LAMBERTSON (A representative from the First Congressional District of Kansas) —I would like the Superintendent to give us some explanation of the decrease in the number of children in the schools, with an increasing population.

RISE OF CONSUMER MOVEMENT

DR. BALLOU (Superintendent of D.C. Public Schools) — There are a number of factors, Mr. Chairman, and members of the committee, that contribute to this decrease. One of them is the decrease which is observed throughout the nation, due to the reduction in the number of children between 5 and 6 years of age and the declining birth rate. . . .

MR. RABAUT—Are there any statistics on it?

DR. BALLOU—The Office of Education has those statistics.

MR. RABAUT—Could they be placed in the record?

DR. BALLOU—Yes.

MR. RABAUT—It might serve as a notice to America that they are passing out.

DR. BALLOU—I shall be glad to submit such a statement.

* * * *

And here is the substance of the statistics—that in 1915, there were 25.1 live births per 1,000 of population in this stalwart country, and that in 1938 the rate was down to 17.6 live births per 1,000. This was no sporadic drop, but the consequence of a steady decline.

* * * *

Well, as they say in New England, how does that signify? For one thing, it signifies we don't need to spend any more money building elementary schools. Only in maintaining them and replacing worn-out units. That is not good for contractors. It means that baby doctors have things to think about. Also baby-clothes makers. Also dealers industries on behalf of juvenility.

But couple with the declining birth rate the lengthening life span. As a nation we are slipping into middle age, with all the wisdom, crotchets, and conservatism that implies. Less cannon fodder. Less raw muscles in the mills.

THE BOTTLENECKS OF BUSINESS

Less springing enthusiasm for exciting words and causes. (Don't mention the Townsend Plan, please. Only another part of whole.)

More skill. More seasoned understanding. More placidity.

*   *   *   *

There are just a few of the vast changes in our habitation for living implicit in Mr. Rabaut's surprise at the difference in the number of children attending D.C. elementary public schools in 1938, compared with the number in 1930.

What else occurs to you?

In a nation dominated by the idea of security on a small income rather than success stories, the hard practical question of how many necessities may be exchanged for farm products or services becomes of tremendous importance and this means interest in prices.

Whether farm subsidies are right or wrong—whether relief should be cut down or raised are questions which I do not wish to argue here, because I am discussing the pressures behind these movements as political facts. I am not arguing whether in an ideal world these pressures are good or bad things. It is important to point out that in the history of every business civilization in the past, we find that free markets have disappeared in the absence of some positive and continuing government force to maintain them.

The question before us today is whether the consumers' movement in America is strong enough to compel an adequate enforcement organization so the government can effectively function as a referee. I, personally, believe that the movement has the necessary force behind it provided it can be turned in the right direction by the education of consumers. There are, today, fourteen hundred active consumers' organizations. They are found in labor, in women's organizations, in churches—in fact in every group that has to think of prices. The Antitrust Division is, today, the focal point of their complaints, and hence this interest.

Consumers' interest, of course, is not confined to consumers' organizations as such. For example, such widely separated organizations as the National Retail Grocers' Association, the National Association of Real Estate Boards, and the Illinois Agricultural Association each passed resolutions endorsing extended enforcement of the Sherman Act. The endorsement of the Agricultural Association is peculiarly significant because a number of its members belonged to the Pure Milk Association of Chicago which was under indictment for violation of the Sherman Act. Why did these powerful groups endorse the Act? It was because the Real Estate Board realized the need for a free market in building, the retail grocers wanted to free the distribution of food, and the Agricultural Association wanted farm subsidies spent in a free market.

I think, therefore, that the consumer movement is strong enough today. The only question is whether it can be sufficiently informed about available procedures to insist on practical action.

THE BOTTLENECKS OF BUSINESS

Future of the Antitrust Law

This year marks the fiftieth anniversary of the Sherman Act. On this anniversary there is a larger organization devoted to enforcement than ever before, and there is more public interest in the Act than ever before. The question arises whether this is just another sporadic crusade like those of the past, or whether it is the beginning of a nationwide organization which is actually adequate to protect the interests of the consumer. The answer to that question will depend on whether the great mass of consumers, who are the chief sufferers in the failure of our system to distribute goods, can be educated to demand a free domestic market.

If the American consumers can be educated in the real causes of the economic disease which is depriving them of food and shelter in a land of plenty, they can unite to cure it. The chief difficulty is that there are too many people who believe that economic distress can be cured by preaching and too few who are willing to take practical measures industry by industry. The failure of the democracies in Europe was due to too much democratic philosophy and too little effort to pull out one by one the weeds that were choking democracy.

Men do not, and cannot, choose their system of government and at the same time ignore the business organizations on which modern government must rest. Government either adapts itself to the needs of the social organization on which it rests or else it does not

282

govern at all. Government depends upon the economic structures which it finds when it comes into power. Therefore, the practical man who wants democracy must direct his effort toward maintaining an economic structure which allows a free government to exist. The only type of economic structure in which government is free and in which the human spirit is free is one in which commerce is free. The Renaissance began with the rebirth of commerce. The Dark Ages of the human spirit were the days when men were not able to meet each other in a free market place. The suppression of democratic freedom always follows suppression of the free exchange of goods. Out of commercial civilizations have come not only experiments in industry and production, but experiments in art and literature. Free commercial enterprise breeds free dissemination of ideas. Freedom from intellectual tyranny is impossible without freedom from commercial tyranny. It is for this reason that an industrial democracy is the only economic structure that has any permanence, whether the head of the political government is called a King or an Emperor or a President.

Therefore, the practical problem before us is to preserve a commercial civilization in a world that is being compelled to revert to a more primitive type of culture because the free market places of the world have been closed and men cannot get food and shelter and security from them.

There is nothing new about the Fuehrer principle or about the unity of Fascism. It is the old idea of an Indian chief at the head of a tribe which cannot hunt or make war without him. It does not work except in desperate situations where men are unable to think beyond the minimum requirements of life. It goes to pieces when an economic level is obtained on which men can think of other things than a bare existence. It is for this reason that it flourishes only in the dark ages of economic disaster. It is for this reason, also, that, to preserve itself, a totalitarian system instinctively turns toward war. Without war a totalitarian economy cannot maintain the low level of economic opportunity necessary to preserve its rigid discipline.

For that reason dictatorships are fragile and short-lived in spite of their apparent strength, just as all vigilante systems are short-lived. When in San Francisco the police failed to function, vigilantes preserved peace within the city. In the same way, where economic law and order fail, economic vigilantes fill the gap. Men give up their freedom not through a free-will choice, but because there is no choice between the food and shelter and security offered by a dictator and the starvation and unemployment offered by the anarchy which follows when the free market is gone.

Therefore, in the long run we need have no fear about the rebirth of commercial civilization after rigid dictatorships have shaken themselves to pieces. Indeed, if we take a long enough view we can see that tyrannies of the past have been like purges which cleanse the arteries of a nation from the accumulated rubbish of its monopolies. After the purge is over dictatorships fall. Hitler's army is a great example of the cold, cruel, competitive efficiency which can grow up during a period of preparation for war. But the trouble with the army form of social organization is that it freezes particular people into power and these people, who may have originally won their places by competitive merit during the period of war preparations, are allowed to rest on their oars when peace comes. It may liberate initiative rapidly but it freezes it even more rapidly. When competitive pressures of war cease, army control becomes inefficient and corrupt. It cannot stand prosperity. It cannot long be maintained in time of peace because the pressures that require it are gone.

Therefore, we need not worry about the ultimate future of commercial freedom within the next twenty years. It is the next ten years that present to us the only problem we can do anything about. That problem is preserving industrial democracy at home. I recall a phrase which was repeated over and over again by English and American orators prior to the War. It ran as follows: "One by one the lamps of reason are going out in Europe and they shall not be lighted again in this generation." The men who were repeating this phrase so lugubriously were doing nothing to preserve in their own countries the only type of civilization where the lamps of reason have ever shone, a free commercial civilization. In that social structure dying of auto-intoxication they refuse to clean out the accumulated poison of the little business monopolies.

The forces which make it difficult to clean out the channels of trade are always the same. They consist in resistance of vested interests which have put money value on restraints of trade and called them national wealth. That resistance is backed by the fear of deflation of investments on which the livelihood of thousands depends. When a capitalized commercial bottleneck is destroyed, those who make their living out of it must lose. These bottlenecks exist in every area of economic life—in labor, in business and in agriculture. Therefore, we find businessmen, farmers and unions all fighting for the preservation of the particular bottlenecks they control. We find them turning to price-fixing to protect their investment and then to subsidies in order to maintain their prices.

The progress of the disease is not pleasant. It first creates a major depression. If it goes on too long it ends in revolution. Such revolutions are not revolts—they are only the dying agonies of thousands of little monopolies which have tried to insulate themselves against competitive progress.

Every time men try to maintain a capital structure against the free competitive enterprise that might otherwise get rid of its dead tissues, sooner or later they find that they are protecting a corpse. This is true even where the government regulates the prices so that a fair return on that capital structure may be maintained against the ups and downs of competitive, commercial life.

Years ago we decided to regulate the railroads and preserve their capital structure. Rates were always fixed at a point where the railroads could get a fair return. Today we wake up to find that the capital structure of the railroads has disappeared in spite of all this protection. Theoretically, if a dollar were invested in a capitalistic system in the time of George Washington and received compound interest at a fair return, it would amount to a huge sum today. Actually, it is impossible to preserve that dollar and let it accumulate its increment while the person who owns it rests on his oars. We may try to preserve it, but it either gradually disappears or it blows up with a bang to the astonishment of the people who thought it represented security.

Another way by which a frozen system of distribution destroys itself is by arming its enemies. Great Britain armed Germany because it could not sell goods at home. The process is difficult for the abstract theorist to understand. Therefore, during the rise of Hitler to power, economists were predicting that he would fail because he had no foreign exchange. What was wrong with this theory?

The trouble with it was that it did not take into account the fact that supplies which cannot be sold at home because of a rigid price structure at home will be forced abroad, even if taxes have to be levied to do it. A short illustration is found in our own plumbing industry. We were committed to high cost distribution of plumbing which our low income groups could not support. One great corporation engaged in the manufacture of plumbing and heating equipment had accepted the high level of prices caused by the wasteful distribution system in plumbing (now the basis of an indictment of 102 persons and firms in Cleveland) as the only way that the plumbing business could be profitably carried on. Because it could not distribute its product, the corporation had idle capital. It was using part of that capital to build a plant in Germany instead of increasing distribution at home through competitive prices. The vice-president of the company was explaining this to me. He said that Hitler would allow his company to make money in Germany. I said, "But you can't get your profits out of Germany." He replied, "Oh, that will work itself out when things settle down."

The building of that plant in Germany was the result of the pressure of dammed up productive capacity of a product essential to decent housing which could not be utilized in America even though we sorely needed the houses. When such pressures force goods abroad the rationalization comes afterwards. This conversation took place just before the war.

Of course the corporation now knows that the net result of its enterprise was simply to build Hitler a plant at the expense of its American stockholders. Nevertheless, the same pressure operating again will create the same results. An economy that can distribute goods at home will always drain away the lifeblood of an economy that cannot distribute them, even though in money terms it is insolvent.

The reason is that in a country where men think that business bottlenecks are wealth, they fear the real wealth of material goods. Today in America we fear that we are about to be flooded with cheap manufactured products from Germany or cheap agricultural goods from South America. And so we are still talking about export subsidies to protect our pretended wealth from real wealth. We are talking about the necessity of lowering our standard of living in order to pay to export goods which would raise that standard if we could only distribute them. We cannot remedy this economic disease through legislation. Destruction of capitalized restraints of trade is a painful process. Pressure on the legislation will always be in the direction of softening the effect of deflation, of unreasonable combinations. Such adjustments are probably necessary. This makes it all the more essential that the organization which attacks the bottlenecks of business be removed from these political pressures or its efforts will fail. The idea of the separation of powers of the government is one of paramount practical utility in such situations. The administration of justice in every civilized country is the only balance wheel against political pressure. For that reason it is the only organization that can perform a painful operation.

This is a difficult lesson to teach to economic planners who seek the simplicity and symmetry of new legislative brooms that never work because they are wielded by a body too close to the pressure groups who are immediately affected. This is nowhere better illustrated than in the collapse of the attempt of the Weimar Republic to legislate balanced prices into Germany. That government understood the problem and based its political program upon the necessity of deflation. The reason why its program failed is described by Dr. Gustav Stolper in his recent book "German Economy."

Speaking of the efforts of the Weimar Republic to

THE BOTTLENECKS OF BUSINESS

stem the tide during the critical period when German free enterprise was being destroyed, he says (p. 194):

In theory, the deflationary policy really seemed to open a path that in due time could lead out of the crisis, once the hurricane sweeping over the world markets (and particularly over the United States) had abated somewhat. *Politically, however, it proved one of the strongest contributing factors in the downfall of the Republic.*

To understand the scope of the deflationary policy as inaugurated by Bruening's government, it is well to remember that in Weimar Germany already, not only later in Hitler Germany, prices and wages were largely controlled by the state or by organizations under direct or indirect state influence. *Prices were largely "political prices," wages largely "political wages."* Tied up as the price system was with government decisions on the one hand and with monopolistic organizations or companies on the other hand, it had lost much of the flexibility that prices display in a free capitalistic economy. In further consequence of this rigidity the pressure on prices fell much more heavily on the narrow free sector of business than on the controlled sector—another disturbing factor in the economic balance.

The objective of the deflationary policy was to force the political prices down to the very level they would have reached automatically in an elastic system. *But the difference between a natural and a politically enforced price decline is that nobody can find whom to make responsible for the former, whereas the blame for the latter is directed with full weight against the Government.*

There is a tremendous amount of sound political observation packed into these brief paragraphs. Here in a nutshell is stated the reason why "planned economy" by the legislative branch never works. The legislature is too near the force of pressure groups to resist the political forces which protect capitalized restraints of trade.

It is never a clear cut issue between monopolies and the "plain people." A restricted market does not have any such clean cut line of cleavage. Often the worst restrictions are the main support of millions of "plain people." And the taxing and the spending powers on which the planners rely to create balanced prices never work. They are wielded by the governmental bodies responsive to political pressure. To continue our quotation from Dr. Stolper (p. 195):

Deflationary policies are necessarily unpopular. It is true that the "consumers" are benefited. But since everybody is a consumer, most individuals are more concerned with their fate as producers than as consumers. Moreover, the business organizations and pressure groups center around producer interests. The cooperative movement, strong and excellently organized in Germany, had weighty producer interests.

Here is a clinical description of the pressures which defeated free enterprise in Germany until a dictatorship became the only way out, and war the only way out for the dictatorship. How strong are the same pressures in this country. It is obvious that there are many similarities. Our own wages and prices are gradually becoming political wages and political prices, as more and more forces of government are called in to bolster them up. Even our own cooperative movement is "weighted with heavy producer interests." Therefore, the pessimist has some grounds to predict that America *could* go the way of Germany under the possible economic pressures of the next ten years.

Against this unhappy fate however there are balance wheels in our own economy which were not present to help Bruening over his crisis. Let us list them.

In the first place, we are not very far along the road which Weimar Germany had taken in 1930. Our own "political prices" and "political wages" are as yet only tendencies. There is tremendous popular opposition to them. Their position is still insecure.

In the second place, we have before us today the object lessons of the European economic revolution. We know now what happens to a political government which lets free commercial enterprise die. We are learning that lesson not only from Germany but from England and France. We now know that the failure of democracies to produce at capacity during the war was not the fault of Baldwin and Chamberlain and Laval and Daladier but of the frozen economic system that kept these men in power. The English themselves know this today—and through them we are beginning to know it also. What we see in Europe is the explosion which inevitably follows closing the safety valve of commercial enterprise. We are still sitting on the safety valve in this country, but the reverberations of the detonation in Europe should jar us off before it is too late.

And finally, as a balance against our growing system of "political prices" and "political wages," we are fortunate in possessing the strongest tradition in favor of free enterprise of any country in the world enforced by an agency of government the further removed from political pressure of any branch. The Sherman Act has become so woven into our habits of thought that it is today our economic common law. No other country in the world has such a balance wheel backed by such a tradition. The difference between the United States and Europe in this respect is well stated in the following quotation from Dr. Stolper's book (p. 83):

> The trend of modern industrialism has been determined in all countries by two conflicting tendencies: the one toward liberation of the individual from ties and codes inherited from the Middle Ages and the mercantilistic era; the other toward integration on a more or less monopolistic basis. The whole Western world has experienced this conflict. But, with the sole exception of Germany, the individualistic tendency was defended by the policies of the various countries, and monopolies were torn up or at least made as difficult as possible. *The Anti-Trust Laws in the United States were the extreme expression of this individualistic philosophy. Free competition was the only recognized economic policy. Infringement of free competition was made a criminal offense.* The western European countries did not go as far as that. But England, France, Austria, and, following them, the smaller industrialized countries declared agreements in restraint of trade void and therefore unenforceable in the courts. In Germany alone cartel agreements had "legal status"; that is, they were treated by the law like any other private contracts. Any contravention of the contractual provisions among members of a cartel could be brought into court or penalized

by the forfeiture of bonds provided for this purpose under the agreement. Not until 1923, at the end of the inflation period, was a cartel law enacted. This we shall have to deal with in a subsequent chapter.

Nothing shows more clearly how little liberalism had taken root in the German mind than this special treatment of cartels. Liberalism was never recognized as the basis of a free capitalist system. As early as 1883, Professor Kleinwachter, an Austrian economist, who wrote the first scientific book on cartels, approved them as "the pioneer foundation of a state-controlled economy." The mercantilistic spirit, which all too readily merged later with the collectivist spirit of the labor movement, was strong even in the liberal era. The result of this merger was Hitlerism.

America has not gone so far along the road toward a rigid economic structure that its traditions of free trade are not strong enough to swing it back. The only question is whether Congress is going to support that tradition with funds and men to enforce it.

To arm ourselves against the hazards which confront us, we must first understand what they are. It is not the capitalistic system which is in danger. In essence all that capitalism means is that goods are distributed through the payment of money instead of by army quartermasters in accordance with military necessities. The moment that money becomes the medium of exchange we can't keep some people from making more of it than others. These people become the capitalists. Hitler made such an ingenious use of the capitalistic system that his money and credit was cheerfully accepted even by his enemies who dumped into Germany the goods from which he built his army. His method of accomplishing this capitalistic legerdemain was much the same as that of the American automobile industry in its circulation of notes based on the value of second-hand cars. Hitler issued currency on the productive capacity of his empire.

You may call this state capitalism if you like. But the real meaning of state capitalism is only that the process of centralization has gone on to its ultimate conclusion.

Therefore, the fear of the downfall of capitalism is really only the fear that money will stop being the root of all evil—a worry which we will do well to class with such worries as the geological prediction that the sun will burn out in the next hundred years.

The real hazard that confronts us is the disappearance of free commercial enterprise. The available remedy is to stamp out restraints of trade.

Will we seize our opportunity? As this book is written we have at least made a start, inadequate though it is. At the same time there are great pressures to keep down appropriations for actual antitrust enforcement and to salve our conscience by research and reports on prices which emit feeble roars like a toothless lion. Which set of pressures will win? I am not a prophet. I can only point out the following possible alternatives:

First, the Sherman Act and the ideals which it represents may be thrown into the discard, as was done in France. That country, prior to the war, was a mass of economic restrictions. These restrictions prevented France from even arming herself. Articles are being written today blaming labor restraints for the failure of France to produce airplanes. To the freezing of wages and shortening of hours is attributed the failure of France to produce armament on a large scale.

I have shown in this book that labor restraints follow business restraints—they do not cause them. Once an industrial system is so organized that it restricts new enterprise to protect its capital structure, the investors, labor and the farmer all commence to organize also for the same purpose. When the industrial system is slowing down at the top, the same brakes begin to have their effect at the bottom. The freezing of labor organizations in incompetent hands follows the freezing of industrial organizations in incompetent hands.

The Sherman Act was swept aside in the last war. It had just been revived in the Wilson administration by the passage of the Clayton Act and then everybody got in a hurry and forgot it. We are, today, paying the price for forgetting it. And so is France paying her price for abandoning the country to the monopolists.

The second possibility is that through the democratic process we will build such private organizations as we need in order to prepare for national defense, and at the same time we will develop a large enough government organization to keep these private organizations from becoming permanent in time of peace and from being capitalized as an integral part of our economy. We will do this by enforcement of the Sherman Act on a nationwide scale, breaking down all restraints of trade which cannot be positively justified in the interest of efficiency of production and distribution. If we can do this, the necessity of preparing for defense and the employment of millions of men in that effort, may be the greatest stimulus that we have ever had toward creating a new America.

Appendix I.

THE TEXT OF THE SHERMAN ACT [1]

*AN ACT to protect trade and commerce against
unlawful restraints and monopolies.*

Sec. 1.[2] Every contract, combination in the form of trust
or otherwise, or conspiracy, in restraint of trade or commerce among the several States, or with foreign nations, is hereby declared to be illegal. Every person who
shall make any such contract or engage in any such combination or conspiracy shall be deemed guilty of a mis-

[1] Act of July 2, 1890, c. 647, 26 Stat. 209.
[2] Section 1 was amended by the Miller-Tydings Act of
August 17, 1937, c. 690, 50 Stat. 693, by adding two provisos
at the end of the first sentence. The first proviso states that
"nothing herein contained" shall render illegal agreements
prescribing minimum prices for the resale of a commodity
which bears the trademark, brand, or name of the producer
or distributor and which is in free and open competition with
other commodities of the same general class, when agreements
of that description are lawful as applied to intrastate transactions in the State in which resale is to be made. The second
proviso qualifies the first by stating that the first shall not
make lawful any minimum resale price agreement between
manufacturers, between producers, between wholesalers, between brokers, between factors, between retailers, or between
persons in competition with each other.

THE BOTTLENECKS OF BUSINESS

demeanor, and, on conviction thereof, shall be punished by fine not exceeding five thousand dollars, or by imprisonment not exceeding one year, or by both said punishments, in the discretion of the court.

Sec. 2. Every person who shall monopolize, or attempt to monopolize, or combine or conspire with any other person or persons, to monopolize any part of the trade or commerce among the several States, or with foreign nations, shall be deemed guilty of a misdemeanor, and, on conviction thereof, shall be punished by fine not exceeding five thousand dollars, or by imprisonment not exceeding one year, or by both said punishments, in the discretion of the court.

Sec. 3. Every contract, combination in form of trust or otherwise, or conspiracy, in restraint of trade or commerce in any Territory of the United States or of the District of Columbia, or in restraint of trade or commerce between any such Territory and another, or between any such Territory or Territories and any State or States or the District of Columbia, or with foreign nations, or between the District of Columbia and any State or States or foreign nations, is hereby declared illegal. Every person who shall make any such contract or engage in any such combination or conspiracy, shall be deemed guilty of a misdemeanor, and, on conviction thereof, shall be punished by fine not exceeding five thousand dollars, or by imprisonment not exceeding one year, or by both said punishments, in the discretion of the court.

Sec. 4. The several district[3] courts of the United States

[3] Section 4 as enacted gave "circuit" courts the jurisdiction specified, but the Act of March 3, 1911 (36 Stat. 1087), abolished the circuit courts and conferred their powers upon the district courts.

APPENDIX I

are hereby invested with jurisdiction to prevent and restrain violations of this act; and it shall be the duty of the several district attorneys of the United States, in their respective districts, under the direction of the Attorney-General, to insitute proceedings in equity to prevent and restrain such violations. Such proceedings may be by way of petition setting forth the case and praying that such violation shall be enjoined or otherwise prohibited. When the parties complained of shall have been duly notified of such petition the court shall proceed, as soon as may be, to the hearing and determination of the case; and pending such petition and before final decree, the court may at any time make such temporary restraining order or prohibition as shall be deemed just in the premises.

Sec. 5. Whenever it shall appear to the court before which any proceeding under section four of this act may be pending, that the ends of justice require that other parties should be brought before the court, the court may cause them to be summoned, whether they reside in the district in which the court is held or not; and subpoenas to that end may be served in any district by the marshal thereof.

Sec. 6. Any property owned under any contract or by any combination, or pursuant to any conspiracy (and being the subject thereof) mentioned in section one of this act, and being in the course of transportation from one State to another, or to a foreign country, shall be forfeited to the United States, and may be seized and condemned by like proceedings as those provided by law for the forfeiture, seizure, and condemnation of property imported into the United States contrary to law.

Sec. 7. Any person who shall be injured in his business or property by any other person or corporation by reason

301

of anything forbidden or declared to be unlawful by this act, may sue therefor in any district[4] court of the United States in the district in which the defendant resides or is found, without respect to the amount in controversy, and shall recover threefold the damages by him sustained, and the costs of suit, including a reasonable attorney's fee.

Sec. 8. That the word "person," or "persons," wherever used in this act, shall be deemed to include corporations and associations existing under or authorized by the laws of either the United States, the laws of any of the Territories, the laws of any State, or the laws of any foreign country.

[4] See note 3, *supra,* p. 300.

Appendix II.

LEADING DECISIONS INTERPRETING THE SHERMAN ACT

Introductory Statement

THE Sherman Act sets up no detailed code of proscribed conduct and its prohibitions, directed against restraints of trade and monopolies, have the "generality and adaptability comparable to that found to be desirable in constitutional provisions." The courts in performing the judicial task of giving reality to this broad declaration of legislative policy, have been called upon to pass an economic judgment upon the acts and practices brought into question under the Act and decision has usually turned more upon this economic judgment than upon application of strictly legal principles. Since it is the underlying facts and the courts' appraisal thereof which have largely governed decision and since the same pattern of facts is seldom repeated, a summary statement of Sherman Act decisions presents peculiar difficulties.

The cases which established, slowly and somewhat tortuously, the main outlines of the law's incidence will first be reviewed. This bird's-eye view of the law's scope gives useful perspective in attempting more detailed exami-

THE BOTTLENECKS OF BUSINESS

nation of the decisions dealing with particular types of
restraint of special importance.

Cases Establishing the Major Outlines
of the Act's Application

U. S. v. E. C. Knight Co., 196 U. S. 1 (1895), the first
case under the Act to come before the Supreme Court, involved a combination under one ownership of every important sugar refiner of the country. The Court, ignoring
the fact that when production is monopolized, commerce
in the product of manufacture is likewise monopolized,
said that the combination was concerned solely with
manufacture, that manufacture is not commerce, and that
there was therefore no violation of the Act. This decision
has no present judicial vitality but it had the effect of
blocking prosecution of industrial combinations under
the Act, for almost a decade.

U. S. v. Trans-Missouri Freight Ass'n, 166 U. S. 290
(1897), and *U. S. v. Joint Traffic Ass'n*, 171 U. S. 505
(1898), condemned as unlawful agreements on the part
of competing railroads to maintain uniform freight rates.
The Court said that since the statute prohibited restraint
of trade in absolute terms, the alleged reasonableness of
the rates charged and of the restraint itself was not a
defense.

Addyston Pipe and Steel Co. v. U. S., 175 U. S. 211
(1899), held unlawful an agreement by which certain
manufacturers of cast-iron pipe eliminated competition
among themselves in the submission of bids for the sale of
cast-iron pipe. The Court stated that all the facts and circumstances must be considered in determining the funda-

304

APPENDIX II

mental question whether the necessary effect of the combination is to restrain interstate commerce.

In *Montague & Co. v. Lowry,* 193 U. S. 38 (1904), the Supreme Court first applied the Act to a commercial boycott, holding it illegal. The case also ruled that the quantum of commerce which is restrained is immaterial. *Northern Securities Co. v. U. S.,* 193 U. S. 197 (1904), held that the acquisition by a holding company of majority control of the stock of two competing railroads violated the Act. Dissolution of the holding company was directed. By this decision it was settled that the prohibitions of the Act are not limited to restraints flowing directly from consensual arrangements, but include those flowing from property transfers.

In *Swift & Co. v. U. S.,* 196 U. S. 375 (1905), the leading meat packers had agreed that in buying cattle at the stockyards they would act concertedly to depress prices. They had also agreed to act together in raising, lowering, and fixing the sales price of meat. The combination was held to violate the Sherman Act. The decision establishes that price manipulation or other artificial interference with a free market is illegal whether the objective be higher or lower prices and whether the combination be one of buyers or one of sellers.

Loewe v. Lawlor, 208 U. S. 274 (1908), was the first case in which the Supreme Court applied the Act to a labor combination. The case held that when a national union, in the course of a campaign to unionize the factories of a hat manufacturer, engages in an interstate boycott of those purchasing hats produced by this manufacturer, such secondary boycott is in illegal restraint of trade.

Standard Oil Co. v. U. S., 221 U. S. 1 (1911), held that the group of oil companies which the Rockefeller interests had brought under common control and formed into a single business organization unlawfully restrained and unlawfully monopolized interstate commerce. The Court also held that the only adequate measure of relief was dissolution of the combination and return of the stock of the subsidiary corporations to their former stockholders. Since common control over the various companies had been largely obtained prior to enactment of the Sherman Act, the holding was that continuance of such control constituted, under the circumstances existing in this case, a continuing violation of the Act. The circumstances which the Court emphasized in reaching this conclusion were the dominant position in the industry attained by the combination, the monopolistic purposes of its management, and the oppressive use it had made of its power in crushing competitors.

The Court in this case adopted the so-called "rule of reason." The Court said that the words "restraint of trade" were used in the Sherman Act in the light of the meaning which they had acquired at common law and that since only unreasonable restraints were unlawful at common law, only unreasonable restraints are within the interdiction of the Sherman Act. Notwithstanding the extensive legal literature which this rule of statutory interpretation provoked, it is doubtful whether it has had any very great effect in determining the actual decisions rendered in subsequent cases.

American Tobacco Co. v. *U. S.,* 221 U. S. 106 (1911), was likewise a business organization which had been formed and enlarged by merging, consolidating, or otherwise eliminating former competitors. Most of these had voluntarily come into the fold, tempted by the lure of monopoly profits or by the high prices offered for their properties. Ruthless price wars were directed at other competitors, until they were forced to come to terms. The Court, finding the combination illegal, directed the lower court to work out and put into effect a plan for dissolving the combination which would recreate, out of its constituent elements, "a new condition which shall be honestly in harmony with the law."

In *Standard Sanitary Mfg. Co.* v. *U. S.,* 226 U. S. 20 (1912), competitors, under the cloak of an exercise of patent privileges, had agreed upon the prices they would charge and upon the channels through which they would distribute their products. The case holds that where a restraint of trade condemned by the Sherman Act is effected by an agreement between a patent owner and others, the agreement is illegal and will be struck down if it transcends what is "necessary" to protect the privileges of exclusive manufacture, sale, and use which the patent law confers.

Nash v. *U. S.,* 229 U. S. 373 (1913), upheld the validity of the penal provisions of the Act and rejected the contention that its prohibitions are so vague and indefinite that, when applied in a criminal proceeding, they offend the requirements of due process.

Mergers and Like Consolidations of Competitors

Comparatively few cases involving a merger of competitors or other like union under single ownership or control have come before the Supreme Court, and none since 1927. Some of the decisions have given controlling weight to considerations which seem to have been ignored in other decisions. Of the entire field of the application of

THE BOTTLENECKS OF BUSINESS

the Sherman Act, this is the area in which the decisions
are least enlightening. Curiously enough, the law appears
to have been applied more rigorously to railroad combinations or acquisitions of control than to industrial combinations.*

Where one railroad had acquired control over another,
the acquisition was held to effect an illegal restraint of
trade even though the two roads had been competitive as
to only a part of their traffic and even though, as to this
traffic, other railroads offered effective competition. *U. S.
v. Union Pacific R. R. Co.,* 226 U. S. 61 (1912); *U. S. v.
Southern Pacific Co.,* 259 U. S. 214 (1922). Where a railroad's purchases of anthracite coal mines or of the stock of
companies owning such mines had brought under its control a large but minority part of the total national production of anthracite, the power to control commerce in
anthracite thus obtained was held to constitute a menace
to and an unlawful restraint upon interstate commerce,
"regardless of the use" made of this power. *U. S. v. Reading Co.,* 253 U. S. 26 (1920). See also *U. S. v. Lehigh
Valley R. R.,* 254 U. S. 255 (1920).

The cases of industrial mergers subsequent to the
Standard Oil and *Tobacco* decisions present a different
picture.

In *U. S. v. United Shoe Machinery Co.,* 247 U. S. 32
(1918), a merger of manufacturers of shoe-making machinery which conferred an almost complete monopoly

* In 1920 the Interstate Commerce Act was amended so as
to prohibit, without the approval of the Interstate Commerce
Commission, railroad mergers, acquisitions of control, etc.
Since the Commission's approval exempts the transaction
from the prohibitions of the Sherman Act, that Act is, for all
practical purposes, no longer applicable to mergers of competing railroads.

was allowed to stand, upon the ground that the machinery which the merged concerns respectively manufactured was complementary, not competitive.

In *U. S.* v. *U. S. Steel Corp.*, 251 U. S. 417 (1920), a holding company had been formed to acquire the stock of various independent steel companies. By this deal about half the country's steel production was brought under one control. The Court said that the legality of the combination was not to be tested by the circumstances existing when it was formed, but by those existing ten years later when suit to dissolve was filed. The Court, after finding that at this later time the Steel Corporation had neither the power nor the purpose to exact monopolistic prices, held that the size of the corporation, its ability to exercise effective price leadership, and its earlier price-fixing agreements with competitors did not establish that it illegally restrained or monopolized commerce.

The authority of *U. S.* v. *International Harvester Co.*, 274 U. S. 693 (1927), is doubtful because the decision turned upon the construction of the provisions of a consent decree. The defendant company was formed by a merger of competitors. A consent decree gave the Government certain relief. Later it filed suit alleging that it was entitled under the terms of the decree to further relief. The Court held that the legality of the original merger was not before it and that a showing that the corporation presently controlled about 64% of the trade was not in itself sufficient to establish that interstate commerce was being unlawfully restrained.

THE BOTTLENECKS OF BUSINESS

Price-Fixing and Related Combinations
in Restraint of Trade

Decisions under the Sherman Act dealing with the legality of price-fixing admirably illustrate development of the law by the case by case method. Definitive decisions of the Supreme Court have gradually limited the number of questions remaining unsettled and have clarified the tests by which application of the statute is determined. In this respect, a notable advance was made at the very last term of Court.

As we have previously noted (*supra*, p. 304), the Court at an early date held that an agreement to maintain uniform rates or prices imposes a restraint of trade prohibited by the Sherman Act and that the alleged reasonableness of this restraint cannot be set up as a defense. This holding was approved when the Court later interpreted the Act as prohibiting only unreasonable restraints. *Standard Oil Co.* v. *U. S.,* 221 U. S. 1, 64-65, *supra.* The Court there said that price-fixing agreements "operated to produce the injuries which the statute forbade" and thus fell within the interdiction of the statute, and that this statutory ban left open no question of reasonableness for consideration by the courts.

American Column and Lumber Co. v. *U. S.,* 257 U. S. 377 (1921), and *U. S.* v. *American Linseed Oil Co.,* 262 U. S. 371 (1923), show the illegality of agreements which, while falling short of direct price-fixing, produce the same effects. In the former case the members of a trade association, constituting a minority of an industry, not only disclosed to each other detailed information as to current prices and sales, but the association's executive officer added interpretative comments and recommendations de-

310

signed to induce the members to raise prices and limit production. In the latter case most of the producers of a commodity agreed to exchange their current price lists and agreed not to quote lower prices without immediately making a detailed report thereof to the other members. The agreement also provided pecuniary penalties for non-observance.

Maple Flooring Mfrs. Ass'n v. *U. S.,* 268 U. S. 563 (1925), and *Cement Mfrs. Protective Ass'n* v. *U. S.,* 268 U. S. 588 (1925), held that collection and dissemination of extensive statistical data among the members of an industry did not, in the absence of agreement upon prices or production, violate the Act. The Court said that trade was not illegally restrained merely because the exchange of data, by enabling producers to exercise a more informed judgment, would tend to stabilize the trade and to bring about uniformity of price and trade practice. The *Cement* case also held that exchange of information concerning particular contracts was permissible where the purpose was to "enable sellers to prevent the perpetration of fraud upon them."

U. S. v. *Trenton Potteries Co.,* 273 U. S. 392 (1927), held that where those controlling a substantial part of an industry agree upon the prices which they will charge, this is a restraint forbidden by the Sherman Act and the alleged reasonableness of the agreed prices or the good intentions of the combining parties are no defense. The case confirmed the dicta and clear intimations of prior cases, but it necessarily left unsettled the important question of whether the price-fixing which the Act directly prohibits is limited to agreements of the kind then before the Court, that is, to agreements (a) providing for sales or purchases at uniform prices and (b) conferring upon those combining the power to "control" market prices.

In *Appalachian Coals, Inc.* v. *U. S.,* 288 U. S. 344 (1933), a minority but substantial group of bituminous coal producers had agreed to market their coal exclusively through a common selling agency. There remained ample outside competition and the power to fix market price was neither sought nor within the grasp of the parties. The principal objectives were promoting the consumption of bituminous coal and eliminating, as far as the parties were concerned, certain marketing methods which put the seller at an unfair disadvantage. The Court held that the plan did not illegally restrain trade merely because it had the incidental effect of eliminating price competition among those marketing through the common selling agency. Furthermore, the case was presented to the Court before the plan had gone into effect. The trial court was directed to retain jurisdiction in order that it should be free to grant relief if the plan in actual operation should prove to be in undue restraint of commerce.

In *Sugar Institute, Inc.* v. *U. S.,* 297 U. S. 553 (1936), a dominant group in an industry had agreed, not to eliminate all price competition among themselves, but to stamp out every trade practice in any way conducive to actual competition. Since sugar refiners openly announce their prices in advance of sale, the lowest price announced by any refiner fixes the maximum price at which the others can sell and published prices are, at any given time, uniform. But secret concessions from published prices and variation in subsidiary terms of sale, such as freight allowances, cash discounts, guarantees against future decline in price, etc., may give rise to competition. The Court held that the elaborate structure of agreement which the re-

APPENDIX II

finers had erected in order to prevent secret departures
from published prices and in order to make the cost of
sugar the same for all purchasers (thereby reducing the
pressure upon refiners to sell competitively), imposed restraints which were unreasonable and therefore illegal.
The Court also held that the fact that one of the purposes
of the agreement was elimination of a competitive evil—
secret price concessions—was not sufficient to save the restraints from the condemnation of the statute.

The salient facts in *Socony-Vacuum Oil Co.* v. *U. S.*, 60
S. Ct. 811 (1940), were these. Most of the gasoline con-
sumed in a large area in the Middle West is produced and
marketed by major oil companies and they base their selling prices on the Mid-Continent spot market price of gasoline. Sales by Mid-Continent independent refiners to jobbers and consumers determine this spot market price.
The majors agreed to join in a program to purchase such
part of the output of the independent refiners as would be
likely, if sold in the ordinary course on the spot market,
to depress spot market price. The total amount to be purchased was divided up among the participating majors,
each assuming responsibility as to a certain portion. For
gasoline bought under this program, the majors agreed to
pay approximately the spot market price on date of purchase. The Court held that this was a price-fixing combination illegal *per se* under the Act and therefore not open
to the defense that the restraint was reasonable.

The decision establishes that the price-fixing agreements
thus illegal *per se* are not confined to agreements to buy
or sell at uniform prices, but include all those in which
purchases or sales are to be made within an agreed price
range, or at a certain price level, or at ascending or descending scales, or by applying some formula to market

313

prices. The decision also establishes that such price-fixing agreements are *per se* illegal even though the combining parties lack the power to "control" the market. The decision further establishes that the statutory prohibition is not escaped by a showing that the price-fixing agreement eliminates so-called "competitive evils."

Restraints Imposed under a Claim of Patent or Copyright Privilege

The Sherman Act's prohibition of undue restraint of trade does not extend to restraints resulting from the exercise of rights conferred by the patent law. Accordingly, when a claim of patent right is set up as a defense to a restraint which would otherwise be illegal under the Sherman Act, the Court's decision turns primarily on the scope of the patent privilege rather than on the meaning of the Sherman Act itself. The cases where this issue has been presented nevertheless deserve review. For one thing, these cases indirectly involve the meaning of the Sherman Act since the impact of this Act upon rights claimed under patent law is one of the chief factors given consideration in determining the true bounds of those rights. For another thing, the problem of reconciling the differing objectives of the Sherman Act and of the patent law is of current and increasing importance.

Since the nature of the issue is the same where a restraint of trade is defended under a claim of copyright privilege, the copyright cases will be considered *pari passu* with the patent cases.

The Court has held that a patent owner is within his patent rights when he licenses another to sell a patented article and fixes the price at which the licensee may sell,

APPENDIX II

and that these price restrictions therefore do not violate
the Sherman Act. *Bement* v. *National Harrow Co.,* 186
U. S. 70 (1902); *U. S.* v. *General Electric Co.,* 272 U. S.
476 (1926). The basis for the holding is that such control
over sales price is "normally and reasonably adapted to
secure pecuniary reward" for the exclusive right of sale
which the patent law confers upon the patentee. But since
sale of the patented article exhausts this right, an agreement fixing the price at which the purchaser may resell is
outside any patent privilege and constitutes a restraint of
trade illegal under the Sherman Act. *Standard Sanitary
Mfg. Co.* v. *U. S.,* 226 U. S. 20 (1912), *supra; U. S.* v. *A.
Schrader's Son, Inc.,* 252 U. S. 85 (1920); *U. S.* v. *General
Electric Co., supra,* at p. 488.

When different copyright owners, each engaged in selling articles on which he holds valid copyrights, agree with
each other to sell or distribute their copyrighted articles
upon the same terms and conditions, such agreement and
concert of action is outside any privilege conferred by the
copyright law and the resulting restraint of trade, if unreasonable, is prohibited by the Sherman Act. *Straus* v.
American Publishers' Ass'n, 231 U. S. 222 (1913); *Interstate Circuit, Inc.* v. *U. S.,* 306 U. S. 208, 230 (1939). Likewise, if competing process patents are pooled or cross-
licensed for the purpose of fixing the price of the product
manufactured or otherwise unduly restraining trade
therein, this *united* exercise of the individual monopolies
granted by the patent law is beyond the privileges conferred by that law and falls within the prohibitions of the
Sherman Act. *Standard Oil Co. (Indiana)* v. *U. S.,* 283
U. S. 163, 174 (1931).

When the owner of a copyright makes an agreement
with one to whom he grants a license under the copyright

315

as to the terms upon which he will grant licenses to others under the same copyright, the inclusion of the agreed terms in subsequent licenses is outside the owner's copyright privilege and effects a restraint coming within the purview of the Sherman Act, at least if the agreement is entered into at the demand of the first licensee and for the purpose of restricting the business of its competitors. *Interstate Circuit, Inc. v. U. S.*, 306 U. S. 208, 228-230 (1939), *supra.* The case thus holds that, just as the copyright law does not authorize restraints which are the product of agreement between two copyright owners, so it does not authorize restraints which are the product of agreement between a copyright owner and one who holds no copyright.

In *Ethyl Gasoline Corp. v. U. S.*, 309 U. S. 436 (1940), the defendant corporation owned patents covering a fluid which, when mixed with gasoline, increased its value. It also owned a patent covering the fuel produced by mixing this patented fluid with gasoline. It sold the fluid to refiners under licenses authorizing mixture of the fluid with gasoline and sale of the resulting product, but sales could be made to jobbers only if they were licensed by the corporation. It generally refused to license jobbers who had engaged in price-cutting and it administered the jobber licensing system so as to promote maintenance of gasoline prices. Jobber licenses were issued royalty-free. The Court held that since the corporation had chosen to exploit its patents by selling the patented fluid at a profit and since the agreements with refiners prohibiting sale to unlicensed jobbers were used, not to increase the patentee's reward, but to maintain prices and suppress competition in the interstate distribution of gasoline, the jobber licensing device was not embraced within the corporation's patent

rights and effected a restraint of trade prohibited by the
Sherman Act.

The Application of the Act to Activities
of Labor Organizations

The application of the Sherman Act to organized labor
has long been the subject of political as well as judicial
controversy. In the political arena, this has led to legislation giving labor partial and somewhat indefinite relief
from the provisions of the Act. In the judicial arena, the
practical effect of the decisions would seem to be to free
large segments of customary labor activity from the hazards of the Act.

A strike for terms or conditions of employment has been
held not to violate the Sherman Act even though it stops
the production of a mine or factory which ships most of its
product in interstate commerce, and even though the demands of the workers are enforced by lawless conduct.
Prior to *Apex Hosiery Co.* v. *Leader,* 60 S. Ct. 982 (1940),
the reason the Court gave for this conclusion was that the
restraint operated immediately upon production and not
on commerce. In other words, the restraint on commerce
resulting from curtailing the supply of goods available for
interstate shipment was considered only incidental in its
effect on interstate commerce. *United Mine Workers* v.
Coronado Coal Co., 259 U. S. 344, 408-413 (1922); *United
Leather Workers* v. *Herkert & Meisel Trunk Co.,* 265 U. S.
457, 464-465, 470-471 (1924); *Levering & Garigues Co.* v.
Morrin, 289 U. S. 103 (1933).

This doctrine was, however, subject to the qualification
that if the *intent* of the strike was to control the supply or
the price of goods in interstate markets, it was illegal un-

THE BOTTLENECKS OF BUSINESS

der the Sherman Act. *Coronado Coal Co.* v. *United Mine Workers*, 268 U. S. 295 (1925). Of course, in every case of a strike by those engaged in production, the labor unions intend to better working conditions. They also intend to accomplish this end by affecting the supply of goods. Whether this latter intent also embraces the supply of goods moving in interstate commerce is not a question of fact in any real sense. Therefore the distinction is practically unworkable.

Two types of situations have been held by the Court to be violations of the Act regardless of the intention. One is the case where a labor union used coercive action against third parties by sympathetic strike or secondary boycott. In *Duplex Printing Press Co.* v. *Deering*, 254 U. S. 443 (1921), *Bedford Cut Stone Co.* v. *Stone Cutters' Ass'n.*, 274 U. S. 37 (1927), and *U. S.* v. *Brims*, 272 U. S. 549 (1926), the Court held that boycotts or like coercive combinations which limited or suppressed the interstate trade of third parties were illegal under the Sherman Act. Another case where intention is immaterial is where labor is a party to a price-fixing combination which restrains interstate commerce. *Local 167* v. *U. S.*, 291 U. S. 293 (1934).

Apex Hosiery Co. v. *Leader, supra,* reexamined the question of whether labor unions are exempt from the application of the Sherman Act and held that they were not exempt. In that case, a union had closed down a factory in order to enforce its demand for a closed shop. Such a situation, the Court declared, was not a violation of the Act because it did not restrain competition. By this test the Court apparently meant that the coercion must not extend to third persons not parties to the labor dispute.

The Court left open the question as to whether a legiti-

APPENDIX II

mate labor objective would in certain cases justify a secondary boycott.

The result of the *Apex* case appears to be to support the prosecution policy of the Department of Justice against labor unions which is described in Chapter X.

Notes

CHAPTER I

[1] Moulton, *Income and Economic Progress* (Brookings, 1936) , pp. 27-28.

[2] *Hearings Before the Temporary National Economic Committee.* Part I, "Economic Prologue," Exhibit No. 5, p. 194.

[3] Kreps, "Welfare Levels in American Life," Ch. 7, *Social Education,* Stamford Education Conference, (The Macmillan Company, 1939) .

[4] *Consumer Incomes In the United States,* National Resources Committee, p. 18.

[5] *Hearings Before the Temporary National Economic Committee,* Part I, "Economic Prologue."

[6] Cartel Decree of Nov. 2, 1923.

[7] *Verhandlungen und Berichte des Unterausschusses für allgemeine Wirtschaftsstruktur.*

[8] The most recent as well as the most descriptive book on the rigid control of distribution in Germany is found in Lothrop Stoddard's *Into the Darkness,* (Duell, Sloan and Pearce, 1940) .

[9] See Miriam Beard's *The History of the Business Man* (The Macmillan Company, 1938) .

[10] There were 7,000,000 registered unemployed in Germany in 1933. The totalitarian method of getting rid of unemployment is described in Chapter XI, "The Army of the Spade," Stoddard, *supra,* fn. 10.

[11] Source for decrease of farmer share in consumer dollar.

CHAPTER II

[1] For a description of the admirable method of cross-licensing of patents which made the rapid competitive development of the automobile possible after Henry Ford became established see *Hearings Before the Temporary National Economic Committee,* Part 2, "Patents," pp. 286-313.

[2] *Ethyl Gasoline Corporation* v. *United States,* 27 F. Supp. 959, 60 Sup. Ct. 618 (1940) .

[3] Gypsum Wallboard.

NOTES

[4] *United States* v. *American Optical Co.,* Nos. 417-420, Dist. Ct. S. D. N. Y. (1940).

[5] *Hearings Before Temporary National Economic Committee,* Part 11, "Construction Industry," pp. 4935-4972.

CHAPTER III

[1] *United States* v. *Socony-Vacuum Oil Co.,* 23 F. Supp. 531, 105 F. (2d) 809, 60 Sup. Ct. 811 (1940).

CHAPTER IV

[1] The statements in this and in the following paragraph are taken from the indictment in *United States* v. *Bausch & Lomb Optical Co., et al.,* returned in the District Court of the United States for the Southern District of New York, No. 107-169 (March Term, 1940).

[2] To set out in detail the monopoly situation in war industries would require a lengthy technical exposition too long for this book. To summarize them would lead to the kind of misrepresentation that comes from half statements.

CHAPTER V

[1] Arnold, *The Symbols of Government* (Yale University Press, 1935), pp. 203, 205-206.

[2] *Sunshine Anthracite Coal Co.* v. *Adkins,* 60 Sup. Ct. 907 (1940).

[3] *United States* v. *Socony-Vacuum Oil Co.,* 60 Sup. Ct. 811 (1940).

CHAPTER VI

[1] *Chicago Conference on Trusts* (1900), p. 283.

[2] *Hearings Before the Temporary National Economic Committee,* Part 2, "Patents," pp. 256-285.

[3] *Ethyl Gasoline Corporation* v. *United States,* 60 Sup. Ct. 618 (1940).

CHAPTER VII

[1] Act of October 15, 1914, 38 Stat. 730.

[2] Act of June 3, 1937, 50 Stat. 246, reenacting Section 8b of the Agricultural Adjustment Act.

[3] Act of August 17, 1937, 50 Stat. 693.

[4] *Decrees and Judgments in Federal Anti-Trust Cases,* 1918, Volume 1, p. 341.

[5] See release of May 18, 1938.

[6] *Appalachian Coals, Inc., et al.* v. *United States,* 288 U. S. 344 (1933).

NOTES

Chapter VIII

[1] See *Baush Machine Tool Co.* v. *Aluminum Co. of America*, 79 F. (2d) 217 (1935).

[2] *Hearings Before The Temporary National Economic Committee*, Part 2, "Patents," pp. 425, 432.

[3] *Id.* at 613-614.

[4] *Id.* at 589-590.

[5] *Id.* at 600-601.

[6] *Id.* at 621-623.

[7] *United States* v. *Hartford-Empire Company, et al.*, No. 4426, Dist. Ct. N. D. Ohio (1939).

[8] *Hearings Before The Temporary National Economic Committee*, Part 5, "Development of The Beryllium Industry," p. 2038.

[9] *United States* v. *National Container Association, et al.*, Dist. Ct. S. D. N. Y., indictment returned August 9, 1939.

[10] Annual report of the Attorney General for the year ending June 30, 1938, pp. 59-60.

[11] *United States* v. *Borden Co.*, 28 F. Supp. 177 (1939).

[12] *United States* v. *American Medical Ass'n.*, 28 F. Supp. 752 (1939).

[13] 308 U. S. 188 (1939).

[14] 110 F. (2d) 703 (1940).

[15] 60 Sup. Ct. 618 (1940).

[16] *Apex Hosiery Co.* v. *Leader*, 60 Sup. Ct. 982 (1940).

Chapter XI

[1] *United States* v. *William L. Hutcheson, et al.*, Dist. Ct. E. D. Mo., indictment returned November 3, 1939.

[2] *United States* v. *Michael Carrozzo, et al.*, Dist. Ct. N. D. Ill., indictment returned June 24, 1940.

[3] *United States* v. *Joseph M. Schenck, et al.*, Dist. Ct. S. D. N. Y. indictment returned June 3, 1940.

[4] *Apex Hosiery Co.* v. *Leader*, 60 Sup. Ct. 982 (1940).

[5] *United States* v. *The Tile Contractors' Association of America, Inc., et al.*, No. 1761, Dist. Ct. N. D. Ill. (1940).

Chapter XII

[1] *Schechter Corp.* v. *United States*, 295 U. S. 495 (1935).

[2] *Id.* at 532-533, 537.

[3] *Id.*, at 553.

[4] *Nebbia* v. *New York*, 291 U. S. 502 (1934).

[5] *Appalachian Coals, Inc., et al.* v. *United States*, 288 U. S. 344, 359 (1933).

[6] *United States* v. *E. C. Knight Company*, 156 U. S. 1 (1895).

Index

INDEX

INDEX

Cartelization, 74, 106, 126
Cartels, 15-6-7, 32, 71, 79, 80, 112, 117, 126, 168, 173, 293-4
Catton, Bruce, 199
Ceiling profit, 62
Cement industry, 58
  Manufacturers' Protective Association, 311
Centralized government, 17
Central Labor Union, 248
  Trades Council, 243
Chain stores, 238
Chamberlain, Neville, 292
Chamber of Commerce, 278
Charity, 2, 21, 46
Cheap goods, 17, 82-3-4, 125, 288
Checks, 95, 97, 106-7, 109, 110
Cheese, 220-1-2-3, 230-1, 233-4
Chemical industry, 58
Chicago, 117, 127, 192, 194, 201, 213, 221, 233, 243, 257-8
  Milk case, 192, 238, 251, 260, 281
  University of, 193
Chinese Bandit system, 184, 244
Chiseler, 16, 58, 120, 264-5
Chrysler Corp., 24, 154, 160
Church, 98, 102, 281
Churchill, Winston, 80
Cigarettes, 34, 128, 229
C.I.O., 244
Civil Aeronautics Authority, 171
  proceedings, 134-5, 142-3, 150-1-2, 154
  Service, 80
  War, 97
Clayton Act, 136, 296
Cleveland, 184, 201, 221, 287
  Grover, 272-3
Clothes, 1, 5, 21-2, 28, 225
Coal, 104, 308, 312, 317
Code provisions, 65, 157, 258, 266
Coercion, 209, 249
Coffee, 86
Collective bargaining, 109, 136, 161, 190, 240-1-2-3-4, 248-9, 250, 252, 257
  states, 15

Collectivism, 94
College, 46, 93, 215
Collusion, 198, 200
Columbia Gas & Elec. Co., 154
Comer, George, ix
Commerce, 263, 266, 283, 304-5, 312
Commercial empire, 88
  system, 81
Commission merchant, 218
Common law, 104-5-6, 138, 270, 293
Communist, 94
Competition, 5, 12-3, 15, 24, 27, 33, 38-9, 43, 47, 51-2, 58, 83, 87-8, 113, 117-8-9, 120-1, 128-9, 135-6-7, 140, 142, 159, 175, 190, 230, 244, 265
Competitive, 1, 12, 14, 17-8, 25, 61-2, 64, 76, 80, 84, 117, 148, 168, 170, 176, 188, 194-5, 214, 219, 228, 271, 284-5-6, 288, 314
Concrete, 127, 243
Congress, 25, 57, 62-3, 73, 93, 98, 104-5-6-7, 110-1, 126, 137, 141, 143, 163, 171, 175, 182, 187, 190, 215, 240, 256, 266, 269, 270, 272, 294
Congressman, 52-3
Consent decree, 141-2-3-4, 153-4, 156, 158-9, 161, 309
Conservative economy, 276
  Party, ix, 89
Conspiracy, 71, 195, 200, 205, 208, 232, 237-8, 257-8, 299, 301
Constitution, 100, 137-8
Constitutional law, 97, 138
Construction, 37, 43-4, 198, 205
Consumer, viii, 1, 2, 3, 4, 5, 16, 18, 20-1-2-3, 25, 28, 30, 34-5, 46, 48-9, 57, 59, 60-1, 64-5-6, 73-4-5-6-7, 88, 100, 111, 114, 120, 122-3-4-5-6-7-8, 130-1, 154, 159, 165, 172, 192, 196, 201-2, 219, 260, 263, 277, 281-2, 291
Containers, 231, 233, 236, 275
Contempt, 161, 259
Contractor, 36-7, 41-2-3, 197-8, 243
Controlled market, 12

INDEX

INDEX

INDEX

INDEX

INDEX

INDEX

INDEX

157, 188-9, 190, 194, 238, 247, 250, 256, 264
Sweden, 15, 240
Swift & Co., 221, 305

Tanks, 79, 90
Taxes, 11, 25, 28, 37, 45, 48-9, 50, 57, 128, 194, 287
Taxpayers, 21, 35, 74
Teamsters' Union, 118, 132-3, 141
Technical, 118, 132-3, 141
Technicians, 5, 14, 69, 169
Technological, 30, 34, 84, 130-1, 250
Temporary National Economic Committee, 9, 36, 38, 175, 180
Ten-cent stores, 28, 123
Thomas, Norman, 112
Tin Lizzie, 23, 119, 121
Tobacco, 34, 128, 229, 230-1, 306, 308
Totalitarian, 14, 77-8-9, 84, 87-8, 284
Townsend Plan, 280
Trade Associations, 15-6, 38, 89, 173, 181, 200, 203, 205, 266
  Free, 20, 124
  restraint, 16, 20, 25, 35-6-7-8, 40-1-2-3-4, 46-7, 52, 71-2, 75, 84, 89, 104, 112, 124, 127, 129, 133-4-5, 143, 145-6, 149, 173, 183-4, 187-8, 194-5-6, 201, 203-4, 207, 213, 215-6, 219, 220, 228-9, 248, 252, 258, 270, 286, 289, 291, 293, 295-6, 299, 300, 303-4, 306-7, 310, 312
  unions, 42, 82-3, 257
Tradition, 91-2, 95-6, 98, 100, 103, 111, 151, 269, 272-3, 275, 293-4
Trans-Missouri Freight Association, 304
Trenton Potteries Co., 311
Trueblood, Howard J., 85
Trust-buster, 122, 124, 262
Trusts, 66, 123, 133, 262, 272

Underwood, R. R., 178
Unemployment, 2, 11, 17, 55, 57, 89, 96, 126, 130, 142, 203, 275, 277

Union Pacific Railroad Co., 308
Unions, 16, 39, 42, 58, 149, 150, 160, 193, 198, 207, 240-1-2, 254, 286, 305
United Mine Workers, 317-8
United Shoe Machinery Co., 188, 308
United States, 1, 2, 5, 26, 28, 36, 44, 52, 63, 68-9, 70, 72, 76, 81, 85-6, 95, 98, 114, 126-7-8, 133, 175, 194, 196, 211, 220, 226, 268, 278, 284, 290, 293, 300-1-2
  District Court, 34, 258-9
  Treasury Dept., 48, 54, 68, 212
  U. S. v. American Medical Association, 190
  v. Borden Co., 189
  v. Socony-Vacuum Oil Co., 190
  Steel Corporation, 275, 309

Vigilantes, 166, 284
Vinson, Representative, 63
Vitamins, 225-6

Wages, 2, 16, 32, 45, 57, 66, 82, 116, 161, 220, 223, 249, 250, 256, 277
Wagner Act, 240-1, 245, 268
Waldrop, Frank, 278
Wall Street, 123, 262
Walsh-Vinson Bill, 62
War, 35, 49, 59, 67, 77-8-9, 81, 83, 89, 90-1, 95, 118, 284-5
  "babies," 75
  boom, 2, 66, 74
  Department, 73
  industries, 62, 67-8, 71, 74, 90
  materials, 27, 43, 61, 68, 74, 77, 181
  pattern, 79, 80
  present, 68, 81, 88-9, 120, 288, 296
  World, 2, 7, 15, 62, 64, 66-7-8-9, 73, 75, 285
Washington, George, 287
Washington
  Daily News, 28
  Post, 50, 54-5-6, 214

INDEX

Printed in the United States
125040LV00001B/85/A